M Fahy

Enterprise Resource Planning Systems

Leveraging the benefits for business

CIMA

First published in 2001 by:
The Chartered Institute of Management Accountants
63 Portland Place
London
W1B 1AB

ISBN 1 85971 463 3

Printed in Great Britain

Acknowledgements

We are grateful to Martin Fahy for taking on the role of editor and contributing to this book, and to the following organisations for their contributions and support.

PRICEWATERHOUSECOOPERS

Articles have been contributed by Martin Osborn, John Blackburn and Jens Larsen. PricewaterhouseCoopers (www.pwcglobal.com) is the world's largest professional service organisation. Drawing on the knowledge and skills of more than 150,000 people in 150 countries, PricewaterhouseCoopers helps clients solve complex business problems and measurably enhance their ability to build value, manage risk and improve performance in an ERP and Internet-enabled world.

Many independent commentators perceive PwC to be the world leader in ERP implementation with strong practices in SAP, Oracle, Peoplesoft, JD Edwards and other leading ERP solutions. PwC are heavily involved at the forefront of Supply Chain, CRM, E-market and private exchange developments and helping major organisations realise the full benefits of the e-markets revolution.

PricewaterhouseCoopers refers to the member firms of the worldwide PricewaterhouseCoopers organisation.

Partners for Change

Articles in this book have been contributed by John Perry with the assistance of Mark Smith, John Tiller, Ricardo Rodrigues and Paula Marriott.

Partners for Change is one of the fastest-growing consultancies in the UK and ranked 29 in the 2000 Virgin Atlantic/Sunday Times Fast Track 100, up 9 places from 1999. The company has strong values and a completely different attitude to clients, based on putting clients' interests above its own. It makes this real by employing grown-up people who share its values passionately.

Partners for Change's services include programme management, design, sourcing, implementation and benefits realisation of:

- Structural change: outsourcing, shared service centres, merger integration;
- Technology change: Enterprise Resource Planning, Customer Relationship Management and e-business;
- Process change and performance improvement.

The differentiator in all that it does is delivering sustainable business benefit.

Partners for Change has a very strong track record in large-scale ERP implementation. It has also helped clients integrate following mergers, set up shared service centres, and in 'business implementation' of other technologies such as e-procurement. The company has helped clients launch new e-business products and set up 'incubators' to encourage creativity. Recent clients include Standard Chartered Bank, CGNU, GlaxoSmithKline and Cable & Wireless.

Partners for Change is pioneering new approaches to resourcing, knowledge sharing and partnering arrangements.

Contents

Foreword

At different times over the last decade, the reputation and contribution of ERP implementations have been challenged. More recently people have said, 'ERP is dead. Today is the age of the Internet!'. In such a time of flux and uncertainty I was very pleased to be invited to contribute to this work with CIMA and to encourage the debate.

At times ERP implementations have deserved their bad press. Many organisations are now looking back, realising the mistakes they made in their implementation approaches, and deciding to re-implement. Others are realising that they can do more to gain greater benefits from their current investments. Some are using the ERP platform to drive on to a shared-services approach that has the potential to give significant economies of scale, and to eliminate a complex variety of legacy systems and diverse corporate practices. When you add the contribution that ERP made to controlling the Y2K problem, and the improved availability and quality of information, this does not suggest that ERP has failed, although it has given, and still gives, much grief and pain en route.

Our firm conviction is that ERP is not dead. When ERP and e-business extensions are properly implemented they support and supercharge each other. A well-implemented and integrated ERP system is central to the provision of quality information, efficient processes and adequate integration both within and across enterprises. Companies that try to integrate within an extended value chain before implementing their own ERP systems will find the benefits of value chain integration elusive. Organisations that decide not to integrate the enterprise and the market will lose the chance to compete. Victory goes to the most efficient and speediest competitor. Therefore this debate is essential and timely.

CIMA brought together Martin Fahy, Partners for Change Ltd and Pricewaterhouse-Coopers to contribute on various basic and significant subjects. These include the scope of ERP, implementation approaches and lessons, change management, benefits realisation, management accounting and strategic enterprise management. PwC were pleased to support with some of the basic ERP chapters and to lay out PwC's viewpoint on strategic enterprise management and the way that new pressures and developments are transforming the enterprise.

I hope that you get great value from dipping into this debate!

John Blackburn
Partner In Charge
UK SAP Practice - PricewaterhouseCoopers

Enterprise Resource Planning Systems

Introduction

The term enterprise resource planning (ERP) was originally coined by the Gartner Group in the early 1990s. In the early days ERP was viewed as the next generation of MRP II software, with the added functionality of quality control, process operations management, and regulatory reporting. These rather simplistic systems quickly evolved to extend their scope to include not just material resources but also production processes, equipment, financial resources and supply chain activities.

In simple terms ERP systems use database technology and a single interface to control all the information related to a company's business including customer, product, employee and financial data. ERP software is designed to model and automate many of the basic processes of a company, from finance to the shop floor, with the goal of integrating information across the company and eliminating complex, expensive links between computer systems. The software has become the means to support and speed up the entire order supply chain process and to automate and integrate the business and production process. In addition ERP is increasingly seen as a transaction backbone and data source for ancillary decision support systems as well as emerging e-business applications. More recently, functionality has been added to support the specific needs of vertical industry segments, such as consumer packaged goods, automotive manufacturers and pharmaceuticals. As well as addressing particular industry requirements, ERP systems vendors have also turned their attention to process improvement in the form of specialist supply chain management, customer service, field service, CRM, and WEB-based order processing. In addition ERP vendors have also started to address the needs of small and medium-sized organisations with the development of the so-called 'Mid Market ERP Solutions'.

Enterprise Resource Planning has been one of the major driving forces of technology change over the last 10 years, with worldwide sales in the billions of pounds a year and related hardware, software and consultancy costs accounting for many times more than this again. Year 2000 issues have driven market growth over the past few years and now the majority of the top 500 companies in the USA, UK and Germany have implemented ERP. The cost of implementing ERP has limited its adoption by companies with a turnover of less than £250 million; however, there are now market offerings that make ERP more attractive to the small and medium-sized enterprise (SME) market. SAP, the German supplier, currently dominates the market with 31 per cent market share worldwide, followed by its main competitors – JD Edwards, Peoplesoft and Oracle.

An ERP system can be an important catalyst for organisational change by providing tighter integration of functions to support process based management. It also enables the enterprise to manage multiple sites as a single entity and better co-ordinate cross-site processes. It forces companies to implement a set of proven processes, e.g. build-to-order vs. build-to-inventory approach (as employed by Compaq) allows them to benefit from industry-based solutions and adopt best practices. In addition ERP software can provide an organisation with a powerful foundation to support growth. Its flexibility, scalability and functionality allow enterprises to open new areas of business and provide improved customer service. In addition well-implemented ERP systems can improve profitability, productivity and effectiveness. They can result in cost reductions, revenue enhancements, improvements in management reporting and control, improved efficiency and more timely access to accurate information. Where previously manual processes were automated, savings can be achieved from reducing the time and errors involved in processes. Other benefits which firms have achieved are as follows:

- By optimising information, savings can be achieved from better demand forecasting, production and distribution scheduling, or just-in-time replenishment can reduce plant capacity and inventory requirements;
- Eliminating non-value-added activities in processes and applying automated workflow capabilities can remove inefficient or optimise necessary processes;
- Structural changes, such as multiunit enterprises, can establish shared service centres for processing administrative transactions (e.g. cheque and invoice processing, cash applications, etc.);
- Workflow technology and electronic commerce can reduce transaction processing costs;
- The disbanding of legacy systems can solve EMU readiness issues;
- The termination of hardware and software support and maintenance contracts associated with legacy systems can reduce costs.

In theory ERP systems allow companies to replace their existing information systems, which are often incompatible with one another, with a single, integrated system. Commercial ERP software packages promise the seamless integration of all the information flowing throughout a company. While it is clear that ERP systems provide the potential for significant business process improvement, vendors have also claimed that their products would yield significant improvements in decision support and related management reporting and control activities. Davenport (1998)) predicted a number of benefits from the implementation of ERP systems. In particular he suggested that ERP systems would provide the following benefits to the finance function:

- Support for strategic planning and organisational change in the form of tighter integration of functions to support management by process. Multiple sites could be managed as a single entity using proven processes;
- Enterprise-wide integration of systems and information through standardisation, yielding improvements in data integrity and site headquarter reporting;
- Cost reduction and revenue enhancements from improvements in management reporting and control as well as improved efficiency and more timely access to accurate information;
- Data rationalisation through the use of universal transaction codes, and consolidation procedures;
- Improved forecasting for production, distribution and other purposes based on real-time integration with suppliers and customers;
- Improvement in transaction processing in the form of better cash flow control, payables accounting, etc.

ERP systems, it is suggested, streamline a company's data flows and provide management with direct access to a wealth of real-time operating information. For many companies, these benefits have translated into dramatic gains in productivity and speed. In addition to having important strategic implications, ERP systems also have a direct, and often paradoxical, impact on a company's organisation and culture. On the one hand, by providing universal, real-time access to operating and financial data, the systems allow companies to streamline their management structures, creating flatter, more flexible and more democratic organisations. On the other hand, they also involve the centralisation of control over information and the standardisation of processes, which are qualities more consistent with hierarchical, command-and-control organisations with uniform cultures. In addition ERP systems offered an escape from legacy systems and their associated Y2K problems to a more integrated system based on a single data repository that supports data mining and other data warehousing derivatives. In particular ERP systems promised to eliminate the need for spreadsheets, shadow systems and expensive manual integration of data from different legacy systems.

Despite these claims and developments there is evidence of a significant gap emerging in terms of the satisfaction of business users and technology managers with ERP implementations. The business case for investment in ERP has been fairly clear. The benefits that can be derived from better integration, better quality data and the standardisation of business processes can be significant. But there is evidence to suggest that many companies investing in ERP have not delivered the benefits that the business case suggests are available. A recent survey by Peoplesoft revealed that 27 per cent of their clients did not attempt to measure the business benefits of the ERP implementation. Gartner Group found that less than 30 per cent of firms achieved the expected benefits from their ERP implementation. Many firms find themselves spending a large amount of resources post-implementation in an attempt to realise the benefits of their ERP implementation. A growing number of horror stories about failed ERP projects have appeared in recent years. FoxMeyer Drug argues that its system helped drive it into bankruptcy. Mobil Europe spent hundreds of millions of dollars on its system, only to abandon it when its merger partner objected. Applied Materials gave up on its system when it found itself overwhelmed by the organisational changes involved. Dow Chemical spent seven years and close to half a billion dollars implementing a mainframe-based enterprise system; now it has decided to start over again on a client-server version. In addition there are numerous examples of companies that pull out of ERP projects because of functional or even philosophical problems. Schneider (1999) points out that from an organisational viewpoint, ERP concepts are especially tricky because they go against the mantra of decentralisation, which many companies adopted in the '70s and '80s to spur innovation among business units. These sophisticated enterprise systems require a switch from a functional to a process orientation because modules often cut across traditional departmental lines.

While ERP systems appear to be addressing a range of technological problems in organisations, business managers continue to experience data access and decision support problems. Schneider (1999) suggests that, in its brief history, ERP is more often identified with out-of-control budgets and questionable returns than with business transformation. Replacing dozens of legacy systems with a single integrated one for managing operations across every discipline – finance, human resources, procurement, materials management, sales and distribution, production, order management – is challenging even for companies with generous IS budgets and a hefty staff. While technology and systems are a vital enabler, the successful implementation of these systems requires a much wider perspective than many practitioners have suggested to date. In particular a purely technological approach will not lead to the efficient, knowledge sharing, and learning enterprise that focuses on creating value.

Shorter windows of opportunity and the emergence of speed/time as a competitive dimension have led to a situation where managers are expected to make and implement decisions in shorter and shorter time periods. At the same time managers are faced with a deluge of information from both inside and outside the organisation. While the systems which organisations have implemented in the past have been effective in providing the hard quantitative information needed for operational control, they have been of limited value in supporting the activities of senior managers.

Companies toiled for years and spent billions of dollars installing enterprise resource planning systems to automate key back-office business processes. But the ERP movement is far from over. A second, more powerful wave of ERP development promises to increase efficiency in handling transactions, improve decision-making, and further transform ways of doing business. Now being built onto ERP platforms are applications more attuned to engaging customers and driving profits than the manufacturing, financial, and human resources applications that first defined the market. Some of these post-ERP applications – such as sales-force automation, customer-relationship management, data mining, and supply-chain management systems – have already emerged. Newer ERP add-ons focus on areas such as demand planning, component management, product data management, and transportation management.

Modern ERP systems currently provide organisations with an integrated solution for planning, executing and controlling operational business activity. As companies deploy ERP applications to improve their back-office and manufacturing operations, these systems are generating vast amounts of data on employees, customers, finances, products, inventory and other business fundamentals. These systems, e.g. those from Peoplesoft, SAP, Baan or Oracle, have, in their defence, done much in improving performance efficiency within the companies in which they have been installed by using a set of applications which incorporate modern-day best practices. Through this process they have forced these companies to modify and update their processes to meet defined standards. But ERP systems work at an operational, rather than a strategic, level. They do not show how a business can best create value for customers and meet its objectives, from maximizing shareholder value to fulfilling responsibilities to employees, business partners and the communities in which it operates.

In response to this shortcoming the last eighteen months has seen the emergence of strategic enterprise management (SEM) software offerings from the top three ERP vendors. As currently conceived by the major vendors SEM is designed to improve the effectiveness of strategic management processes by providing managers with business performance monitoring, consolidation, and data warehousing/business intelligence capability. Alongside this data and information management capability, vendors such as SAP and Peoplesoft are also attempting to include techniques such as shareholder value management, balanced scorecard and activity-based management as part of their SEM offerings. Over the next twelve months SEM is likely to become an established part of the corporate lexicon. In particular the coming months will see a plethora of management conferences, and technology offerings centred on SEM. SEM systems will sit on top of the ERP systems widely introduced in the early 1990s by large corporations. ERP systems, such as those from SAP, Oracle, Peoplesoft and Baan, have helped to improve efficiency in big companies by using a set of system applications which deploy existing industry best practices. But ERP systems work at an operational, rather than a strategic, level. They do not show how a business can best create value for customers and meet its objectives, from maximising shareholder value to fulfilling responsibilities to employees, business partners and the communities in which it operates. SEM attempts to bridge the gap between strategy and operations by making shareholder value the key criteria in decision-making and by providing the tools and information to support.

This book examines the impact of ERP systems on organisations and in particular on the management accounting function. Many of the arguments put forward for ERP systems have been centred on the automation of data gathering processes rather than the real strategic information requirements of executives. There is a trend among vendors of adding new application areas to their products, mainly in the form of front-office applications, business intelligence and decision support capability. These capabilities are designed to extend the reach of ERP systems beyond transaction processing and process management to a more strategic role in decision-making. For a number of years ERP vendors have been criticised for the inadequacy of the DSS capability within their systems. Trends such as EIS, data warehousing, balanced scorecards, etc., have prompted vendors such as SAP to focus on analytical applications including SEM which are designed to support top managers in their decision-making.

Based on the history of the ERP market to date, we have to ask the basic question, 'Have we learned from the lessons of the past and are we equipped to take advantage of the undoubted opportunities to deliver tangible and lasting business benefits from past and future investments in ERP?'

M Fahy

Chapter 1

ERP Systems

INTRODUCTION

As we enter the new decade there is increasing evidence that the life cycle of the business model is getting shorter and shorter. Where previously firms expected their business model to remain essentially unchanged for ten to fifteen years, we now see firms making fundamental changes to their business model every twelve to eighteen months. Shorter business and product life cycles, increased competition, globalisation and a continuous stream of new technologies have led to a dramatic increase in the velocity of organisations and decision-making. Where, previously, senior executives were expected to undertake a handful of strategic initiatives in their ten years at the top, they are now expected to execute a variety of strategic initiatives every year. These initiatives have in recent years taken the form of acquisitions and mergers, vertical and horizontal integration strategies and the ubiquitous e-business. Alongside this headlong rush to create shareholder value, firms have invested large amounts of resources in the supporting IT/IS infrastructure. In particular, firms will have embraced the notion of competitive advantage from IT as a core part of their strategic posture.

While most of the hype and excitement of the last two years has focused on the Internet and e-business the reality is that ERP systems have accounted for a much large portion of expenditure in many firms in the last six to seven years. In particular, firms have replaced a large number of standalone (and often non-Y2K compliant) legacy systems with ERP offerings from the major vendors. In addition the future is likely to see ERP systems providing the core transaction processing capability of many firms' e-business strategies. In particular, successful exploitation of the business-to-business (B2B) opportunities of the web will require a well-established ERP architecture. So while e-business, B2B, B2C and other buzz-words grab the media attention the reality is that ERP systems will remain a key element of firms' IT/IS strategy and will continue to consume large amounts of resources.

If we are to successfully exploit the potential of the ERP investments made to date we need to fully understand the landscape they inhabit. In particular we need to gain an appreciation of the factors that gave rise to the current difficulties associated with ERP and why so many organisations remain disappointed with the return on their ERP investment. The purpose of this chapter is to explore the nature of ERP systems as they were originally conceived and then to examine the realities of ERP implementations. In particular the chapter will focus on providing insights into the potential contribution which ERP systems can make to protecting the existing shareholder value and in exploiting opportunities for new value in the form of the new virtual market spaces of the web.

The chapter begins with a review of the experiences and evolution of ERP by Kumar and Hillegersberg. Their piece from the communications of the ACM provides interesting insights into the factors that drove many firms to invest in ERP systems in the early 1990s. They discuss how the ERP vendors quickly recognised the potential of the market place and began adding new functionality to their product offerings. They suggest that many practitioners, consultants and academics have been 'asleep' at the wheel with respect to the changing ERP landscape and that the time has come to revisit the ERP investment and begin to finally exploit it in pursuit of shareholder value.

The main body of this chapter will explore the architecture of ERP, especially the functionality it offers to firms. In particular we will attempt to gain an understanding of the incredible reach and range of ERP offerings and the enormity of the task of implementing them across multi-site organisations. The chapter concludes by looking at the importance of ERP for the finance function and the challenge of e-business for ERP.

ERP EXPERIENCES AND EVOLUTION: Introduction

Kuldeep Kumar, Jos van Hillegersberg, *Communications of the ACM*, April 2000, Volume 43, No. 4 © 2000 ACM. Reprinted by permission.

Enterprise resource planning systems are configurable information systems packages that integrate information and information-based processes within and across functional areas in an organization. The current generation of ERP systems also provides reference models or process templates that claim to embody the current best business practices.

Integration has been the holy grail of MIS since the early days of computing in organizations. As early as 1969 Blumenthal proposed an integrated architecture and a framework for organizational information systems [1]. However, due to the high level of organizational and technical complexity associated with their development and implementation, integrated enterprise-wide systems have been difficult to achieve in practice. For example, in the late 1980s and early 1990s, several attempts to develop integrated enterprise-wide corporate data models did not succeed because of a lack of development and resource continuity over the long time horizons typically needed to build and implement these systems.

While these attempts for creating in-house integrated systems were floundering in various organizations, first-generation ERP systems packages were beginning to appear in the manufacturing industry. SAP and Baan, both European companies with backgrounds in industrial engineering, manufacturing, and operations, laid the groundwork for large-scale adoption of ERP systems in manufacturing organizations such as Boeing, Mercedes-Benz, BMW, and Ford. The development of these ERP systems was an inside-out process of evolution starting from standard inventory control (IC) packages, to material requirements planning (MRP), manufacturing resource planning (MRP II), further expanding to include other enterprise processes such as sales and order management, marketing, purchasing, warehouse management, financial and managerial accounting (finance), and human resource management. The evolution to extended-ERP systems continues to include inter-organizational processes such as supplier and customer relation management.

ERP and ERP vendors were the major success stories of the mid-1990s. In addition to the European stalwarts (SAP and Baan), companies such as Oracle, PeopleSoft, and JD Edwards were beginning to make inroads in the ERP market. ERP revolution was in full swing with market capitalization of major vendors such as SAP and Baan approaching astronomical heights. Mid-1998 saw a severe correction in the market with Baan stock plummeting to one-tenth of its highs and SAP suffering a decline in stock value. By mid-1999 articles such as “ERP R.I.P.” [3], “ERP: staying out of trouble” [2], and “ERP’s fight for life” [4] in influential business and trade press were predicting the imminent demise of ERP. Market analysts observed that by this time most of the Fortune 500 companies had already installed ERP systems. As some of the growth in ERP sales was presumably due to Y2K problems, with the approach of 2000 the bloom on the ERP rose was considered to be over. Moreover, the complexity of ERP and associated high costs and problems of ERP implementations were causing organizations to reexamine their plans for acquiring and implementing enterprise-wide systems.

However, current evidence suggests that news of the demise of ERP has been somewhat premature. The large, relatively untapped market of midsize companies is now beginning to embrace ERP. Also, while ERP is relatively well established in the U.S., Germany, Scandinavia, and The Netherlands, it has only recently started making inroads in developing countries such as India, Brazil, and China, as well as in industrialized nations such as Singapore, Japan, the U.K., and Spain. Furthermore, ERP from its traditional base in manufacturing and logistics is now expanding into industries traditionally relying on in-house development or specialized packages. These include industries such as wholesale, service, maintenance and repairs, project industry, finance, banking, and insurance. The move into these new markets and industries requires new software products, knowledge, and competencies that do not currently exist in the present generation of ERP vendors with their origins in manufacturing and logistics.

ERP is now considered to be the price of entry for running a business, and at least at present, for being connected to other enterprises in a network economy. Furthermore, ERP is becoming a platform for applications such as executive information systems, data mining, and supply chain management. Therefore the market for ERP is likely to continue to expand and grow. However, a number of organizational and technical issues remain to be resolved before the potential of ERP can be fully realized. Willcocks and Sykes, in their provocative article, "The Role of the CIO and IT Function in ERP," observe that most CIOs and their IS/IT departments seem to have been "asleep at the wheel" in understanding and dealing with the ERP phenomenon.

Typically, ERP initiatives in organizations are motivated by senior executives other than the CIO. Furthermore, usually senior business executives do not perceive the IS department and the CIO as having the right strategic vision and capabilities for implementing ERP initiatives. Consequently, these initiatives are often implemented using expertise from outside the organization. The CIO and the IS/IT department are sidelined in these initiatives – relegated to the supporting role of maintaining and operating systems developed and implemented by others. Willcocks and Sykes suggest how the CIO and the IS department can transform themselves in dealing with the challenges of adopting, implementing, and if necessary, adapting enterprise-wide systems to the specific needs of their organization.

In keeping with their practitioner counterparts, academics in business school IS departments also seem to have been asleep at the wheel of the school bus. Coming out of industrial engineering schools, ERP itself, and the research on ERP has primarily been shaped by the engineer's view of organizations. Up until 1998, when the ERP phenomenon first appeared on the radar of the trade press, most IS academics were not aware of this revolutionary change. On the side of research, IS academics now seem to be catching up, and interesting preliminary results are beginning to appear in specialized, usually vendor-sponsored conferences and workshops, and in mini-tracks in IS conferences. However, most of the early research has not examined the implications and complexity of enterprise-wide information integration and the normative nature of reference models. In education, some universities, recognizing the multidimensional, integrative, and normative nature of ERP, are using ERP to integrate their business curriculum.

A key premise of ERP systems is the underlying, sometimes unstated, but often implicitly promoted notion that the reference models in ERP systems embody best business practices. Reference models supposedly reflect preferred business models including underlying data and process models as well as organizational structures. As Soh et al. eloquently point out, there can be considerable mismatches between the actual country, industry, and company-specific business practices and the reference models embedded in the ERP systems. While at the abstract level the idea of "universal" best practices may be seductive, at the detailed process level these mismatches create considerable implementation and adaptation problems.

Mismatches can also occur between the assumptions about organizational structure implicitly embedded in the reference models of the ERP software and the actual organization. The current generation of ERP packages is based upon a traditional hierarchical, functional view of organizations. Consequently, adaptations may be needed at both organizational as well as the system and software levels, leading to complex and difficult trade-offs. In addition, work in organizations can be distributed over many geographically and/or organizationally dispersed locations. Depending upon the level of decentralization and autonomy at these sites, integration of information and processes, and therefore ERP systems becomes an important issue.

ERP systems are continuously evolving in terms of technology and functionality. ERP vendors are regularly introducing new versions of their packages. Often these versions are quite different from the previous versions (for example, Triton, Baan IV, and Baan ERP) and sometimes not backward compatible. The problem of migrating between versions is further compounded if the user organizations have made modifications to the software or built custom interfaces between the ERP system and their in-house applications. Next, given the packaged nature of ERP, a disconnect can exist between specifying the organization's information requirements and the solution proposed by ERP. Traditionally this disconnect is addressed by using people who have ERP configuration expertise in the detailed capabilities, options, and parameters of the ERP package. However, there is no guarantee that such knowledge is sufficient to understand the requirements from the organization's perspective.

Thus the solution finally implemented may be determined more by the capabilities and options inherent in the ERP package rather than the organization's underlying information requirements. In order to address this dilemma, enterprise-modeling tools such as ARIS for SAP and Baan's DEM have been developed. However, given the monolithic nature of current ERP packages, these tools do not resolve this dilemma and end up being tools for selecting options and parameter setting.

The preceding problems have their genesis in the monolithic architecture of ERP systems. The design of the current generation of ERP systems is based upon the assumption that the requisite variety and complexity in organizations can be best accommodated by increasing the number of parameters, options, and configurable functionality in the ERP system (as in the transition from Baan IV to Baan ERP). However, variety and complexity can also be managed through an alternate minimalist strategy. This strategy relies on composing large systems from largely independent components that are assembled to meet situation specific requirements.

The idea of software components has evolved from object-oriented systems modeling. Components hide their internal complexity, communicate through clearly defined interfaces, and are both configurable and extensible. Similar to the concept of browsers that provide a platform for third party plug-ins, a component-based strategy would rely on a minimal ERP backbone supplied by few key ERP vendors together with a variety of domain specific components supplied by third party software houses. In those cases where the needed components are not available, the user organization will need to adapt or develop its own components. The organization is further responsible for selecting, assembling and when necessary, installing new versions of these components.

Such a component strategy would address the issues identified previously. First, firms would be able to gradually acquire and assemble component-based ERP solutions customized to their specific needs. This would reduce the problem of mismatch between organizational requirements and ERP solutions. It should also lower the cost of acquiring and implementing reasonably customized ERP solutions for small- and medium-size enterprises. Migrations will become more gradual as outdated components are upgraded individually instead of the whole system. Moreover, in multi-site implementations, the versions implemented at each site can be tailored to the site itself. Modeling toolsets, instead of being mainly configuration tools, will need to evolve to incorporate support for selecting, configuring, and extending components and for wiring components together. Finally this strategy should give the CIO and the IT department a renewed central role in identifying the organization's information requirements and implementing the ERP system.

What of the future? At present, ERP focuses mainly on structured transaction data in organizations. As we move to a more Web-based multimedia world, enterprise-wide information is also likely to expand to include multimedia documents such as engineering drawings, scanned documents, and audiovisual product descriptions. Second, ERP has focused primarily on transaction processing. The extensive databases provided by ERP are likely to provide the platform for decision support, data mining, and executive information systems. Finally, so far the development of ERP has been an inside-out process. On the other hand, supply chain management software such as i2, Manugistics, and SC21 aim to foster outside-in inter-organizational integration. As we move closer to a network economy, these two initiatives will need to converge. A component-based ERP architecture is likely to facilitate these developments.

References

1. Blumenthal, S., *Management Information Systems: A Framework for Planning and Development,* Prentice Hall, NJ, 1969.
2. Dempsey, M., ERP: Staying out of trouble, *Financial Times* (23 July 1999).
3. ERP R.I.P., *The Economist* (26 June 1999).
4. Stein, T., ERP's fight for life, www.informationweek.com (12 April 1999), 59–66.

THE ABCs OF ERP
Compiled from reports by Christopher Koch, Derek Slater and E. Baatz, www.cio.com. Reprinted through the courtesy of CIO.

What is ERP?
Enterprise resource planning software, or ERP, doesn't live up to its acronym. Forget about planning – it doesn't do that – and forget about resource, a throwaway term. But remember the enterprise part. This is ERP's true ambition. It attempts to integrate all departments and functions across a company onto a single computer system that can serve all those different departments' particular needs.

That is a tall order, building a single software program that serves the needs of people in finance as well as it does the people in human resources and in the warehouse. Each of those departments typically has its own computer system, each optimized for the particular ways that the department does its work. But ERP combines them all together into a single, integrated software program that runs off a single database so that the various departments can more easily share information and communicate with each other.

That integrated approach can have a tremendous payback if companies install the software correctly. Take a customer order, for example. Typically, when a customer places an order, that order begins a mostly paper-based journey from in-basket to in-basket around the company, often being keyed and re-keyed into different departments' computer systems along the way. All that lounging around in in-baskets causes delays and lost orders, and all the keying into different computer systems invites errors. Meanwhile, no one in the company truly knows what the status of the order is at any given point because there is no way for the finance department, for example, to get into the warehouse's computer system to see whether the item has been shipped. "You'll have to call the warehouse," is the familiar refrain heard by frustrated customers.

How can ERP improve a company's business performance?
ERP automates the tasks involved in performing a business process – such as order fulfillment, which involves taking an order from a customer, shipping it and billing for it. With ERP, when a customer service representative takes an order from a customer, he or she has all the information necessary to complete the order (the customer's credit rating and order history, the company's inventory levels and the shipping dock's trucking schedule). Everyone else in the company sees the same computer screen and has access to the single database that holds the customer's new order. When one department finishes with the order it is automatically routed via the ERP system to the next department. To find out where the order is at any point, one need only log into the ERP system and track it down. With luck, the order process moves like a bolt of lightning through the organization, and customers get their orders faster and with fewer orders than before. ERP can apply that same magic to the other major business processes, such as employee benefits or financial reporting.

That, at least, is the dream of ERP. The reality is much harsher.
Let's go back to those in-boxes for a minute. That process may not have been efficient, but it was simple. Finance did its job, the warehouse did its job, and if anything went wrong outside of the department's walls, it was somebody else's problem. Not anymore. With ERP, the customer service representatives are no longer just typists entering someone's name into a computer and hitting the return key. The ERP screen makes them business people. It flickers with the customer's credit rating from the finance department and the product inventory levels from the warehouse. Will the customer pay on time? Will we be able to ship the order on time? These are decisions that customer service representatives have never had to make before and which affect the customer and every other department in the company. But it's not just the customer service repre-

sentatives who have to wake up. People in the warehouse who used to keep inventory in their heads or on scraps of paper now need to put that information online. If they don't, customer service will see low inventory levels on their screens and tell customers that their requested item is not in stock. Accountability, responsibility and communication have never been tested like this before.

How long will an ERP project take?

Companies that install ERP do not have an easy time of it. Don't be fooled when ERP vendors tell you about a three or six month average implementation time. Those short (that's right, six months is short) implementations all have a catch of one kind or another: the company was small, or the implementation was limited to a small area of the company, or the company only used the financial pieces of the ERP system (in which case the ERP system is nothing more than a very expensive accounting system). To do ERP right, the ways you do business will need to change and the ways people do their jobs will need to change too. And that kind of change doesn't come without pain. Unless, of course, your ways of doing business are working extremely well (orders all shipped on time, productivity higher than all your competitors, customers completely satisfied), in which case there is no reason to even consider ERP.

The important thing is not to focus on how long it will take – real transformational ERP efforts usually run between one to three years, on average – but rather to understand why you need it and how you will use it to improve your business.

What will ERP fix in my business?

There are three major reasons why companies undertake ERP:

To integrate financial data. As the CEO tries to understand the company's overall performance, he or she may find many different versions of the truth. Finance has its own set of revenue numbers, sales has another version, and the different business units may each have their own versions of how much they contributed to revenues. ERP creates a single version of the truth that cannot be questioned because everyone is using the same system.

To standardize manufacturing processes. Manufacturing companies – especially those with an appetite for mergers and acquisitions – often find that multiple business units across the company make the same widget using different methods and computer systems. Standardizing those processes and using a single, integrated computer system can save time, increase productivity and reduce headcount.

To standardize HR information. Especially in companies with multiple business units, HR may not have a unified, simple method for tracking employee time and communicating with them about benefits and services. ERP can fix that.

In the race to fix these problems, companies often lose sight of the fact that ERP packages are nothing more than generic representations of the ways a typical company does business. While most packages are exhaustively comprehensive, each industry has its quirks that make it unique. Most ERP systems were designed to be used by discreet manufacturing companies (who make physical things that can be counted), which immediately left all the process manufacturers (oil, chemical and utility companies that measure their products by flow rather than individual units) out in the cold. Each of these industries has struggled with the different ERP vendors to modify core ERP programs to their needs.

Will ERP fit the ways I do business?

It's critical for companies to figure out if their ways of doing business will fit within a standard ERP package before the checks are signed and the implementation begins. The most common reason that companies walk away from multimillion dollar ERP projects is that they discover that the software does not support one of their important business processes. At that point there are two things they can do: they can change the business process to accommodate the software, which will mean deep changes in long-established ways of doing business (that often provide competitive advantage) and shake up important peoples' roles and responsibilities (something that few companies have the stomach for). Or they can modify the software to fit the process, which will slow down the project, introduce dangerous bugs into the system and make upgrading the software to the ERP vendor's next release excruciatingly difficult, because the customizations will need to be torn apart and rewritten to fit with the new version.

Needless to say, the move to ERP is a project of breathtaking scope, and the price tags on the front end are enough to make the most placid CFO a little twitchy. In addition to budgeting for software costs, financial executives should plan to write checks to cover consulting, process rework, integration testing and a long laundry list of other expenses before the benefits of ERP start to manifest themselves. Underestimate the price of teaching users their new job processes can lead to a rude shock down the line. So can failure to consider data warehouse integration requirements and the cost of extra software to duplicate the old report formats. A few oversights in the budgeting and planning stage can send ERP costs spiraling out of control faster than oversights in planning almost any other information system undertaking.

What does ERP *really* cost?

Meta Group recently did a study looking at the Total Cost of Ownership (TCO) of ERP, including hardware, software, professional services, and internal staff costs. The TCO numbers include getting the software installed and the two years afterward, which is when the real costs of maintaining, upgrading and optimizing the system for your business are felt. Among the 63 companies surveyed – including small, medium and large companies in a range of industries – the average TCO was $15 million (the highest was $300 million and lowest was $400,000). While it's hard to draw a solid number from that kind of a range of companies and ERP efforts, Meta came up with one statistic that proves that ERP is expensive no matter what kind of company is using it. The TCO for a "heads-down" user over that period was a staggering $53,320.

When will I get payback from ERP – and how much will it be?

Don't expect to revolutionize your business with ERP. It is a navel gazing exercise that focuses on optimizing the way things are done internally rather than with customers, suppliers or partners. Yet the navel gazing has a pretty good payback if you're willing to wait for it – a Meta group study of 63 companies found that it took eight months after the new system was in (31 months total) to see any benefits. But the median annual savings from the new ERP system was $1.6 million per year.

The hidden costs of ERP

Although different companies will find different land mines in the budgeting process, those who have implemented ERP packages agree that certain costs are more commonly overlooked or underestimated than others. Armed with insights from across the business, ERP pros vote the following areas as most likely to result in budget overrun.

1. Training
   Training is the near-unanimous choice of experienced ERP implementers as the most elusive budget item. It's not so much that this cost is completely overlooked as it is consistently underestimated. Training expenses are high because workers almost invariably have to learn a new set of processes, not just a new software interface.

2. Integration and testing
   Testing the links between ERP packages and other corporate software links that have to be built on a case-by-case basis is another often underestimated cost. A typical manufacturing company may have add-on applications for logistics, tax, production planning and bar coding. If this laundry list also includes customization of the core ERP package, expect the cost of integrating, testing and maintaining the system to skyrocket.

   As with training, testing ERP integration has to be done from a process-oriented perspective. Instead of plugging in dummy data and moving it from one application to the next, veterans recommend running a real purchase order through the system, from order entry through shipping and receipt of payment – the whole order-to-cash banana – preferably with the participation of the employees who will eventually do those jobs.

3. Data conversion
   It costs money to move corporate information, such as customer and supplier records, product design data and the like, from old systems to new ERP homes. Although few CIOs will admit it, most data in most legacy systems is of little use. Companies often deny their data is dirty until they actually have to move it to the new client/server setups that popular ERP packages require. Consequently, those companies are more likely to underestimate the cost of the move. But even clean data may demand some overhaul to match process modifications necessitated – or inspired – by the ERP implementation.

4. Data analysis
   Often, the data from the ERP system must be combined with data from external systems for analysis purposes. Users with heavy analysis needs should include the cost of a data warehouse in the ERP budget – and they should expect to do quite a bit of work to make it run smoothly. Users are in a pickle here: refreshing all the ERP data in a big corporate data warehouse daily is difficult, and ERP systems do a poor job of indicating which information has changed from day to day, making selective warehouse updates tough. One expensive solution is custom programming. The upshot is that the wise will check all their data analysis needs before signing off on the budget.

5. Consultants ad infinitum
   When users fail to plan for disengagement, consulting fees run wild. To avoid this, companies should identify objectives for which its consulting partners must aim when training internal staff. Include metrics in the consultants' contract; for example, a specific number of the user company's staff should be able to pass a project-management leadership test – similar to what Big Five consultants have to pass to lead an ERP engagement.

6. Replacing your best and brightest
   It is accepted wisdom that ERP success depends on staffing the project with the best and brightest from the business and IS. The software is too complex and the business changes too dramatic to trust the project to just anyone. The bad news is, a company must be prepared to replace many of those people when the project is over. Though the ERP market is not as hot as it once was, consulting firms and other companies that have lost their best people will be hounding yours with higher salaries and bonus offers than you can afford – or that your HR policies permit. Huddle with HR early on to develop a retention bonus program and to create new salary strata for ERP veterans. If you let them go, you'll wind up hiring them – or someone like them – back as consultants for twice what you paid them in salaries.

7. Implementation teams can never stop
   Most companies intend to treat their ERP implementations as they would any other software project. Once the software is installed, they figure, the team will be scuttled and everyone will go back to his or her day job. But after ERP, you can't go home again. You're too valuable. Because they have worked intimately with ERP, they know more about the sales process than the salespeople do and more about the manufacturing process than the manufacturing people do. Companies can't afford to send their project people back into the business because there's so much to do after the ERP software is installed. Just writing reports to pull information out of the new ERP system will keep the project team busy for a year at least. And it is in analysis – and, one hopes, insight – that companies make their money back on an ERP implementation. Unfortunately, few IS departments plan for the frenzy of post-ERP installation activity, and fewer still build it into their budgets when they start their ERP projects. Many are forced to beg for more money and staff immediately after the go-live date, long before the ERP project has demonstrated any benefit.

8. Waiting for ROI
   One of the most misleading legacies of traditional software project management is that the company expects to gain value from the application as soon as it is installed; the project team expects a break, and maybe a pat on the back. Neither expectation applies to ERP. Most don't reveal their value until after companies have had them running for some time and can concentrate on making improvements in the business processes that are affected by the system. And the project team is not going to be rewarded until their efforts pay off.

9. Post-ERP depression
   ERP systems often cause havoc in the companies that install them. In a recent Deloitte Consulting survey of 64 Fortune 500 companies, one in four admitted that they suffered a drop in performance when their ERP systems went live. The true percentage is undoubtedly much higher. The most common reason for the performance problems is that everything looks and works differently from the way it did before. When people can't do their jobs in the familiar way and haven't yet mastered the new way, they panic, and the business goes into spasms.

How do you configure ERP software?

Even if a company installs ERP software for the so-called right reasons and everyone can agree on the optimal definition of a customer, the inherent difficulties of implementing something as complex as ERP is like, well, teaching an elephant to do the hootchy-kootchy. The packages are built from database tables, thousands of them, that IS programmers and end users must set to match their business processes; each table has a decision "switch" that leads the software down one decision path or another. By presenting only one way for the company to do each task – say, run the payroll or close the books – a company's individual operating units and far-flung divisions are integrated under one system. But figuring out precisely how to set all the switches in the tables requires a deep understanding of the existing processes being used to operate the business. As the table settings are decided, these business processes are reengineered, ERP's way. Most ERP systems are not shipped as a shell system in which customers must determine at the minutia level how all the functional procedures should be set, making thousands of decisions that affect how their system behaves in line with their own business activities. Most ERP systems are preconfigured, allowing just hundreds – rather than thousands – of procedural settings to be made by the customer.

How do companies organize their ERP projects?
Based on our observations, there are three commonly used ways of installing ERP:

The Big Bang – In this, the most ambitious and difficult of approaches to ERP implementation, companies cast off all their legacy systems at once and implement a single ERP system across the entire company.

Though this method dominated early ERP implementations, few companies dare to attempt it anymore because it calls for the entire company to mobilize and change at once. Most of the ERP implementation horror stories from the late '90s warn us about companies that used this strategy. Getting everyone to cooperate and accept a new software system at the same time is a tremendous effort, largely because the new system will not have any advocates. No one within the company has any experience using it, so no one is sure whether it will work. Also, ERP inevitably involves compromises. Many departments have computer systems that have been honed to match the ways they work. In most cases, ERP offers neither the range of functionality, nor the comfort of familiarity that a custom legacy system can offer. In many cases, the speed of the new system may suffer because it is serving the entire company rather than a single department. ERP implementation requires a direct mandate from the CEO.

Franchising strategy – This approach suits large or diverse companies that do not share many common processes across business units. Independent ERP systems are installed in each unit, while linking common processes, such as financial book keeping, across the enterprise.

This has emerged as the most common way of implementing ERP. In most cases, the business units each have their own "instances" of ERP – that is, a separate system and database. The systems link together only to share the information necessary for the corporation to get a performance big picture across all the business units (business unit revenues, for example), or for processes that don't vary much from business unit to business unit (perhaps HR benefits). Usually, these implementations begin with a demonstration or "pilot" installation in a particularly open-minded and patient business unit where the core business of the corporation will not be disrupted if something goes wrong. Once the project team gets the system up and running and works out all the bugs, the team begins selling other units on ERP, using the first implementation as a kind of in-house customer reference. Plan for this strategy to take a long time.

Slam-dunk – ERP dictates the process design in this method, where the focus is on just a few key processes, such as those contained in an ERP system's financials module. The slam-dunk is generally for smaller companies expecting to grow into ERP.

The goal here is to get ERP up and running quickly and to ditch the fancy reengineering in favor of the ERP system's "canned" processes. Few companies that have approached ERP this way can claim much payback from the new system. Most use it as an infrastructure to support more diligent installation efforts down the road. Yet many discover that a slammed-in ERP system is little better than a legacy system, because it doesn't force employees to change any of their old habits. In fact, doing the hard work of process reengineering after the system is in can be more challenging than if there had been no system at all, because at that point few people in the company will have felt much benefit.

How does ERP fit with electronic commerce?
After all of that work inventing, perfecting and selling ERP to the world, the major ERP vendors are having a hard time shifting gears from making the applications that streamline business practices inside a company to those that face outward to the rest of the world. These days, the hottest areas for outward-looking (that is, Internet) post-ERP work are electronic commerce, planning and managing your supply chain, and tracking and serving customers. Most ERP vendors have been slow to develop offerings for these areas, and they face stiff competition from niche vendors. ERP vendors have the advantage of a huge installed base of customers and a virtual stranglehold on the "back office" functions – such as order fulfillment. Recently ERP vendors have begun to shrink their ambitions and focus on being the back-office engine that powers electronic commerce, rather than trying to own all the software niches that are necessary for a good electronic commerce Website. Indeed, as the niche vendors make their software easier to hook into electronic commerce Websites, and as middleware vendors make it easier for IS departments to hook together applications from different vendors, many wonder how much longer ERP vendors can claim to be the primary software platform for the Fortune 500.

THE REACH AND RANGE OF ERP SYSTEMS

John Blackburn and Martin Osborn, PricewaterhouseCoopers.

Introduction
An Enterprise Resource Planning system is software that allows a company to automate and integrate its business processes in order to share common data and processes across the enterprise. It streamlines a company's data flows and provides management with direct access to real-time operating information. At its core is a single comprehensive database. The database collects data and supports virtually all of a company's business activities – across functions, across business units and across its world.

This section provides a basic introduction to the process and functional scope of traditional ERP applications and outlines the newer areas of ERP development.

ERP's Process, Nature and Scope
A key feature of ERP software is that it is process-oriented, not task-oriented. It forces standardisation of codes, processes and hierarchy and eliminates cross-system reconciliation. It increases information flow, promotes workflow automation and provides a cohesive internal environment. These processes and data are integrated across modules in one enterprise-wide system (see Figure 1).

Figure 1: The Reach and Range of ERP Systems Across the Business Processes (illustrated from the J D Edwards Suite of Processes). © J.D. Edwards & Company, used by permission.

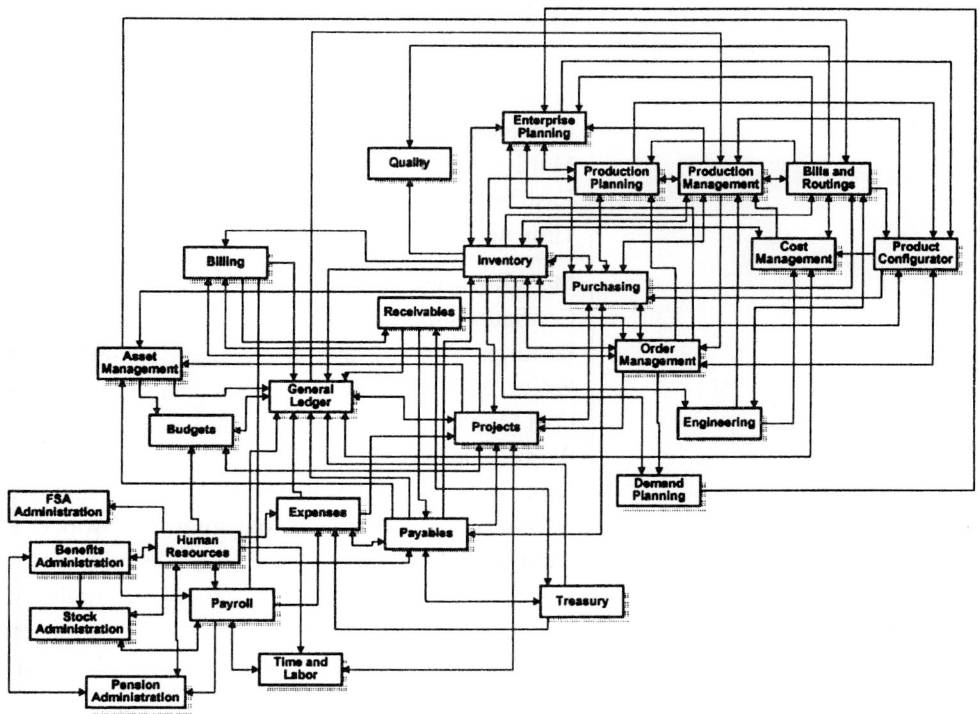

Contemporary ERP systems permit organisations to manage resources across the enterprise and enable the integration of sales management, component procurement, inventory management, manufacturing control, project management, distribution, transportation, finance and other functions.

Traditionally ERP systems have embraced four major processes:

- Finance
- Logistics, sales and marketing
- Manufacturing
- Human resources.

The functional scope of these is illustrated in Table 1.

Finance

Table 1 shows the typical range of applications within a financial module. The applications are designed to meet the core data processing and information needs within the area. They also integrate together and into the manufacturing, logistics, sales and other business processes. When compared to legacy systems, ERP software significantly reduced the cost of financial record keeping by eliminating cumbersome reconciliation processes in areas such as the costs of bill of material items and inventory management transactions.

Table 1: The typical range of applications within a financial model

Financial Suite	**Human Resources Suite**
General Accounting Accounts Payable Accounts Receivable Fixed Assets Financial Modelling & Budgeting Multi-Currency Processing Cash Basis Accounting Time Accounting	Human Resources Maintain personnel data Payroll Time & Labour Recording Pensions Administration Benefits Administration
Manufacturing Suite Configuration Management Routings & Bill of Material Project Management Cost Management Product Data Management Capacity Planning & Scheduling Advanced Maintenance Management Shop Floor Management	**Logistics/Sales and Marketing Suite** Forecasting Requirements Planning Enterprise Facilities Planning Sales Order Management Advanced Pricing Procurement Work Order Management Inventory Management Quality Management Advanced Warehouse Management Transportation Management

The consistency of ERP system data provides improved information for analysis and a seamless reconciliation from the general ledger to sub ledgers. The data is updated in real time throughout the month. With innate ERP integration, a physical transaction cannot be booked without the resulting financial effect being shown. This visibility of activities across finance and operations gives operational managers the ability to better understand the effects of their decisions. With ERP systems the company's financial organisation are better equipped to:

- provide decision support to corporate leadership
- create strategic performance measures
- engage in strategic cost management.

Manufacturing

Typical manufacturing functionality is illustrated in the table above. An integrated ERP system also enables better order-to-production planning by linking sales and distribution to materials management, production planning, and financials. It gives visibility of customer orders and customer demand; and modelling of anticipated orders. The software provides:

- a consistent set of product names across all systems;
- a consistent way of looking at customers and vendors;
- integration of sales, production and purchasing information;
- a way to calculate availability of product for sales, distribution, and materials management.

With ERP, sales opportunities are turned into orders-based stock availability, deliveries and production schedules. Stock is adjusted by sales transactions and detailed manufacturing resource planning can be performed actively. All of this is linked with the financial systems and an enterprise can easily show related financial performance.

ERP also supports companies operating multiple sites around the world. For instance, a company's U.S. sales office may be responsible for marketing, selling and servicing a product assembled in the U.K. but using parts made in Germany and Singapore. ERP enables the company to understand and manage the effect of sales orders placed across the world on the plants in Germany and Singapore.

In addition to improving integration between business units, ERP systems are also improving integration across the supply chain. Many companies have created links from their ERP software to the Internet to provide manufacturing production schedules, inventory levels and other important information to key suppliers in an attempt to make suppliers responsible for monitoring their own inventory levels. This also reduces inventory and shortens the replenishment cycle. The supplier can replenish depleted stock without being notified directly.

Logistics

A well-implemented ERP system can provide tighter integration of functions in the logistics area to support management. It also enables the enterprise to manage multiple sites as a single entity and better co-ordinate cross-site processes. It forces companies to implement a set of proven processes, and benefit from industry-orientated solutions. Also, ERP systems can provide a platform to achieve significant reengineering and process change within logistics.

The table shows the functionality that spreads across the logistics and sales processes. Typically the software provides an integrated basis for managing the data that support distribution and offers:

- picking and packing
- product substitution
- shipping documentation
- simple route planning
- load planning
- purchasing
- materials management.

Each of these processes can be driven from forecasted demand produced using actual order information, or forecasts from historical data or re-order level/re-order point data.

There are many examples of firms using ERP to improve the logistics process. One CPG company introduced streamlined communications with suppliers to help achieve its goal of cutting costs by $1.5bn annually. A leading maker of computer-aided design software took an average of two weeks to deliver an order to a customer. After having installed an ERP system, it now delivers 98% of its orders within 24 hours.

Sales and Marketing

The sales functionality in ERP software is aimed at enhancing an enterprise's sales efforts in a number of ways. At a management level, performing profitability analysis and determining contribution margins by market segment requires real-time data for costs, revenue, and sales volumes. It is also possible to design sophisticated pricing procedures that include numerous prices, discounts, rebates, and tax considerations. Any pricing element can be maintained by many specific criteria, including combinations of customer, customer group, material, material group and sales channel.

Sales organisations are using ERP to project much more accurate delivery dates for orders. The systems can check the company's finished-goods and work-in-process inventories, as well as materials availability to determine how quickly an order can be filled.

A furniture manufacturer created an extranet to provide its retail partners with access to its ERP software via browser-based PCs. The tighter integration, between sales force automation software and ERP, allowed consumers and business customers to configure and order online for the first time.

Human Resources

Human resources modules support human resource planning, development, and compensation areas. It provides an integrated database of personnel (employed or contracted), maintains salary and benefits structures, supports planning and recruiting, and keeps track of reimbursable travel and living expenses. ERP can also complete payroll accounting for a wide variety of individual country requirements and allows a company to centralise or decentralise the payroll function by country or by legal entity.

Typically the HR suite will:

- record individual qualifications and requirements used for resource planning and leading to enhanced career and succession planning;
- co-ordinate training programmes;
- maximise time management, from planning to recording and controlling time and time reporting for cost allocation to specific projects or service orders.

Industry-Based Solutions

As ERP systems have evolved, functionality has been introduced to support the specific needs of vertical industry segments, such as consumer packaged goods, automotive manufacturers, utilities, retail and oil and gas. These industry solutions have included special industry functionality (such as category management which is an essential feature for product life cycle management in the Retail sector).

The example in Figure 2 shows the typical functionality found in an ERP system implemented in the automotive sector. The system supports a full range of processes including those which are unique to the automotive sector.

Figure 2: The Architecture of ERP – An example from SAP™ and the Automotive Industry, edition 2001

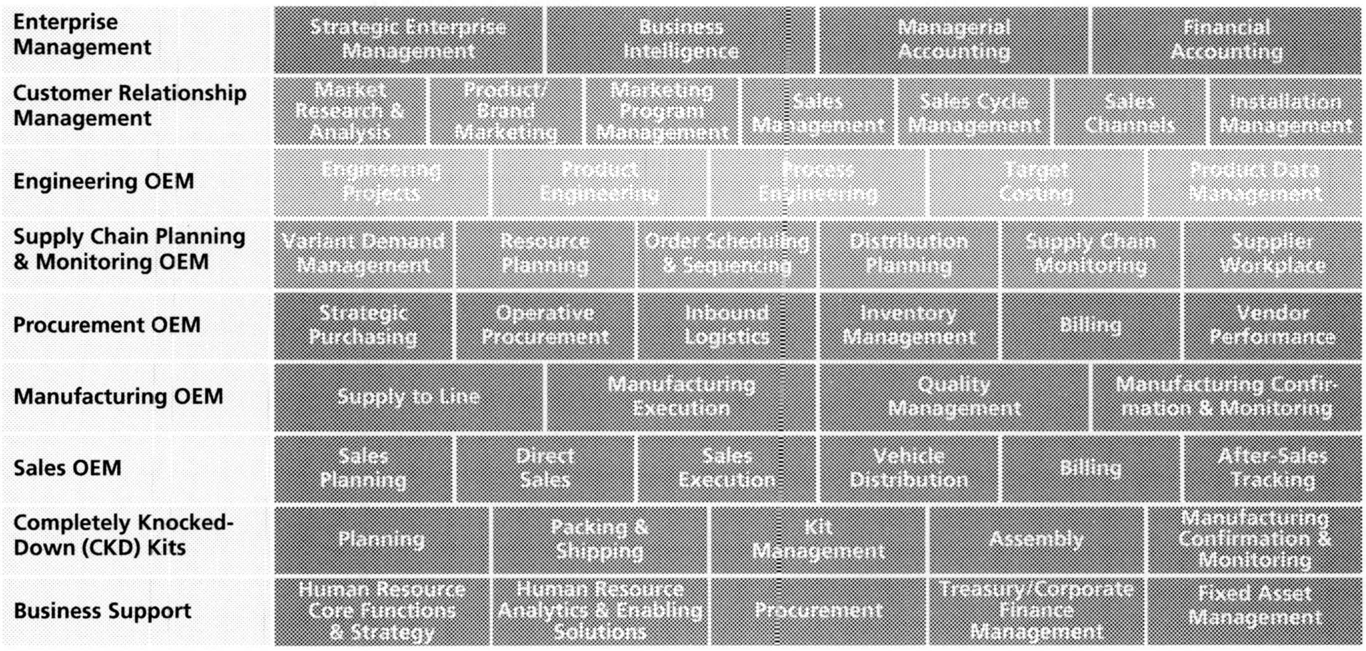

In the addition to the high-level business process functionality ERP vendors also offer solution maps for the detailed processes. These solution maps typically take the form of extensive libraries of standardised business processes fine tuned for specific industry sectors. As Figure 3 illustrates, the level of detail/prescription in these processes is extensive.

The International Nature of ERP

ERP systems are increasingly designed to be multi-site, multi-company and multi-currency systems running over distributed client server environments.

The international nature of products extends to many aspects of the applications, such as the support of multiple, simultaneous currencies (including the Euro) and the automatic handling of country-specific import/export, tax, accounting, legal and language requirements.

Emerging Functionality of ERP

Initially Y2K requirements gave a tremendous boost to ERP sales. The ERP route seemed to be the only viable and cost effective way to bring a portfolio of legacy applications systems to the required standard. Often this gave the added benefit of overcoming known legacy restrictions and improving business processes.

As the year 2000 approached ERP sales declined. Two reasons were suspected:

- fear of the Year 2000 transition meant all non-essential development was halted.
- classic ERP had penetrated into many of the organisations who had the hunger to use ERP systems and the pockets to afford them!

In response ERP vendors started looking for other opportunities. This led to initiatives aimed at meeting the further needs of senior management or of decision support. These initiatives have now been significantly joined by the drive to respond to internet opportunities that link to customers or suppliers.

Figure 3: A solution map

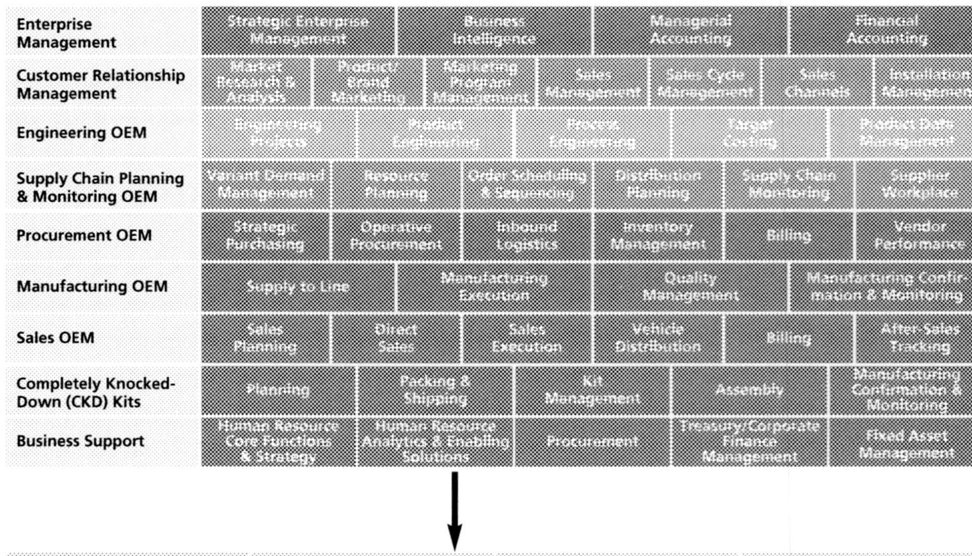

Human Resource Management	Procurement	Treasury	Fixed Asset Management
Payroll Accounting Time & Attendance Compensation & Benefits Administration Personnel Cost Planning Recruitment Personnel Administration Organisational Management Personnel Development & Training Expense & Travel Administration	Vendor Management Contract Management/ Scheduling Agreements Requisition/Purchase Order Management Goods Receipt Invoice Verification Catalogue Management Third Party Integration External Services e-Procurement	Cash Management & Electronic Banking In-house Cash Liquidity Planner Financial Investment & Debt Management Portfolio Analyser Mortgage Loans Foreign Exchange Management Market Risk Analysis & Simulation Credit Risk Analyser & Limit Management Interfaces	Capital Investment Budgets Capital Investment Planning & Analysis Capital Investment Measure Controlling Fixed Asset Inventory Management Simulation Functions Leasing

ERP is now being developed in three directions.

- Supplier facing – to meet the needs of E-Supply Chain (E-SCM)
- Customer facing with Customer Relationship Management (CRM) enhancements
- Management facing to support the requirements for the effective management of enterprises (SEM).

Most major ERP vendors are developing their own solutions in each of these areas but they are also providing functionality through integration with 'best of breed' products in each area. Figure 4 illustrates the evolution in the SAP environment.

Figure 4: Extending the ERP Footprint.

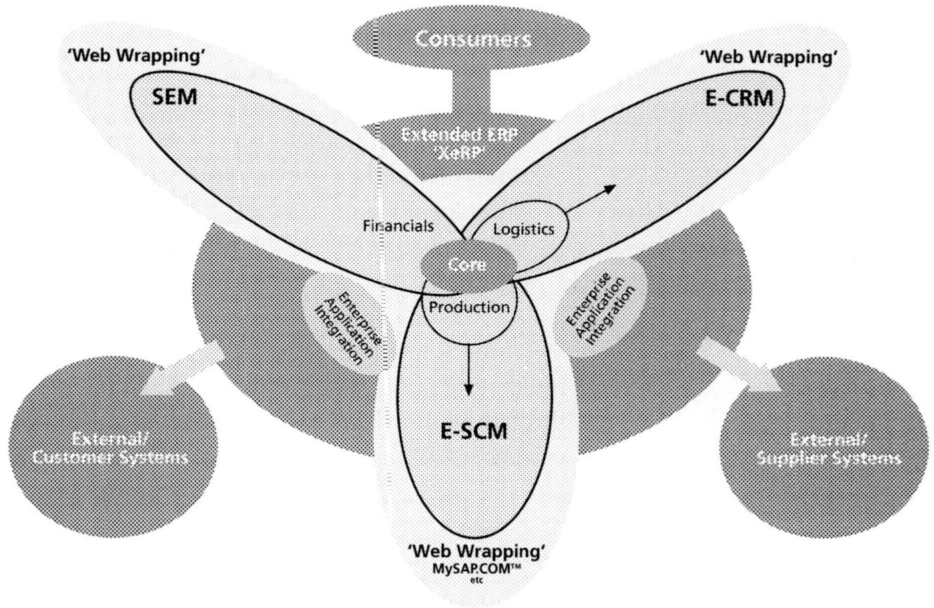

E-Supply Chain

A major area of current investment appears to be in E-supply chain. Electronic supply-chain management (e-SCM) enhances business-to-business processes and improves speed, real-time control, and customer satisfaction. E-SCM is also about cultural change and changes in management policies, performance metrics, business processes, and organisational structures across the supply chain.

The success of an e-supply chain depends on two major factors:

- all companies in the supply chain must view partner collaboration as a strategic requirement and a 'must do' in terms of operational priorities. It is this tight integration and trust among trading partners that generates agility and reduced costs.
- information visibility across the supply chain information is critical and must be managed with strict policies, disciplines and active monitoring.

The e-supply chain consists of six components:

1. Supply-chain replenishment
2. E-procurement
3. Collaborative planning
4. Collaborative product development
5. E-logistics
6. Supply webs.

This area of development also includes the development of functionality to link into E-markets and private exchanges. E-markets usually focus on either a vertical market or on a cross industry basis. They consolidate demand from multiple buyers in order to gain greater purchasing power and speed integration between buyers and sellers. They also can facilitate various types of auctions to sell excess capacity or to buy at more competitive rates. The private exchanges carry out the same functionality but without aggregating the demand with other purchasers.

Customer Relationship Management (CRM)

In addition to looking for opportunities in the area of inbound logistics ERP vendors are also enhancing their core offerings to help companies to:

- Respond to new markets via the internet
- Work with distribution business partners and consumers to reduce costs and cycle times of products, and to provide better order-tracking information
- Build loyalty and some degree of lock-in. Without this a company is vulnerable to losing customers to a competitor with whom the customer finds it easier to do business.

These ERP enhancements are aimed at strengthening customer relationships by integrating sales, product configuration, planning, and design processes with customers through both existing and new channels. The CRM application additions enhance the company's 'front office', focusing on sales, marketing, and customer service. However, in order to be truly successful, CRM must also be seen as a combination of people, processes, and systems, rather than as a narrowly defined IT application. CRM focuses on outward-facing processes, tying them together with the inside-the-enterprise transaction-processing engine of the original ERP systems.

To support these requirements the ERP vendors are integrating both telephone and internet into their core ERP applications. The Internet links allow direct access to order or inquire and can support access to product catalogues, order taking, on-line credit checking and integration to banks and credit card companies. They also have:

- strong security features;
- auto response and auto forwarding of emails;
- the ability to request a telephone contact to discuss content on the web site.

Telephone integration or CTI (Computer Telephone Integration) allows queue management, auto response, fax back, caller identification, changed routing or system processing driven by the number dialed and automatic access to basic customer information.

All the above processing is typical of what is required by businesses and in major call centres. It could be backed up by an integrated customer database pulling all internal information together and merging it with external information.

Data warehouses and data mining tools are being developed to store and analyse more information about the customer, their history and the market place, in order to understand customer needs and reactions and to target services more effectively.

The CRM systems should also support the full range of outbound telephone customer contact required, whether by diary managed calling, response calling, or planned outbound campaigns. They should also integrate with the supporting actions with paper or electronic mail. The systems all integrate into fulfillment and distribution functionality to give quick response.

Modern CRM solutions have significant field or service management capability. Many ERP providers are developing handheld functionality that will allow field operatives or the sales force to handle customer queries and transactions and to automatically link to ERP systems for key information and to process transactions.

All the above functionality is being developed as add-ons to core functionality or by integration with market leading products.

Strategic Enterprise Management (SEM) Enhancements

Traditionally, strategic decisions and policies have not been supported adequately or enforced by the legacy or ERP systems:

- Strategic objectives are not converted into the operational objectives of the business units. They are not understood or optimised at all levels.
- Information is not available to measure performance in a way that is consistent with strategic ways of looking at the organisation.
- Performance measures are not embedded within system logic and need separate manual and retrospective monitoring.

Many ERP vendors are evolving their solutions to support management decision making and provide best practice in support of senior management. The purpose is to focus the system to provide information that encapsulates key management information and assists the manager to make strategy happen. The information should cover the whole value system including the extended organisation, its suppliers, customers and partners.

SEM solutions typically provide an integrated framework to support the following core processes:

- Corporate strategy planning and modelling
- Resource allocation and planning
- Performance management
- Compensation and rewards
- Stakeholder relationship management
- Communication
- Consolidation
- Business information sourcing.

The applications pull together the technologies of data warehouse, decision support, integration into application systems, remote data capture and conversion and analytical analysis, simulation or modeling to support the processes.

They also support techniques such as Value Based Management, Activity Based Costing, Balanced Score Card, Critical Success Factors or Key Performance Indicators.

The Development of Enterprise Portals

The increased use of web browsers and ISPs by the wider population has created the awareness and acceptability of the metaphor of the 'desktop' where each user has their screen 'desktop' applications and data arranged as they desire.

ERP providers have seen this as an opportunity to:

- escape from criticism about the ease of use of their existing user interfaces
- create role specific views of their systems and hide irrelevant detail from the users who don't need it
- reduce high training costs by moving to the more 'intuitive' interfaces
- improve integration between legacy systems
- improve the integration between internal and external systems and data sources.
- hide the variations of screen presentation when using multiple, disparate legacy systems.

This has coincided with realisations that self-service by staff is viable and cost effective and that the portal can be used as a knowledge manager across the enterprise community.

ERP providers are therefore increasingly using portal (or workplace) technology to enable the creation of a personalized workplace or portal on the computer of each user. These portals already contain integration into the ERP provider's systems and supply the toolset to facilitate integration into other systems.

The workplace is role specific and can be further tailored by the user to their own preferences. This customisation can add new information sources and systems or can remove existing items.

In addition the workplace can be customised so that data retrieved from one source can be related into another system simply by 'dragging and dropping' the item into the icon or window for the other system. The workplace can be set up so that it will automatically translate the data from the original source so that it is usable to access the second source. This greatly facilitates ease of use and integration.

In a B2E application (Business to Employee - Self Service) the portal approach can be used to standardise business practices across the full geographic split of the organisation as well as gain efficiencies by self service and improved processes.

This same portal approach is used to create portals available across the external internet to facilitate customer, supplier, investor, analyst or general public self-service capability as appropriate.

Conclusions

ERP solutions attempt to allow a company to integrate its business processes and to establish common data and processes both within and outside the enterprise. They have the potential to streamline a company's data flows and give visibility in order to support and manage the value chain right from cradle to grave.

ERP providers are also providing solutions that meet individual industry's needs and international requirements in order to improve their acceptability & penetration.

ERP is now being developed in three further directions.

- Supplier facing - to meet the needs of E Supply Chain;
- Customer facing with Customer Relationship Management enhancements;
- Management facing to support the requirements for the effective management of enterprises.

There is also a more general development of the user interface to mimic browser desktops and facilitate integration of systems and data both within and outside enterprises. These portals are used to improve the user interface and for wider employee, customer, supplier, investor and general public self-service.

ERP vendors will often meet these immediate market needs by integrating 'best of breed' solution into their products but will eventually develop their own solutions in order to offer greater and easier integration and to maximise the ERP vendor's future business revenues.

Survey – Enterprise Resource Planning: Going live is end of the beginning: Second wave ERP.

Mark Vernon, *Financial Times*, 15th December 1999. Reprinted by permission.

ERP is rather like learning the piano. Every lesson reveals more about how much further you have to go. It is for this reason that many, if not most, organisations with ERP would now consider themselves as embarking upon a second wave of implementation. It may be that the first phase did generate the opportunities expected, and that the company is now able to exploit them further. But the evidence is that for many, the first dabble with ERP has produced ambiguous results at best. What is more likely is that the second wave began with the IT director barking down the phone about the cost of the initial implementation and the effort it took, wondering where the return on investment was to be seen.

The problem runs deep. A recent report from Spikes Cavell for Computasoft Consulting noted that two-thirds of companies have failed to realise the benefits they expected from implementing the leading ERP solution, from SAP. Two thirds of respondents, from a mix of SAP project managers and IT business managers, said that if they had to deliver on return on investment, the challenge facing them was to enhance the flexibility and functionality of SAP and develop a more user-friendly front end. David Duray, partner with global responsibility for the SAP practice at PricewaterhouseCoopers, asks whether these organisations had the right vision to start with. "People openly admit that they did not approach ERP correctly," he says. "Logically, it made sense, but the project fell down because the firm did not have the willpower to see it through."

The situation can be worse than that, at least according to Ray Hobson a managing consultant in the Enterprise Solutions Group at Computer Sciences Corporation. "Quite often, ERP implementations are incomplete and in need of recovery," he says. He notes that much of the second wave work with which his company is involved begins with an assessment of whether or not there is a sufficiently stable ERP system in place on which to move forward or, worse still, whether there is a need for more urgent remedial action.

The point is explored further by Henry Cook, managing consultant, IBM Global Business Intelligence Solutions, Europe, the Middle East and Africa. "ERP helps people do things right, but not to do the right things. ERP packages enable people to bring basic business packages up to a level that defines best practice or lowest common denominator, depending upon who you talk to."

However, the good news is that the marketplace is encouraging innovative vendors seizing the second wave opportunity, and tackling many of the imperatives facing businesses revisiting their ERP investment.

John Hutchinson, senior consultant at IT management consultancy Druid, points to three. "Organisations should examine the barriers to achieving their business goals," he says. "A second area that many companies are now developing is customer relationship processes and performance. The third area of development around ERP is the upstream supply side integration with an organisation's suppliers."

Another second wave type of development is an emerging generation of new ERP applications. PeopleSoft, for example, has coined the phrase Enterprise Performance Management (EPM) to suggest a move beyond traditional ERP. EPM is designed in part to deal with a leading commercial concern, assessing the value of the business for financial markets. These calculations include non-transactional, intangible data to accurately reflect the wide range of variables contributing to corporate success. But perhaps the overriding lesson of the second wave story is that once an ERP system has been installed, no-one can sit back and simply wait for the operational benefits to follow. Maximising return on investment and efficiencies has to be a continuing project. Therefore ERP vendors need to offer additional "after implementation" training services, to ensure that the system is used at its full potential. "In many cases, companies that have installed an ERP solution are not aware of the functionality in all modules of the system," says Richard Bennett, sales and marketing executive at QAD, a US-based ERP and extended supply chain management software vendor. "Second wave ERP fundamentally means better post-implementation customer service from the vendor, the development of strategic relations and an extended supply chain."

CONCLUSION

This chapter examined the evolution and experiences to date with ERP systems. In particular the chapter has highlighted the key role which ERP systems have played in helping corporations respond to the challenges of the global 24 * 7 market space. The chapter has tried to provide insights into the architecture and functionality of ERP and to highlight some of the challenges facing organisations in the coming years in this important area. Unfortunately the chapter has raised as many questions as it has answered. In particular it has highlighted the lessons which we as part of the finance function need to learn if we are to be successful in our attempts to leverage real shareholder value from the investment in ERP systems. These lessons include the following:

- Organisations need to recognise that ERP systems are an established part of the IT/IS infrastructure and will provide the transaction processing backbone for many years to come. In particular, ERP systems will be a key enabling technology in the bid to embrace and exploit the opportunities of e-business;

- The functionality of ERP systems will continue to expand and will embrace such areas as CRM, ABM, SEM and other areas. The future focus of ERP will shift from helping firms do things right to helping firms do the right things;

- The level of investment required to effectively deploy ERP systems will continue to grow. The next five years will see a significant ERP effort in the areas of enterprise application integration arising from e-business initiatives and other changes. The existing ERP infrastructure will also need to be maintained and in some cases renewed. All of this will require a substantial commitment of resources from organisations. Firms which continue to view ERP systems in cost-avoidance terms will find it increasingly hard to justify their ERP investments. As total cost of ownership increases, those instrumental in deploying ERP will have to show a real contribution to shareholder value;

- The finance function will be expected to play a key role in benefits realisation from the ERP investment. CFOs and their support staffs, including management accountants, will be expected to measure and drive out the benefits identified in the original business case for ERP. Accordingly finance will have to move centre stage in leveraging the investment made to date;

- Systems integration issues will continue to consume large amounts of resources. As firms continue to partner, merge and acquire, the requirement to integrate diverse systems across the organisation and its value chain will increase. The emergence of B2B trading hubs and e-business will reopen the systems integration problems which ERP originally set out to solve in the early 1990s;

- The future focus of ERP will be the value chain and in particular ensuring that the firm does not lose opportunities for value creation to other players in the broader supply chain. In this regard ERP systems will play an important role in projecting the firm's market power across the supply chain.

ERP dominated the technological agenda for most of the 1990s. In the coming decade ERP systems will become a key element of the business strategy agenda of many firms. In the twenty-first century, success will come to those firms that enjoy a comparative advantage in information- and knowledge-based processes. ERP systems will be a key element in those processes.

Chapter 2

Successful ERP Implementation

INTRODUCTION

There is overwhelming anecdotal and scientific evidence to suggest that firms have struggled to successfully implement ERP systems. While the promotional material for systems vendors abounds with case studies of successful projects the landscape is littered with ERP projects that drove firms to the brink of bankruptcy. Indeed, as suggested in the introduction to this text, several large global multinational firms abandoned their ERP implementations and incurred significant losses in revenue as a result. Despite this evidence firms continue to embrace ERP projects and roll out multi-site multi-company systems upgrades with alarmingly regularity.

Prior to the introduction of ERP systems, large IS projects were typically functionally based and the resulting changes in processes and operations were by and large confined to the functional stovepipe in which the systems had been implemented. While difficulties inevitably arose they were confined within a single functional area. The second-order effects on other processes and functions were limited. With the advent of ERP systems IS projects became corporate-wide initiatives affecting processes across the supply chain and across business units. As a result the level of co-ordination and the complexity of the implementation grew exponentially. With the exponential growth in the number of sites and functions involved, the opportunities for errors and mishaps grew accordingly.

Since many ERP implementations also brought with them process re-engineering/redesign aspects, implementers were faced with the double challenge of implanting systems while trying to bring about fundamental change in the organisation processes. Changes in systems were occurring alongside changes in structures, value systems and in most cases substantial downsizing. In this climate it was hardly surprising that implementation difficulties arose. In addition as firms absorbed the enormous costs associated with the purchase of licences networks and hardware to support the ERP system, implementation budgets were often overrun. In the pressure to contain costs some firms cut training and change management resourcing and suffered the consequences.

It is difficult to draw cohesive lessons from the last ten years of ERP implementations. In many cases firms themselves were reluctant to discuss the problems they encountered. In other cases the glowing vendor reference sites often disguised a reality of missed deadlines and cost overruns. In this chapter we explore the lessons for firms involved in implementing ERP technologies. While many may feel that these lessons are too little too late the reality is that ERP implementations are never finished and that the process in ongoing. It is clear that ERP implementation is a multidimensional process involving elements of technology, people, systems, processes and organisational development. While a contingency approach is often advocated there appears to be merit in the 'tips and tricks' of those that have undertaken ERP projects before. Experience of and an affinity for change management are key requirements for those managing ERP projects. The evidence to date however seems to suggest that accountants may not be temperamentally well suited to these tasks. In particular the training of many accountants leaves them with an excessively rational perspective of organisational processes and a bias against what they see as the 'touchy feely' approach of the behavioural sciences.

In this chapter we attempt to address some of these shortcomings. In the first section we explore the issue of organisational readiness and ERP systems. In particular we attempt to map out the prerequisites for a successful project launch. This is followed by an in-depth examination of the current best practice approach to ERP rollout. This section reflects the experience of PWC consultants worldwide and is based on their first-hand experiences. The remainder of the chapter explores some more specific aspects of implementation including vendor selection, post-implementation issues and the main causes of project failure.

IS YOUR ORGANIZATION READY FOR ENTERPRISE RESOURCE MANAGEMENT?
Keith J. Launchbury and Carol A. Ptak, *APICS Magazine,* June 1998, Volume 8, No. 6

Buying a piece of ERP software does not ensure success for the business. As with all tools that have evolved before the advent of ERP, the focus is on planning; but the reality is that planning is only one piece of managing the business. Many companies have embarked on major projects to implement ERP systems with very little to show in the way of actual results. We believe that the reason many of these companies have failed to realize the full benefits of enterprise resource planning is because most organizations are not organized in such a way as to benefit from the new information tools provided by ERP systems. Many of the companies attempting implementation of enterprise-wide systems have run into difficulty because the organization is not positioned for integration. Departments work to their own sets of objectives. Measurements are functional not global. People are specialists not generalists. Information is spread out on many systems and platforms. Systems are often fragmented, and there are very few people who have an enterprise-wide view of the organization.

Enterprise resource planning is only part of the challenge facing most organizations today. It is not good enough to just plan the resources required to run the enterprise. These resources need to actually be managed as well. Enterprise resource management (ERM) more accurately describes all planning, control and management functions required to effectively operate the enterprise.

The organizational assessment checklist provides a simple and practical reference to determine if your company is ready for the competitive business environment of today and positioned for tomorrow by assessing your organizational readiness for enterprise resource management.

Checklist

- *Have you transitioned from internally-focused performance measurements to customer-focused performance measurement systems?*
  Customers care only about how their needs are serviced. They care little about the supplier's internal efficiencies and utilization. When a company clearly understands the needs of the customer and aligns its business processes to meet those needs, it enjoys a market advantage against the competition.

- *Have you flattened the organizational hierarchy?*
  An organization with many levels of personnel reduces the speed of communication and the agility of the organization. A flattened organization has nimble communications and can respond more quickly to the needs of the customer.

- *Have you fully educated your personnel in enterprise-wide thinking?*
  Only personnel that understand what the organization is attempting to achieve and why can begin to implement those customer-focused ideas and processes. Silo-based organizational myopia must be replaced with an enterprise-wide focus. Departments are not in competition with each other, but rather must collaborate with an integrated customer focus.

- *Have you successfully moved to a team-based organization?*
  Teams with a clear vision and mission consistently outperform individual efforts. The creativity of a high-performing team can successfully move the organization to significantly higher levels of performance.

- *Have you reengineered your major business processes and eliminated all waste?*
  Waste is any non-value-added activity upon which the organization expends resources. These critical resources can yield consistently higher profits for the organization when they are focused on the desired results only.

- *Have you moved from traditional costing methods to value-added costing?*
  Traditional costing methods spread overhead on direct labor hours. This has caused many organizations to make purchases at the lowest cost, thereby encouraging overseas procurement while at the same time decreasing in-house production. Overall costs rise in accordance with increased inventory and real profits decline. There is no direct cause and effect between overhead charges and direct labor cost. Value-added costing includes only those direct revenues and costs when considering product line costing. Only those costs that would go away are considered when costing a product. More realistic profit contribution information is available using value-added costing.

- *Have you adopted the principles of integrated supply chain management?*
  The information about the available supply and desired demand must be shared from your customer's customer to your supplier's supplier. These principles of integrated supply chain management provide a seamless integration of supply and demand and provide the ability for the company to deliver products that uniquely meet the needs of the market.

- *Have you implemented completely reliable information networks and communication systems (software, hardware and human systems)?*
  The information systems of a company, including software, hardware and human systems, must be completely reliable for the information to be trusted by everyone using it. Sophisticated modern computer tools still require the basic building blocks of information to be accurate for the tool to be effective.

- *Have you changed your evaluation and appraisal systems to recognize both team and individual performance?*
  This is probably one of the most difficult areas in the checklist. Keep in mind that how people are measured will determine how they will behave. Since personnel are expected to function both as part of a team and also as individuals, measurement systems must be changed to measure and reward desired team behaviours.

- *Have you become a customer-focused organization?*
  A key competitive strategy is to focus on the needs, wants and desires of the customer. How well does your organization understand what your customer really wants? How well is your organization aligned to serve these?

- *Have you developed and implemented procedures that ensure standardization of information in all business operations?*
  Only when a process is standardized can it be reliably depended upon and improved. This includes all purchasing, production or distribution processes, together with the delivery of information, products and services.

- *Are your business leaders committed to the principle of lifelong learning?*
  The half-life of education has been reduced to three to five years, and the rate of change is accelerating. New tools and techniques are being developed on a daily basis, so the need for lifelong learning has never been greater.

- *Have you replaced organizational silos with process teams?*
  Cross-functional teams can begin to understand the sources and uses of information and to work across departmental barriers. Process teams require vision and collaboration rather than competition.

- *Have you adopted a single company compensation program?*
  Multiple company compensation programs can cause a great deal of dissatisfaction. Is your compensation program well understood with clear expectations of how increases in pay can be earned? Compensation systems must be perceived to be fair and equitable by all concerned.

- *Have you benchmarked your organizational performance with best-in-class practices by global leaders?*
  Not only must your company improve on what it has always done, but also it must do better than the competition. Only through benchmarking practices with best-in-class companies can you begin to understand what is required for your business to move ahead of the competition.

- *Can you demonstrate total company-wide process capability performance of six sigma or better?*
  Six-sigma quality in all processes virtually guarantees that quality failures statistically cannot happen. Are your business and production processes that reliable?

- *Have you developed business policies and procedures to ensure complete data integrity?*
  Every sophisticated computer system has the same requirement: accurate information input. When the quantities on hand, bills of material, routings, schedules and other inputs are accurate, then the outputs are reliable.

- *Have you prepared your people to operate in a paperless environment?*
  The evolution of sophisticated computers will eliminate the need for paper. Are your people and their management ready for such a drastic change in how they do business?

- *Have you become a truly global organization?*
  Many companies talk about market share in local market terms. In today's business world, you need to get your products to global markets. Your competition is certainly targeting your traditional marketplace. Are you prepared to compete in the global market?

- *Have you adopted an organizational culture with shared vision, values and goals?*
  Shared vision, values and goals enable an organization to nimbly respond to the needs of the market. This culture provides the empowerment needed to quickly adapt to the changing environment.

- *Have you driven out fear?*
  Only when company personnel can take risks without fear of failure can the company move to new levels of performance. Fear is a great limiter of creativity. Empowerment truly occurs when people know that they will be supported when they take ownership of the business processes.

- *Have you developed a truly flexible work force and process capability?*
  Each person in the organization must be truly flexible and focused on constantly improving the process. Are your personnel flexible enough to meet changing requirements and information? Have they been encouraged to develop and use multiple skills?

- *Have you educated all your business leaders in integrated resource management?*
  This includes the integration of sales and marketing management, materials management, human resource management, financial management and production management.

- *Do you have a formal process for identifying and resolving process constraints?*
  Process constraints are those things that limit the ability of the company to increase its output. These can be physical constraints or procedural constraints. Are your personnel trained in how to recognize and resolve these constraints? This is a major key to improved profitability.

- *Have you institutionalized the process of continuous and rapid operational improvement?*
  With the rapid, continual changes faced by companies today, internal processes must also be improved in a rapid and continual manner. Having this process institutionalized in an organization enhances the overall competitive position for the company.

THE ABCs OF ERP IMPLEMENTATION

John Blackburn and Martin Osborn, PricewaterhouseCoopers.

Introduction

Successful implementation of an ERP system requires a well-designed and executed implementation process. In particular it requires a process which is sympathetic to the unique needs of the project and organisation and which leads to a full use of the power of the 'best practice' processes implicit in ERP systems. While no two implementations will be the same, we can identify a number of well-defined phases or steps in the process. In this section we explore the nature of a basic implementation process and provide an insight into both the work to be carried out and the expected deliverables, in each phase. In addition, we discuss roles and skills required around a typical implementation project.

Why follow a method?

The benefits of following a 'tried and tested' method far outweigh the challenges of applying the method intelligently to the particular project or organisation. Using a known method means that:

- The project should start and proceed more quickly since time is spent trying to understand how to apply the method and not designing the method. The team does not need to spend time working out what each deliverable should look like. The deliverables should be in a form that senior managers and key users have been able to use effectively in other situations.
- Information that is required in the project can be collected in an ordered and meaningful way. The early stages of the project should not be delayed collecting too much information. The later stages should not be delayed because required information is not available.
- The team can look at the project from a business viewpoint and focus effort on those areas that offer high payoff. Projects never have enough time to meet every perceived requirement. It is important that the method gives a process that allows prioritisation.
- The lessons from each completed project facilitate learning by management and workers. Each new project should be more effective and efficient because it is using a method that is known and evolving within the organisation.
- Decisions are made in a structured way. At each stage management should be given the 'best available' view of the scope, costs and time to complete the project. This can minimise the exposure of an organisation and delay heavy cost commitment until a fuller picture is available.

Process Overview

The diagram below illustrates the main building blocks in a basic implementation process.

Figure 1 Seven Steps to ERP Implementation

Each phase of this process is discussed in detail below.

Evaluation

Before embarking on an expensive and time consuming process, organisations need to clearly understand the effort involved in migrating to an ERP system and the expected benefits. In particular it is important that the senior executives in the firm are aware of, and have signed off, the scope and size of the project, the benefits that they require and the associated risks.

In the evaluation phase we determine and document the proposed business objectives of the project and how these objectives might be achieved. If there are a number of ways of realising the objectives an overview option analysis may be completed. This phase could also review how the key options align with current business strategies and initiatives.

This phase should include an overview analysis of:

- the gap between the current situation and the proposed ERP solution,
- the risks associated with the project,
- initial project plans and
- an overview migration strategy documenting how to change from the existing to the new systems.

The project must also outline the process that is required to measure and realise the desired benefits. The potential impact of the new ERP system on current organisation, processes, resources and skill should also be reviewed and major requirements and issues documented.

An outline business case is developed including costs, benefits and implementation plan. The purpose is to demonstrate the feasibility of the project, the options that can be evaluated at this stage and to obtain management sign-off for the scope of the project, what it will achieve and the business case.

0 Evaluation Phase
Objective:
Establish the basic scope and business case for the project
Work Packages
Initiate Study Assess Current Situation Analyse Proposed Project Scope Document Alignment with Business Strategy Plan Project Create Business Case Plan Benefits Realization Process
Key Deliverables
Outline Scope Document Fit/Gap Analysis Current Technical Architecture Baseline Project Risk & Mitigation Strategy Business Case Change Management Scope Initial Project Plans & Required Team Structure

Project preparation

Once the initial decision to proceed with the project has been taken, attention turns to preparing in detail for the project.

In the project preparation phase the first phases of the overall project schedule are reviewed in more detail and a detailed work-plan produced covering the Preparation and the Blueprint phases.

Tools, standards, procedures and the project organisation are established and resources obtained. The resources are given initial training. The training should cover:

- overview ERP knowledge;
- general project procedures and tools; and
- training in the project processes and skills for the Blueprint phase.

The initial project hardware and software should be sized and ordered.

Towards the end of every phase within the process it is recommended that some form of quality check be completed. This could use people who are familiar with the:

- business; or
- the ERP system in similar projects; or
- the project method.

This check is required in order to highlight issues that need to be addressed before sign off or during the next phases of work.

In this phase it is essential to get a balance between allowing sufficient time to plan and prepare properly and the pressure to make progress with the analysis. This phase lays the foundation for the way the project team will work together and fills out the focus and priorities for the project. It is important to get this right without losing momentum from the project by spending too much time planning and designing project processes. Other critical processes started at this stage are:

- the formation of an effective steering group to control the scope and priorities of the project and to ensure total business commitment.
- the presentation of Project Charter and approval by the steering group
- the full project team kick-off is carried out. This kick off should involve representatives from all areas of the organisation impacted by the project and should communicate the project organisation, what the project will achieve and the impact of the ERP system on the business.
- the mobilisation of a wider communication processes to win co-operation and understanding from the business and ease the process of change. This should be accompanied by effective communication to all stakeholders or people who may be affected or inquisitive about the project.

1 Project Preparation Phase
Objective:
Perform detailed project planning & establish the project processes and team.
Work Packages
Complete Initial Project Planning Produce Project Procedures Plan Technical Requirements Kick Off Project Check Quality
Key Deliverables
Project Charter including Project Scope Document Detailed Project Plan Project Management Standards and Procedure Project Team Training Project Strategies - Examples include: • Communications Strategy • Knowledge Transfer Strategy Procured Hardware

Business blueprint

Once there is both a detailed plan for the Blueprint Phase and an adequately staffed and trained project team, the Blueprint Phase can start. This purpose of this phase is to produce the 'blueprint' design that meets the business objectives so that the full volume of work is known and it can be signed-off by the Steering Group.

The starting point will typically involve running short, sharp high level workshops that analyse and define the more detailed requirements to meet the business needs in each area. These workshops may use a demonstration version of the ERP system in order to illustrate requirements and potential ways of working. The use of the ERP demo may be very material in giving people a good view of the future and in creating a more detailed gap analysis when comparing ERP capability with what is required. Each gap represents an area which requires either a change to existing processes or some custom development or a manual procedure. The starting point should be to try to eliminate gaps by investigating whether they are real gaps or just traditional ways of working that could be eliminated.

Detailed documentation of the future business processes is obtained through workshops and desk work and is used to create the business blueprint documentation for review and sign off. The definition of processes should also consider the business controls and security requirements in order to ensure future processes are secure and remain acceptable to auditors.

Alongside the documentation of processes, project team training in ERP usage and project processes is continued and the development systems environment is installed.

Both the business and ERP support organisation structures are defined and future organisation and facilities designed. The required changes in terms of resources, skill sets and working policies and practices are defined and a detailed change management plan developed.

The Technical Design is also completed in order to define the technical architecture that is required to support the future systems needs. This will also show how:

- the ERP systems will integrate with existing systems;
- existing system data will migrate from the old to the new systems;
- daily working will transition to the new system at the time of implementation.

2 Business Blueprint Phase
Objective:
Create a detailed description of the required business processes, required development work and update the business case.
Work Packages Produce Updated Project Plans Revise Project Procedures (as needed) Complete Project Team Training (for this phase) Define Business Organisation Structure Define Business Processes Develop System Environment Check Quality
Key Deliverables
Business Blueprint Documentation Business Process Master List Process Definition Documents Organisation Impact Plan System Administration Procedures Business Controls Document Global Parameters & Standards

Realisation

The realisation phase of the implementation typically involves transforming the documented business processes and design from the previous phase into a working system and producing full plans for the cut-over and implementation to the ERP system.

The ERP system is typically configured (built) in two major cycles, Baseline and Final. The objective of the baseline cycle is to build quickly a core working system or proof of concept. This allows the users and core team to see how the system might perform and fit with their designed business processes. The final cycle should fill out the core system to meet the full business requirement and includes the interfaces or integration to existing systems. Most major reports, data conversion programmes and interfaces will be developed and tested in this phase and be made ready for the final integration test.

In parallel with this work, user orientated procedures would be written that tell the users how each business process would be completed at a transaction level. These procedures should be used as an outline for testing and within the user training. Similarly system management procedures can be developed and tested.

3 Realisation Phase
Objective:
To transform the requirements defined in the Blueprint into an approved working system and to build a full implementation plan
Work Packages
Update Project Plans Revise Project Procedures (as needed) Train Project Team (for this phase) Complete Baseline Configuration Complete Final Configuration Develop Reports, Interfaces, Data Conversion Programs & ERP extensions Define System Management Processes Design & Develop End User Documentation Establish Authorisation Profiles Complete Final System Integration Test Plan detailed cut-over Check Quality
Key Deliverables
Cut-over and Production Support Plan Data Conversion Plan Developed User Authorisations Business Process Procedure Documentation Training Schedule and Documentation Tested Baseline & Final Configuration Production ready environment

During this phase User Authorisations are developed. These profiles define who can do what on the system and ensure that audit and control requirements can be met. These will also be tested during the other testing that is completed in this phase.

Training materials are developed and tested. Final Systems Integration Test and a focused volume test on key transactions are also carried out. These activities lead to the creation of the Production Ready Environment. In arriving at a production ready environment significant resources will have been devoted to such issues as data conversion, quality assurance and security.

Final preparation

The dominant features of phase 4 are end-user training and data conversion. The production system administration and help desk are established. Cut-over and production support plans are refined ready for go-live. These should include a contingency plan in case any element of the cut-over plans fails. Phase 4 ends with the cut-over of the system to the production environment and final approval to go-live. The cut-over usually includes a significant data loading and conversion exercise.

4 Final Preparation Phase
Objective:
Complete preparation of the production SAP system, including end user training, system management, and cut-over activities
Work Packages
Update Detailed Project Planning Establish System Management Complete End User Training Cut Over to the production Environment Check Quality
Key Deliverables
Contingency Plan End User Training Help Desk Procedures Technical System Tests Production System Report Conversion Checklist Approval to Go Live

Go-live and Support

In this phase the business transitions from the existing systems to a live and stable operation on the new system. The phase may involve the rollout of the new ERP system to multiple sites and the rollout may occur over many months. This may be essential because of the business risk of rolling out to all locations at once. In addition the roll out may need to be slowed down in order to reach stability on each site before rolling out further.

By the end of this phase the different business process owners in each location should have taken ownership of the new system.

The project can then be closed, with a review of lessons learned and hand over of all documentation to the people who will manage the system in the future.

5 Go Live and Support Phase
Objective:
Transition from a pre-production environment to a stable, productive operation
Work Packages
Handover to Production Support Complete Project Review Close Project
Key Deliverables
Training Effectiveness Report Sustainment Plan Project Closure Document

Sustain

While the go live phase effectively means the end of the project the real task of leveraging the benefits of the ERP system often begins at the hand-over. In this phase post go-live activities such as:

- Review training effectiveness. Do the users understand the system adequately? Are the business procedures working? What mistakes are being made?
- Develop long-term enhancement plans. What further process improvements are required? What needs could not be addressed in the project?
- Complete Post Implementation Review. How effective is the system? Have the business benefits been met?
- Complete systems tuning and upgrade.
- Monitor the growth of data files and complete archiving as needed.
- Operate system.

6 Sustain Phase
Objective:
Ensure that there is a framework in place to sustain and improve the performance of the system after go-live
Work Packages
Complete Post Implementation Review Complete System Tuning Upgrade the system as required Archive data as necessary Operate System Complete Post Go-Live Activities
Key Deliverables
Post Implementation Review Report Executive Blueprint for enhancements Performance Improvement Action Plans Benefits Realization Plan

Skill and Resource Requirements

Many different skill sets need to be brought together to deliver the project. The activities associated with each main skill set can be linked together as project 'themes'. These themes run across all seven project phases and represent the different areas of work specialism needed to produce a complete, integrated solution.

The themes or skill sets include:

- Project Management
- Business Process
- Systems Development
- Technical Infrastructure
- Risk Management
- Change Management
- Benefits Realisation
- End User Education.

Providing a reasonable approach to project estimating has been taken, allocating themes to tasks or activities within each phase allows management to assign the correct volume and type of skills and to build a balanced team. The typical team roles are outlined below.

Title	Role and Contribution
Executive Steering Group	Corporate governance of the programme on behalf of the business. Responsible for the scope and delivery of the programme including business case & benefits. Main programme business champions. Meet monthly or at major programme milestones.
Programme Manager	Full-time experienced programme management responsible for programme mobilisation, monitoring and delivery. Ensures issues are being resolved effectively by Process Owners, management or team. Escalates to programme exec steering group as needed.
Integration Architect	Skilled ERP designer with excellent experience across modules to be implemented. Responsible for the technical design and its performance. Must ensure that decisions in each area are the best compromise to meet the needs of the total system.
Project Office	Completes all project administration on behalf of the programme manager including progress monitoring and reporting, issue monitoring, change control administration, meetings booking and secretariat, project library, document management & version control.
Change Management	Responsible for communication, education and training, organisational design, HR and reward policy and benefits realisation.
Business Process Teams	Joint team including process owners, process experts from the business, ERP process experts and ERP configurers. They may also include external process experts such as supply chain consultants. Responsible for designing the business process, organisation and system to meet the business needs and business case.
Business Process Owner	An authority in business process and policy in a particular area. Responsible for the sign off of the business requirements and evolving solution on behalf of the business. Responsible for issue resolution in the business area or escalation of issue to the steering group.
Business User Team Members	Responsible for the detailed design and implementation of the business process, organisation and system to meet the business needs and business case. They may assist training and data conversion and supply support to users when the system goes live.
Cross Application Teams	These teams include reporting requirements, security & business controls and testing.
Technical Teams	This includes infrastructure design & implementation, custom development, workflow, middleware and technical support.
Super users	These provide additional business support to the project in order to complete testing, training, data conversion and go-live support. They also become a skilled system user in the defined process area to assist organisational learning during the first periods of live use.

Conclusions

This article has provided an overview of a basic approach to implementing ERP systems. It also outlines a project organisation structure that could be used to run a typical ERP implementation.

The use of a known methodology can speed project start up and progress and can ensure that all vital data is acquired in a methodical and timely way. It should help the team focus on big payoff areas and facilitate learning by management and workers. It should reduce risk by giving the 'best available' view of the scope, costs and time to complete the project at each stage. This can minimise the exposure of an organisation and delay heavy cost commitments until the fullest picture is available.

ERP ADOPTION BY EUROPEAN MIDSIZE COMPANIES

Yvonne van Everdingen, Jos van Hillegersberg and Eric Waarts

***Communications of the ACM,* April 2000, Volume 43, No. 4.**

Until recently, the major ERP vendors (SAP, Oracle, Peoplesoft, JD Edwards and Baan) were mainly targeting the high end of the market (companies with more than 1,000 employees), but this market comes close to saturation. Many large companies have already adopted ERP systems and are planning the next step of how to use the installed ERP infrastructures as foundations for e-business [1, 2]. Most of the small and medium-sized companies still have to make the decision to deploy ERP. The midsize market is an interesting market for example, the number of midsize companies (50–1,000 employees) in Europe is estimated to exceed 100,000. Data from our research shows that with average annual IT budgets of more than $500,000, the total European midsize market for IT products and services surpasses a staggering $50 billion per year. This market as a whole is very attractive for the major ERP vendors. However, since the wave of adoption by midsize companies is in its early stages, little is known about developments and drivers that form the basis of ERP adoption decisions. The purpose of this article is to understand developments in ERP adoption within the European mid-market.

The empirical information in this section is based on a large-scale European multi-country/multi-industry survey conducted in mid-1998. Based on the survey data, it addresses a number of issues, such as: How did ERP penetration in the mid-market develop until 1998 and what can be expected in 2000? Furthermore, we explore criteria used by European midsize companies for investing in ERP systems and for choosing an ERP supplier.

ERP penetration development

The survey included questions both on current (mid-1998) adoption of ERP and planned adoption within two years (mid-2000). In 1998 – over all countries and industries – already 27 per cent of the European midsize companies had ERP software installed in one or more functional areas. The functional areas included in the interview were purchase and sales order management, inventory and materials management, production and assembly, transportation, service and maintenance, marketing and sales, warehouse management, financial accounting, and human resource management. Interestingly, a minority (13 per cent) of the adopters used ERP software in just one functional area, while most companies (70 per cent) used it in more than three functional areas. Thus, companies clearly aim at using ERP's main strength: integrating several functional areas. The data further reveals that in nearly all companies, the various functional areas are automated using ERP software of a single vendor. Hence, difficulties in integrating ERP software from different vendors often seen in large companies are not yet an issue for midsize companies. This may change, as midsize companies will increasingly integrate their supply chains, and thus communicate with suppliers that are likely to have adopted different ERP solutions.

With respect to expected further penetration of ERP software our estimations are based on investment indications by the respondents. Among the firms that did not have ERP software installed in 1998, about 40 per cent indicated intention to invest in ERP before mid-2000, yielding an expected average penetration level of 56 per cent over all countries and industries. If we consider average market prices for ERP software, the total European ERP mid-market can be roughly estimated to exceed $5 billion per year for 1999 and 2000. It must be borne in mind that investment intentions are not necessarily equal to actual behavior, but one may cautiously estimate that during this year, a majority of all European midsize companies will embrace ERP.

We've shown average penetration percentages across all countries and industries. However, the data also reveals some interesting differences between European countries and industries. Figure 1 shows the penetration developments for each country.

Figure 1: Penetration development across countries (n = 2647)

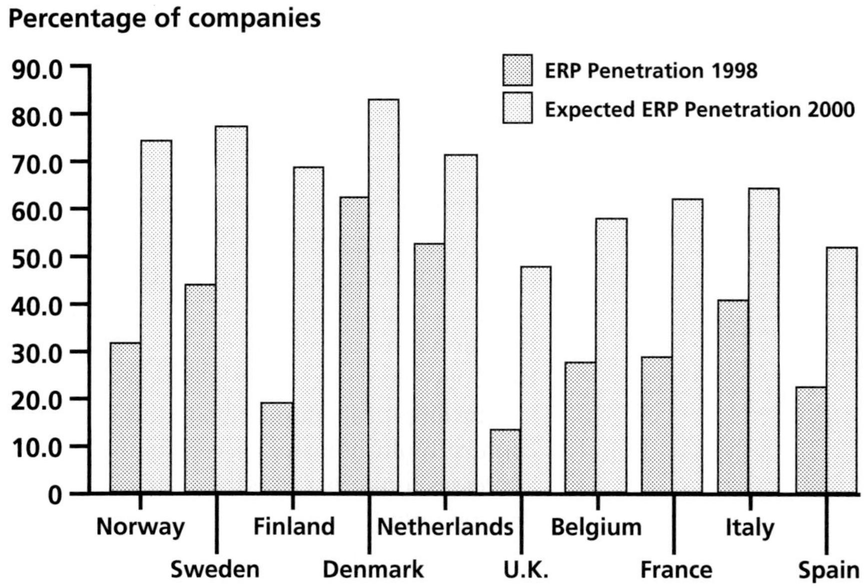

In 1998, Sweden, Denmark, and The Netherlands were far ahead with penetration rates of 45 per cent and higher, while U.K. and Spain were lagging behind with penetration rates less than 20 per cent. The data also shows the penetration of ERP software is expected to grow, especially in countries that showed low 1998 adoption figures. Nevertheless, the expected penetration rates in 2000 still are especially high in the Northern European countries: Norway, Finland, Sweden, Denmark, and The Netherlands. This is an interesting phenomenon, which may be related to certain cultural factors. Cross-cultural research by Hofstede reveals four dimensions of cultural characteristics of a country that can be used to group European countries into three clusters [3, 5]. One of these clusters includes the four Scandinavian countries and The Netherlands, which are characterized as having a low level of uncertainty avoidance, a high level of individualism, a small power distance, and a low level of masculinity. This cluster is recognized as the most innovative cluster with relatively weak resistance to new products and a strong desire for novelty and variety. There is no solid proof of a causal relationship here, but these general cultural characteristics of the Scandinavian countries and The Netherlands may have led to a higher level of ERP trial and adoption. The relatively low ERP penetration in Great Britain could similarly be explained by the fact that Great Britain (together with, among others, Ireland), belongs to a cluster that is described as a fairly risk-averse market. This indicates companies from these countries tend to wait to adopt a new product until a large group of other companies has already adopted it.

Figure 2: Penetration development across industries (n = 2647)

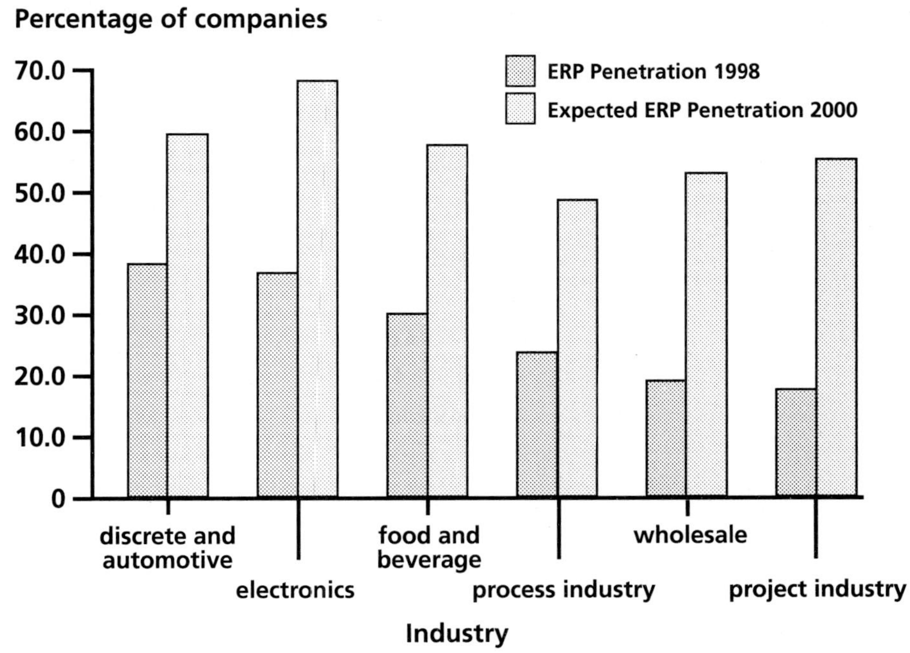

In addition to country differences, the data shows different penetration rates between industries in 1998 (see Figure 2). They run from about 20 per cent in the Project industry and the Wholesale industry up to nearly 40 per cent in Discrete and Automotive. The fact that ERP has its roots in manufacturing is likely to explain these differences. Expected penetration levels for 2000 show, however, that the former industries will make up arrears since many firms in these sectors are planning to implement ERP in the near future. Interestingly, Electronics is expected to become the leader in ERP implementations, with an adoption percentage of nearly 70 per cent.

Information systems selection criteria

When companies consider buying a new product, the perceived characteristics of the product play an important role in the final decision to start using that new product [6]. Thus the characteristics of the ERP software have to match the criteria used by companies to select an information system. In the survey, respondents were asked to indicate the three most important criteria for selecting their current information system (lowest cost, user-friendliness, fit with business procedures, scalability, support, and training). The results show the most important criterion used in selecting an information system is the best fit with current business procedures (see Figure 3).

Figure 3: Criteria for information systems selection (n = 2401)

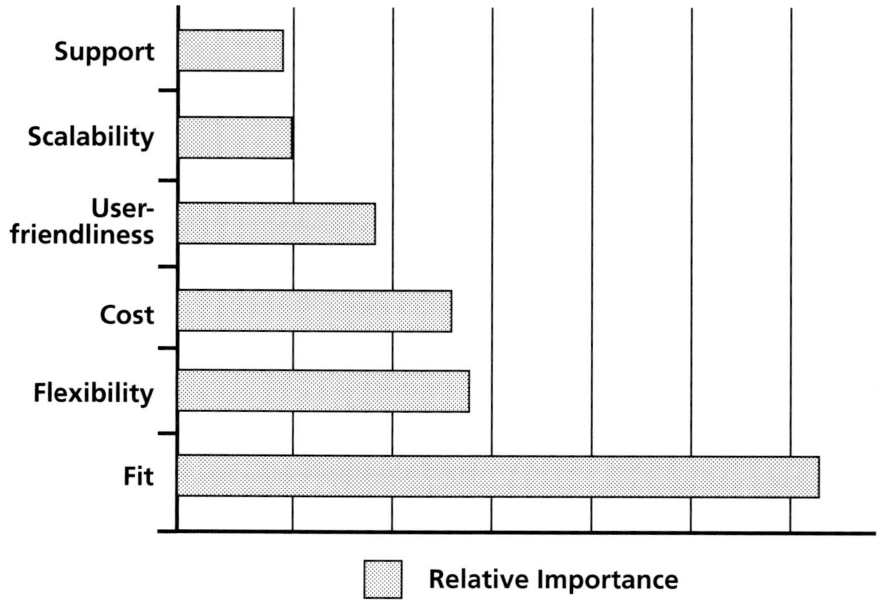

About one-half of the respondents have mentioned the best fit in the top three criteria ranking, while more than one-third mentioned it as the single most important one. Hence, compatibility with the business procedures is the major issue for companies to decide on a new system. Although ERP vendors have given much attention to allow easy configuration of their packages to match existing business processes, several studies have shown that configuring and implementing ERP systems can be costly, and may even require reengineering entire business operations [4] (see also other articles in this special section, for example [7]). Given the large potential of the midsize market and the limited budgets of midsize companies, there is much potential for an ERP package that succeeds in meeting this main selection criterion. Other important selection criteria are flexibility, cost and user-friendliness of the system, and to a lesser extent scalability and supplier support. The importance of criteria is very similar across all industries, but some differences between countries were found. For example, Italian and Swedish companies focus relatively more on user-friendliness, while Spanish companies score the highest on flexibility. Companies from The Netherlands judge the total cost of implementing an information system as important as the fit with current business procedures.

ERP supplier selection criteria

In addition to criteria to select a new system, other criteria may be used to select the supplier of a new information system. The data shows that European midsize companies tend to focus on product characteristics rather than on characteristics of the ERP supplier of the product. It makes little difference whether the vendor is a market leader, an international oriented company, or a company with a superior corporate image.

Companies predominantly look at the functionality and quality of the products and services for evaluating ERP suppliers, which has been found across all lines of business and all countries (see Figure 4). To a somewhat lesser extent, the speed of implementation, the possibilities of the product for interfacing with other applications, and the price of products and services also are important supplier selection criteria.

Figure 4: Criteria for supplier selection (n = 2623)

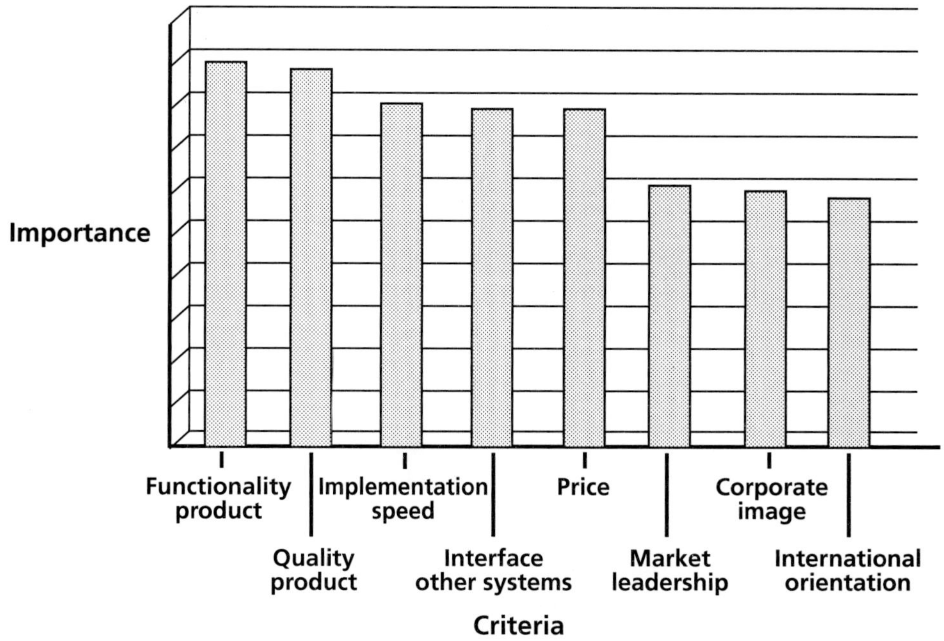

Supplier selection brings us to the final issue in this article, regarding the market positions of the various ERP suppliers. The data provides information about the awareness of the various ERP vendors among the midsize companies in Europe (circa mid-1998), their share of the market, and their nomination as preferred supplier for future investment. It should be noted, however, that since the time of the survey market positions may have changed substantially due to various circumstances. For instance, Baan has had significant negative publicity over the past two years, which may enhance the company's awareness level, but also may have worsened their position as preferred future supplier.

At the time of the survey, the penetration of the five major ERP vendors (SAP™, Oracle, Peoplesoft, JD Edwards, and Baan) in the European midsize market was rather modest. Obviously, the penetration of ERP at that time was in its early stages. About half of companies still preferred their in-house developed, tailor-made information systems to the standardized systems of the large ERP vendors. Among the adopters of ERP, the combined market share of the big five vendors was slightly more than 20 per cent. Regarding specific vendors, SAP had both the highest awareness (that is, it was the most often spontaneously mentioned supplier by respondents) and highest share in the European mid-size market. Roughly 11 per cent of the companies had SAP installed. The European-based ERP vendors (SAP, Germany; Baan, The Netherlands) clearly had a higher level of awareness among the European companies than U.S.-based ERP vendors. SAP and Baan were mentioned spontaneously by 60 per cent respectively 50 per cent of the companies, followed by JD Edwards (33 per cent), and Oracle (28 per cent). Peoplesoft was hardly known in 1998 and had a negligible share of the market.

Based on the respondents' indications concerning preferred suppliers for future investment in ERP systems (see Figure 5), it can be expected that the combined share of the big five vendors will sharply increase to over 60 per cent. SAP is expected to be the most preferred ERP supplier among the European midsize companies; Oracle is expected to strengthen its position.

Figure 5: First considered future ERP supplier (n = 1574)

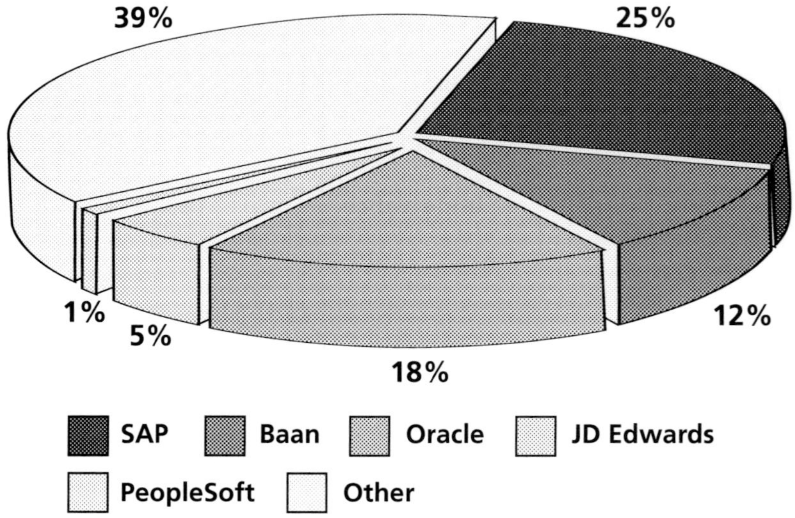

Conclusion

While ERP has been adopted by most of the large companies, the midsize market is now catching up. Given the large number of midsize companies, this adoption wave represents a huge number of ERP implementation projects that have been recently completed, are in progress, or are about to begin. These projects will raise mid-market ERP adoption from our measured 27 per cent in 1998 to the expected 56 per cent this year. Both industries and countries that showed low ERP adoption in 1998 will decrease the gap considerably. This, of course, constitutes a very interesting market for ERP vendors to penetrate. A number of issues emerge from our study that are critical for the development of this market. From the viewpoint of clients, the fit with current business processes is the most important selection criterion for a new system. At the same time, companies within the mid-market rate a low price and short implementation times as highly important. Some of the current ERP vendors are attempting to satisfy these requirements by offering "accelerated" implementation methods. However, these methods are usually based on offering a minimal fit, thus ignoring the number-one wish of small and medium enterprises. Therefore, vendors aiming to penetrate in this market should offer a new generation of ERP systems that is flexible enough to easily handle a wide variety of business procedures. Furthermore, they should have sufficient interfacing capabilities in order to reduce the risk of vendor lock-in and cost of switching. Finally, vendors should take into account that the European midsize business market is not homogeneous. This study shows that significant differences exist in selection criteria among countries. However, for ERP vendors succeeding in satisfying these various requirements, the huge midsize market will be rewarding.

References

1. Foley, J., ERP and E-business: perfect together?, www.information-week.com (13 September 1999), 169.
2. Gilbert, A. and Sweat, J., Reinventing ERP, www.informationweek.com (13 September 1999), 15–20.
3. Hofstede, G., *Culture's Consequences: International Differences in Work Related Values.* Beverly Hills, Sage, 1997.
4. Jarosh, T.J., AS/400: The high scorer in ERP, *Midrange Systems* (April 1999), 36–37.

5. Kale, S.H., Grouping euroconsumers: a culture-based clustering approach, *J. International Marketing 3*, 3 (1995), 35–49.
6. Rogers, E.M., *Diffusion of Innovations,* The Free Press, a division of Macmillan, 1995.
7. Soh, C., Kien, S.S. and Tay-Yap, J., Cultural fits and misfits: is ERP a universal solution? *Communications of the ACM 43*, 4 (April 2000).

THE DOS AND DON'TS OF ERP IMPLEMENTATION

Partners for Change Ltd

Introduction

This article explores the key issues affecting ERP implementations. In particular it examines the key conditions which must be present for a successful rollout of ERP technologies across the organisational value chain. The lists of dos and don'ts provided are not comprehensive, in that particular programmes can – and do – exhibit peculiarities based on individual circumstances. Nevertheless, the comments below reflect programme characteristics that have been observed in many 'first wave' ERP implementations.

Define the business case and manage the benefits proactively

From the outset it is important to have clear objectives for the proposed ERP initiative and to proactively pursue the benefits identified. In many cases firms simply allow competitive pressures to force the company to be a follower rather than a leader in leveraging ERP. For the potential extension of a 'first wave' ERP implementation, firms should look at both the technical implications of extending the system (and changing the configuration) and the change management required to handle the human resource implications (for example, displacement and re-skilling of staff). An effective management of the business case and the benefits management will require that the firm:

- Aligns the business and programme objectives, to ensure that the programme delivers what the business requires;
- Accepts that the business priorities and objectives can change, and tries to identify what changes are likely. Although difficult, business representatives should understand that if they don't do this, project members will make assumptions that may well be wrong;
- Creates a clear business case – ensures the benefits are defined properly (especially the hard-to-measure 'intangible' benefits), and ensures that costs don't exclude the internal implementation costs associated with the participation of the business in the project, including the 'buy in' process for the business case: the key stakeholders will ultimately have to deal with the business impact and address the barriers to effective performance;
- Agrees ownership for the achievement of benefits – the key stakeholders, who will be the project sponsors. Makes their accountability explicit, for example, by putting measurable targets into personal performance appraisal objectives. Considers offering incentives for above target achievement;
- Quantifies the business case and objectives by converting into measurable performance indicators clearly linked to the project features that will enable the programme benefits to be realised;
- Keeps the business case as a 'live' document, so that those involved stay focused on the objectives and benefits. Undertakes regular reviews;

- Ensures responsiveness of the programme to change, to ensure that the solution remains in line with changing business requirements (for example: market and competitive changes, specific customer demands, mergers and acquisitions, legislative change, reorganisation/outsourcing, process improvement, core ERP application upgrades, extended ERP application changes, IT infrastructure changes, new users, problem fixing).

Measure and manage the risks

Risk is an axiomatic part of technology investments. ERP investments are particularly risky because of their wide organisational impact and the critical nature of the business processes they support. Effective risk management will require an assessment of all the programme characteristics – benefits delivery, resources, organisation structure, and the firm's change management capability. In addition to the internal risks, any assessment should include a risk assessment of the business environment outside the ERP programme; for example, other programmes that compete for resources. Include external impacts on the organisation; for example, regulatory changes. It is important that project managers are aware of the risks and that they focus on the high impact, high likelihood risks, *not* on the risks that appear easiest to manage. For the critical risks that cannot be transferred or mitigated, the project team needs to develop a contingency plan, for implementation if the risk materialises or becomes imminent.

Organising the implementation effort

From the outset it is important to establish the right level of programme sponsorship – since ERP typically affects the whole business, the CEO must be the sponsor. Operating sponsors of projects must be senior departmental managers, accountable for the effective use of the new system and processes to achieve specified business objectives. While there are numerous ways of organising the project it is important that each firm chooses, or develops, the organisation form that will ensure the effective direction, control and co-ordination of programme activities and resources, throughout the lifecycle of the programme. Having the right organisation structure is often vital for success; and as a result time spent in defining the organisation and gaining commitment is rarely wasted. It is important that the project team documents clearly: who reports to whom; working relationships between the programme participants; roles and responsibilities; and working relationships between the programme and other parts of the business. To ensure ownership of the project, process owners must be involved during the inception and conduct of the programme in a meaningful way so they can influence it. Finally the firms needs to build a strong network of implementation change managers.

Resource management

ERP projects consume large amounts of resources. There may be a need to take some people out of their line roles completely in order to work on the project. Others will remain in their posts and contribute to the project on a part-time basis. The business will need to be stabilised and positions back-filled with appropriately skilled temporary staff during the project implementation. Any project staffing policy will need to take account of: departmental versus cross-functional issues; the benefits of full-time project personnel (easier planning, better team building, breaks departmental loyalties etc.) versus part-time staff (may access better people, lower cost); and whether there is an operations focus or a technology focus. While a high proportion of the programme investment is normally attributed to human resources, capital resource, and materials and equipment resources, must also be managed throughout the programme (and included in the business case).

The business must determine an appropriate in-house capability – for a first-time ERP implementation, it must decide whether to use an implementation partner for all the ongoing ERP requirements. In-house resources are generally more cost-effective, so the business must be clear about the skills that need to be retained within the organisation and what external expertise needs to be brought in from time to time. When an outside supplier is used, they provide most of the skills the company lacks, but when they go the company is left with little capacity to repeat the process, leaving it dependent on buying in the skills and knowledge about the organisation, again. Building an in-house capability needs more management and may lead to the company being left with surplus skills after the first implementation that may not be easily redeployed. An alternative is to bring in external consultants to work alongside internal staff. In this way there can be skills and knowledge transfer and the company can use the implementation as a means of building its own internal competence centre. When external consultants are used, skills and knowledge transfer must be planned and incorporated in the overall programme plan. The means of effecting capability transfer will vary according to the size of project or programme: methods will vary from coaching in individual skills, through structured training programmes, to full change management skills transfer.

Change management

Managing business change is not a discretionary cost and therefore not dispensable. At an early phase of the project it is important to carry out a change readiness assessment, to understand the history of change in the organisation, and the change skills present that will influence the capacity of the business to implement ERP-related change. In addition firms are advised to carry out an impact-of-change assessment, to identify exactly what will be different as a result of the ERP implementation. In particular there is a need to focus on the big changes and on the business communities with the most change to manage, to help direct resources where they are most needed. 'Change planning' brings together the impact and readiness assessments for each affected community and determines the appropriate package of interventions needed to get the business ready for the system. Interventions can vary from some training and development for those experiencing little impact, to extensive business participation and involvement for those fundamentally affected. The change management plan normally consists of the following activities.

Stakeholder management

One of the key components of well-managed change is the level of participation gained through implementation. Where there has been inadequate participation from the business, the quality of the solution is often poor. It is usually too theoretical and doesn't work in practice, causing people to work 'around' the system rather than with it. In order to get people to take ownership of the solution it is important to get the right people from the business involved from the start. If they have an input to the design, development and testing, they will be more supportive post 'go-live', thus reducing the dip in productivity with detrimental effects on the business.

It is important at the outset to identify *all* the stakeholders, that is 'anyone impacted by the solution' and manage them throughout the programme. This will involve:

- Ensuring there is understanding within the programme of business and user needs, to ensure alignment of expectations between what the business expects and what the programme can deliver;
- Ensuring that users are actively involved in the design of the detail of the technical solution;

- Ensuring that the programme is perceived as open, visible and honest, through effective communication;
- Providing design updates for senior business representatives (without jargon, bringing them up-to-date with current thinking, options, ideas, etc., before decisions are taken).

Ensuring effective business participation in certain stages of the implementation will make a significant difference to the quality and acceptability of the system and new processes. This will complement the change management activity described above. In particular, user acceptance testing should be led by the business and be focused on ensuring the system and processes work in an environment as close to real life as possible. Data management should not only address the process for getting quality data into the new system, but should also address the processes and organisation required in future to ensure new data standards are followed and that weak disciplines do not result in the system being undermined. Cut-over should be planned in detail to ensure there is no discontinuity in business operations. Problems arising from poor cut-over often take a long time to rectify and divert the business from the more important task of getting the business back to stable operations. Handover from the programme team to 'business as usual' should be planned at the outset, to ensure that the programme solution is owned by the business.

Communication

While there is a large body of writing on organisation communication the appropriate communications strategy will vary, depending on: culture and politics; organisational structures; technical constraints; the needs of individual stakeholders and decision-makers. Reporting should be 'bottom up', but with a feedback loop to ensure that decisions, actions and priorities from the programme board and steering group are properly disseminated to project teams. In addition project members should (i) communicate frequently, to ensure that all stakeholders are kept appropriately informed and involved in the programme; (ii) communicate: progress, issues, resolutions, and realisation of benefits; and (iii) develop a communications strategy and plan to deliver relevant information to each constituency, in a timely manner, using appropriate communications media.

Education and training

It is important that staff are adequately briefed and trained in the new systems and processes, so that they are acceptable and workable. Project managers should not allow the period planned for user and technical training to become 'squeezed' between late-running development and testing activities, and the business imperative for a scheduled 'go-live' date.

Don'ts

While the critical success factors for successful ERP implementation are important it is also important that firms learn from the mistakes that have been made in the past. A review of first-wave ERP implementations produces a long list of mistakes made and these are summarised below.

- Do not ignore the opportunity to re-engineer processes or manage change in a bid to save costs; they are not discretionary; do not treat ERP as simply a software implementation project.

- If the ERP system is implemented quickly before re-engineering the business processes, to save cost and reduce risk, don't then cancel the process improvement programme.
- Avoid over-reliance on external suppliers, to avoid always being 'in their pocket'.
- Do not let IT management drive the programme; running the business and satisfying customers is the priority. Get the business to take ownership and to take more of a role in driving projects for business benefit.
- Stakeholders – don't simply identify them at the start, draw them in and then ignore them – communicate all the time. Otherwise, most will have other priorities, get distracted, and give out inconsistent messages.
- An ineffective communications plan leads to risks of: work omitted or duplicated; managers being unprepared; dependencies not identified across projects; programme leaders being unaware of the risks; a lack of stakeholder commitment; programme team members becoming de-motivated.
- Do not assume the drivers for the ERP programme are similar to those for a project – fixed in terms of time, cost and quality. Programmes are focused on achieving benefits for the business by co-ordinating the delivery of the programme portfolio. The required benefits may change over the life of the programme, as priorities or the business environment changes. The approach must be flexible and responsive to these changes.
- Do not plan for the realisation of all the benefits at the end of the programme. The programme destination may change. Further, interim benefits will help to maintain the motivation of the team, and maintain the credibility of the programme within the business.
- Do not ignore the effect of the ERP programme on other business initiatives. The enterprise system may render other projects or programmes redundant.

THE USA PRINCIPLE: THE KEY TO ERP IMPLEMENTATION SUCCESS

Karl M. Kapp, © 1997 by APICS – The Educational Society for Resource Management.
Copied from *APICS Magazine*, June 1997, Volume 7, No. 6.

The decision to purchase an enterprise resource planning (ERP) system is easy; it's effective implementation is difficult. Instances of an ERP project being behind schedule and over budget occur with alarming frequency, as do cases of companies spending thousands of dollars on a system and only using 15 per cent of its features.

Figure 1: The USA Principle implementation flow

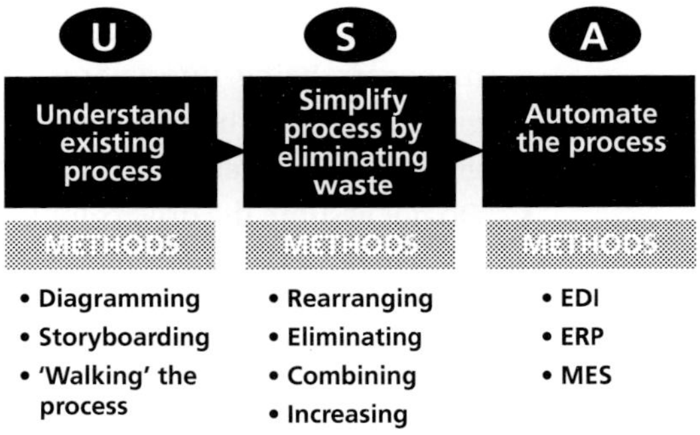

Yet some companies do successfully implement and fully utilize their ERP systems. An analysis of many manufacturing companies in a variety of industries reveals that success is the result of following a simple implementation philosophy. Successful companies strive to first understand their business processes, then simplify them, and then automate their procedures. These manufacturers follow the USA Principle – Understand, Simplify, Automate.

Unsuccessful companies start their ERP implementation effort with automation, bypassing the critical steps of understanding and simplifying their processes. These companies believe that automation alone will improve performance and lead to productivity gains. However, automating complex or non-value-added processes with an ERP system will not increase productivity or improve performance. Automation without simplification or understanding only immortalizes ineffective processes and sustains waste.

Reengineering replacement

The USA Principle is rapidly replacing the paradigm of reengineering as the preferred philosophy for implementing an ERP system. Reengineering, as implemented in many companies and taught by many consultants, ignores the human element in the manufacturing process and assumes all existing processes are completely flawed. Since all processes are assumed to be completely flawed, a "blank piece of paper" mentality is fostered, and every business process is "radically" redesigned.

In order to be successful, reengineering proponents insist that technology and automation are absolute requirements for process improvements. The drive for automation supersedes all other methods of improvement. This means that technology must be applied to the problem whether it is needed or not. The reengineering implementation paradigm is expensive, time consuming, bad for morale and, in some cases, causes the loss of key business.

In sharp contrast, the USA Principle's primary focus is on the human element of manufacturing. Employees are encouraged to examine and improve the processes with which they are involved on a daily basis. Individuals are encouraged to understand and simplify the process of which they are an integral part.

Instead of starting with a "blank piece of paper," the USA Principle builds upon the processes of an organization that is already doing well. Automation occurs only after employees gain an understanding of the process, simplify the process and decide that automation is necessary. The USA Principle leads to increased employee involvement and participation in the ERP implementation, decreased resistance to change, and higher levels of productivity.

Understand

An organization is a collection of rules and procedures. An ERP system is a collection of rules and procedures. When implementing a system, you are replacing one set of rules and procedures with another. If you do not understand the rules and procedures currently operating within your organization, how do you know which ones to keep and which ones to replace? How do you avoid unnecessarily replacing effective, value-added processes?

The goal of the "Understand" step in the USA Principle is for individuals within a manufacturing organization to gain an understanding of the processes of which they are a part and to identify and classify current processes. In fact, a simple awareness of being part of a larger process often leads to process improvement. The "Understand" step involves employees gaining consensus on the steps within a process, classifying the assumptions underlying the process, and finally capturing the process on paper. Several techniques are available to help organizations understand and document their processes.

Diagramming is an excellent tool for understanding internal processes. First, determine what symbols to use for representing different parts of the process. Gather all employees with a part in the process and have them each draw the process. When finished, ask the employees to compare and contrast their separate drawings of the same process. This will typically yield fascinating, and sometimes frightening, results. When the group reaches consensus on the actual process, have the process diagrammed and posted in an area as close to the actual process as possible.

Another powerful technique for gaining process understanding is storyboarding. Start with a stack of index cards in a variety of colors, an area on which to post the cards, and the process participants. Ask participants to write down the underlying assumptions of each step within the process. Each category of assumption should be written on a different color index card. Once categories of assumptions are written on the cards, they should be posted on the display area in the sequence of the process. Move, remove, or combine the cards on the display area as the group discusses and refines the assumptions underlying the process.

A third technique used to gain process understanding is to simply "walk the process." This is done by carrying a customer order, work order, or purchase order through your organization. A member of the implementation team walks the work order from operation to operation until the item is completely manufactured, packaged and shipped. While walking the process, it is important to look for unnecessary wait, move, or queue time. In addition, identify any search and retrieval tasks, extra handling of material, and other non-valued work activity.

The result of the "Understand" step will be a model of the company's present processes and an indication of current areas of strength and weakness. The company now determines which processes to keep, redesign or eliminate.

Simplify

A simplified manufacturing environment provides a company with a clear picture of available material, capacity and labor. Building upon the understanding step, a manufacturing organization needs to examine each internal business process and ask the following questions:

- What is the purpose of this process?
- Is the best methodology for this process being used?
- Why is this process being performed?
- How can we improve the quality of this process?

Answering these questions will lead to a simplification of product design, shop floor layout, manufacturing practices and administrative procedures. Opportunities for simplification come in four different categories.

1. Rearranging. Moving equipment, process steps and personnel into logical groupings is a simple but effective method of reducing complexity. A clothing manufacturer in Virginia rearranged equipment and machinery when converting from a linear layout of the plant floor to a work cell layout. The movement of equipment increased productivity 29 per cent and reduced the amount of floor space required for the assembly line. This eliminated the need to purchase additional manufacturing space and allowed for a less cramped and more open atmosphere.

Changing the ordering of a processing step saved a laser drive manufacturer in Pennsylvania thousands of dollars. Simply testing a subassembly earlier in the process allowed for the detection of flawed material before more expensive parts were added.

The rearrangement of personnel into office work cells can also be beneficial. For example, if order entry personnel are constantly asking engineering for specification information, place an engineer into the office with the order entry department. If purchasing must constantly check with the quality control (QC) department to verify certified vendors, place a QC person side-by-side with the purchasing agent. There is no need to segment an office layout into functional areas when a work cell arrangement could provide the same productivity and performance improvements as similar layouts on the shop floor.

Figure 2: Understand portion diagramming symbols of the USA Principle

SYMBOL	MEANING	EXAMPLES
	Operation	• Inspect the die • Write down the customer order.
	Decision Point	• Does the die need to be recut? • Should the customer be placed on credit hold?
	File or Store	• Return die to tool room. • File a copy of an invoice.
	Wait or Queue Time	• Amount of time a part or paperwork spends waiting to move to the next operation or waiting in line at an operation.
	Move Time	• Amount of time it takes to move or transfer a part or paperwork from one place to another.

2. Eliminating. The removal of material and processes can greatly reduce organizational complexity and result in unanticipated positive results. One computer manufacturing company redesigned a circuit board reducing the number of parts from 270 to 130. This reduction in parts resulted in the added benefit of a reduction of vendors from 120 to 50. This means less purchase orders to cut, less vendor management, less potential quality problems, and more opportunities to develop closer relationships with the suppliers.

Processes can be eliminated through outsourcing. One manufacturer had a motor subassembly with more than 60 parts from different vendors. The kitting of the parts and associated paperwork overwhelmed the manufacturing company. The manufacturer simplified this process by outsourcing the kitting to one vendor. This eliminated multiple purchase orders, receipts, inspections and vouchers.

3. Combining. The combination of multiple procedural steps and the modularization of bills of material can be extremely beneficial during the simplification process. A plastics injection molder in Ohio slightly increased the cycle time on some machines. This was done so employees could apply a subassembly to a just-molded part while the next part is molded. This combination of two operations eliminates unnecessary move time, product handling and employee idle time.

4. Increasing. Although this seems contradictory, an increase in the number of processes actually simplifies daily functions. Many procedures and processes are overly complex, as they must incorporate special procedures, verifications and checks to handle all possible exceptions. This slows the processing of the majority of items which do not require the special checks or procedures. Does every single purchase order, inventory and non-inventory, require a tedious three-way match? Not likely.

The first step in any process should be a classification of the type of response required. If an order is classified as an exception, it can go down a path specifically designed to handle the exception. If the order has no exceptions, it can be processed quickly and efficiently without the added overhead of additional checks. This provides a quick resolution for common situations and a rapid identification of all exceptions. Each path is specific and simplistic.

Simplifying complex processes greatly reduces the difficulty of trying to mold your existing corporate processes into the parameters of an ERP system. Most ERP systems handle simple processes extremely well. It is when a complex process results in inconsistent handling of information that the implementation of an ERP system runs into problems.

Automate

While the USA Principle stresses process understanding and simplification, it does not view automation as a poor second cousin. The proper implementation of ERP technology is critical to a manufacturing organization's long-term success. Automation is neither inherently good nor bad; its application is what makes the difference.

Following the USA Principle provides the proper framework of the application of technology to solving business problems. Organizations that spend time focusing on process understanding and simplification will be a step ahead in terms of implementing their ERP system. However, there are three fundamental automation errors that need to be avoided at the technology implementation stage.

The first mistake companies make is falling into the HAL Syndrome. HAL is the spaceship computer from the movie "2001: A Space Odyssey." In the movie, HAL takes over the ship, killing crew members in the process. But HAL's original mission was to support the ship, not take it over. In an ERP implementation, the mission of the system is the same – to support the company, not control it.

Here is a classic example of the HAL Syndrome at work. A large packaging company halts its entire ERP implementation because the tracking of actual costing for each lot passing through its plant is seen as a must-have capability. The company does not currently use actual lot costing and never has, nor is it required to do so by any regulatory bodies; but because its old MRP system had this functionality, the company feels the new system must have it as well.

This company is trapped by an automation "sizzle" that does not address its actual needs. If the company would have followed the USA Principle, it would not have been seduced by attractive, but unnecessary, software functionality. In fact, using actual lot costing will increase the level of process complexity. Processes should only be automated when the "Understand" and "Simplify" steps reveal opportunities for real productivity improvements via automation.

Figure 3: Before and after the 'Simplification' step of the USA principle

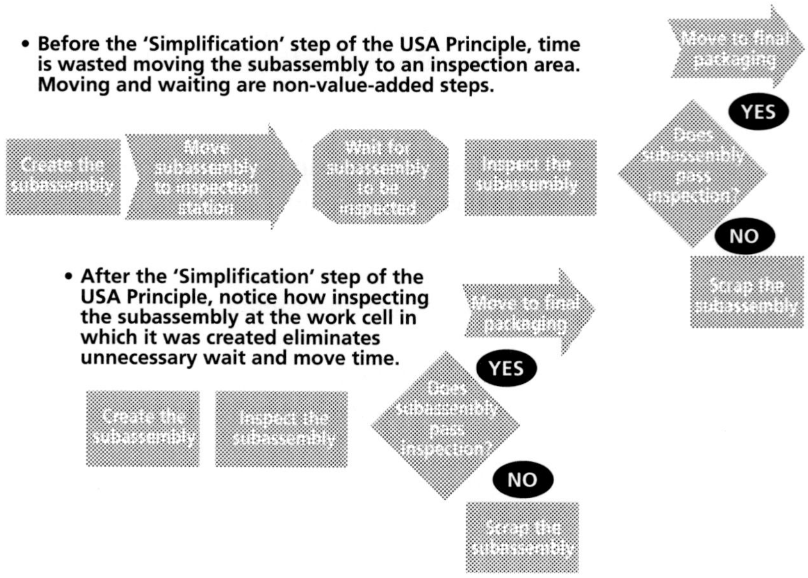

The HAL Syndrome can be avoided by focusing the entire ERP implementation on productive changes to business processes. The drive to automate must not overshadow the primary goal of a company – to make money. Do not let the computerized aspect of the ERP system control your implementation.

The second automation mistake typically made by companies is to implement the ERP system module by module. A company spends months on process understanding and simplification and then fails to implement its ERP system based on business processes. Software is artificially broken into modules. This makes it easy to write, easy to train and easy to document.

However, companies are not made up of individual, well-defined, stand-alone modules. In a fully functional manufacturing organization, purchasing impacts at least inventory, product costing and accounts payable. Order entry impacts several other functions as well. Just because the software is packaged and sold in modules does not mean that is how it should be implemented.

VENDOR AND SYSTEM SELECTION ISSUES

John Blackburn and Martin Osborn, PricewaterhouseCoopers

Introduction

The selection of a system to meet the business needs of an organisation is a time-consuming, complex and risky business. The solutions do not stand still. The vendors live on marketing images and future promises. All of our own organisations have their own built-in prejudices. Even current ERP users do not always tell the truth because of vested interests or a desire to hide their own failings. Recent history is littered with stories about failed projects that did not meet business expectations but consumed significant resources.

This article gives a brief overview of a generic vendor and system selection process (and key decision criteria) that, when applied realistically, should allow an organisation to focus on the key business requirements and find the compromise that best meets their needs.

Focusing on the Critical Business Need

Many of the fundamental drivers of the business case are not affected by the details of package selection. The drivers for any ERP project might include for instance:

- a fundamental initiative around revamping the supply chain to make it more global and to have a picture of the total relationship between each customer or supplier;
- a need to increase responsiveness to customers to meet market pressures;
- establishing a new business or capability in a new market;
- the ability to support internet business including direct delivery to the customer;
- sweeping away a diverse portfolio of legacy systems that have become increasingly difficult to maintain or develop to meet business needs;
- the need to create a shared service facility to improve corporate practices, corporate control and cost effectiveness.

All of these examples are high level business requirements. They do not dictate detailed functional requirements and features. Although it is essential to gain an appropriate understanding of the features and functions of each contending solution, differences do not have a major impact on the key business drivers. Each solution may have variant approaches to meeting the business needs and these may vary from current business practices. The business will need to change its processes to meet those of the selected solution, providing the system's processes are viable. As such, differences between solutions may be irritants not true differentiators. Each solution may well come with its only collection of "irritants". The selection process should be detailed enough to discover functionality and features that are critical to day to day operation but it must not get bogged down in the detail and lose:

- sight of the key business drivers;
- momentum to meet these requirements quickly and effectively.

Why go through the cost and delay of a detailed vendor evaluation?

An evaluation process increases organisational understanding
A selection process is needed to allow the organisation to fully understand or own this decision. There are major benefits in allowing an organisation to go through an appropriate decision process in order to fully understand the decision that is being made. The solutions in the market place are not necessarily dream solutions and each will come with its own pain. Organisations need to believe that they have followed a reasoned process and be given the opportunity to fully understand and plan for the change that they will introduce.

The process must force out the best deals from vendors
There are distinct advantages in keeping the competitive pressure on suppliers for as long as possible. As soon as suppliers believe they are the only horse in the race there will be little further movement on costs or support or on including customer specific needs in development plans. This must be balanced by the need to eliminate suppliers as early as possible in order to minimise evaluation effort.

The process must anticipate the future
It is important to have senior management fully involved in the process such that projected business changes, acquisitions, new ventures and initiatives can be handled within the capacity of the system and planned infrastructure. Average and maximum transaction volumes should be quoted and agreed by senior management and be reflective of known changes.

What issues should drive the vendor or system selection?
Traditionally a Request for Proposal (RFP) or Invitation to Tender (ITT) is developed in order to get specific responses from suppliers to address the critical decision issues. These cover such areas as:

- Can the vendor or system support our key drivers from the business case?
- Does the system support the key functionality and features required by the business processes?
- How well does the system technology fit in with our existing technical infrastructure or desired technical direction?
- How will the solution integrate with our existing applications?
- Do we have the skills and support infrastructure to own and use this solution effectively?
- How does this solution integrate with other existing and planned initiatives?
- Is it easy to use?
- Does it have an appropriate level of sophistication for our key functions?
- What are the project life cycle costs and costs of ownership and upgrade?
- What are the product development plans and market futures for the product and its major competitors?
- What is the commercial standing and stability of the supplier? What are its predicted futures in this competitive market?
- What are the current users and reference sites in appropriate geographies and industry sectors? What volumetrics are available for current users – transactions, file sizes, etc?
- What kind of operational support does the supplier offer? What do current users think about the supplied support?

- What is the contractual basis for acquiring the product and associated services? Are there suitable guarantees, get out clauses and organisational commitment from the supplier?

Some key differentiators?
Many companies have already selected their ERP vendor. If you are currently selecting an ERP vendor then there are only a limited number of contenders for most significant ERP selection exercises. The key differentiators are likely to be:

- the availability of industry-specific and national versions with a track record in the industry and geography that you require;
- the scope and sophistication of the funtionality in the areas that are most important to you;
- the support available in the geography where you work;
- the total life cycle cost of the solution.

If you are seeking an add-on to an existing ERP system (including an e-business extension) then the key decision criteria are likely to be the:

- track record of the solution in similar companies and applications to yours;
- ease of integration with the existing ERP solution;
- stability of the company behind the products;
- quality of support in the geography where you work;
- scope and sophistication of the functionality in the areas that are most important to you;
- capability to handle your projected data and transaction volumes;
- life cycle costs of the full implementation.

What process is required for vendor and system selection?
The efficiency of the selection process is enhanced when early work is undertaken to understand the key business drivers, key functional needs, the main market offerings and what are the key differentiators between products. This information can be used to shape the selection and can be further verified during the selection process. It is important not to allow items at a detailed level to influence unduly the decision. The acid test will always be "does this decision look sensible?". If detail is driving the decision in a direction away from common sense then the findings at a detailed level need to be challenged until it is obvious that they are critical and overwhelming requirements. The history of vendors and systems demonstrates that the best technical products do not always end up as market leaders. There are often other influences or market sentiments or market muscle that choose the eventual market winners.

The generic vendor and system selection process is as follows:

- confirm business case and main drivers;
- identify potential package suppliers;
- develop and weight requirements;
- produce RFP/ITT;
- conduct preliminary evaluation;
- create shortlist of vendors/systems;
- conduct detailed technical evaluation;
- assess suitability of proposed package supplier;
- conduct benchmark;

- conduct detailed contractual review;
- conduct detailed costs review;
- select vendor and system.

The list of potential package suppliers can be drawn up from internal knowledge, discussions with industry watchers (such as Gartner Group), industry groups and consultants. Discussions with these bodies should also provide significant understanding about the main differences between the competing products and what is likely to be material to the organisation. The Request for Proposal or Invitation to Tender should insist that responding organisations say how they will support the functional requirements or features and in which releases. This information needs to be specific in order to be cross checked during site visits, user meetings and demonstrations. Benchmarking solutions, using data that represents predicted transaction volumes and history, is lengthy and expensive. This step may be more effectively handled by site visits to comparable or larger organisations, performance guarantees and by desk based sizing studies.

How should the selection exercise be organised?

The selection process should be organised as a project using normal project management approach and standards. The project has major significance to the business and must be business owned. Senior representatives from the business areas or geographies affected should be represented on the steering group and the business should provide the main business sponsor. The project should include process owners who can speak with authority about the process requirements to meet business area and local geographic processing requirements. The IT director and project manager should also be on the steering group. The project should also be supported by consultancy skills in project management and vendor selection. These can be deployed in the project team or in coaching roles as required. The process will be significantly improved if it can draw from similar exercises conducted by consultants for other organisations. This will greatly speed the process of creating an appropriate RFP and contract.

CONCLUSION

Vendor and system selection is a critical and complex activity that should be exercised as a process in order to;

- allow the organisation to 'own' and understand the decision, and to live with its consequences;
- squeeze the best deal from suppliers.

The efficiency of the process can be significantly enhanced by using experience from previous, similar selection exercises in order to allow the process to focus on the likely significant differentiators.

The process must keep focus on the key objectives of the required business change and not allow immaterial details to slow its momentum.

The best technical products do not always end up as the market winners. Market sentiment and muscle must be considered.

The selection exercise should be organised as a formal project, owned by the business, supported by IT and with adequate involvement from all key functions and geography impacted by the selection.

ERP SETS OUT TO REINVENT ITSELF
Industry is about to reinvent itself
Rod Newing, *Financial Times IT Survey,* December 1999. Reprinted by permission.

Amid the clamour of profit warnings and volatile share prices, it might seem that the enterprise resource planning (ERP) juggernaut has reached the end of the road. However, rather than disappearing, the industry is about to reinvent itself to create virtual supply chains across the internet. The big five vendors, SAP, Oracle, PeopleSoft, J D Edwards and Baan (known collectively as "JBOPS"), enjoyed their heyday between 1995 and 1997. Their customers were seeking integration of business processes and management information across the organisation. They sought both a competitive advantage through more efficient processes and to avoid the prohibitive costs of upgrading their existing mainframe solutions to make them year 2000 compliant.

The ERP vendors' focus is shifting from achieving operational efficiency within the enterprise to trying to increase the organisation's effectiveness outside the enterprise. They are linking across the internet with suppliers, partners, resellers and customers to create virtual supply chains.The ERP vendors see a new set of products to sell to their installed base and have made a number of acquisitions. PeopleSoft of the US purchased supply chain optimisation (SCO) vendor Red Pepper and customer relationship management (CRM) vendor Vantive, while Netherlands-based Baan acquired Aurum for CRM and J D Edwards of the US acquired Numetrix for SCO. Similarly, Oracle, also in the US, has developed its own CRM package and Germany's SAP an SCO package.

"The ERP vendors will be a major force in all their new markets," says Bruce Bond, vice-president for enterprise and supply chain management at Gartner Group, the independent analysts. "However, they will not be fast enough to displace strong competitors in the individual niches, such as i2 in supply chain or Siebel in CRM." The ERP vendors are also in a technology transition from a highly monolithic architecture to a more nimble web-enabled one based on components. "It is a very expensive process and involves rewriting large percentages of the product," says Mr Bond. "Many vendors will not be able to afford to make the move, so we will see market consolidation, but we expect the strong to survive, such as JBOPS."

The manufacturing resources planning (MRP II) market experienced a similar "inflection point" six years ago when the ERP market arrived. Some vendors survived and some did very badly. Tony Friscia, president of AMR Research, the independent analyst, sees the ERP market hitting a similar point. "The market is shifting to business process-oriented extended enterprise suites," he says. "In the next few years, we will see companies like Siebel and i2 expanding their functionality by acquisition or development to compete in head-on collision with each other and with the ERP vendors to 'own' the customer fulfilment process."

This transition is a big issue for end-user organisations, which will have to change their skills. "Support staff must learn about componentisation and object orientation and have web skills," says Mr Bond. "They are skills most people don't have and they are very hard to get. We think that after the year 2000 lock-down we will see more ERP systems being outsourced." One means of outsourcing that attracts much hype at present is the application service providers (ASPs). They can provide organisations, especially smaller ones, with access to an ERP system over the internet, in return for a monthly rental fee. TDS Informationstechnologie has been providing SAP's R/2 and R/3 software on dedicated servers for 25 years and has 100 customers, mainly medium-sized German companies, with a total of 10,000 users. "The most important benefit is helping customers to get to market more quickly," says Gunter Steffan, chairman of TDS. "We are also converting fixed costs into variable costs and saving clients 30–40 per cent per annum over the cost of running and supporting their SAP environment in-house. We can also give smaller companies access to a pool of expertise they wouldn't normally be able to afford."

However, these directly related costs exclude the internal administrative costs of supporting the business process within the organisation, as well as implementation costs. Mr Steffan accepts that implementation costs are the same whether a company uses an ASP or sets up its own installation. These implementation costs are still between three and five times the cost of software licences. "The mid-market isn't learning from what happened in the top end market," Mr Boyd warns. "A lot of people are still pushing rapid implementation to reduce costs when they should look for cost-effective implementation that delivers improved customer service."

As to increasing their market reach, Mr Boyd points out that there are still untapped ERP markets, especially in Asia. There is a market for unsophisticated systems in China, but he predicts that it is only a matter of time before the market explodes. Mr Hochberg sees no change in the line-up of the big five ERP vendors, although he points out that Intentia should also be considered alongside them, because although it is not well known, it ranks fourth in Europe in revenues. He suggests Navision from Denmark, IBS from Sweden and Agresso from Norway are ones to watch.

It is clear that ERP is far from dead, although the market looks set to merge with the supply chain and CRM markets. This merger would create customer-focused software that can support business processes between organisations. The ERP vendors will face a fight with strong competitors such as i2 and Siebel. Dataquest currently puts the combined worldwide market for ERP, CRM and SCO at $11bn, but predicts that it will almost treble in size by 2004 to $29.4bn. ERP provides an essential backbone for business processes within the organisation, but it will have to be extended out across the internet. Linking with suppliers and partners will enable organisations to form a responsive supply chain. But it remains to be seen how easy this will be in practice, because there are formidable technical obstacles to be overcome.

LIVING with ERP

Thomas Davenport, www.cio.com, 1 December 1998. Reprinted through the courtesy of CIO.

The conventional wisdom is that ERP sales will decline substantially after 2000, when organizations are no longer trying to solve their Y2K problems with a fast (right!) ERP installation. Perhaps in anticipation of this problem, several ERP vendors' stocks are disproportionately down. It is important to recognise that ERPs are not purely a result of millennial craziness. For vendor and user companies, they are not a flash in the '90s pan, but rather a long-term phenomenon. Unfortunately, many companies that have bought the packages are treating the systems not as a till-forever-do-us-part marriage but as a brief cohabitation. However, no matter how depressing it may seem, "going live" with an installation is just the beginning (but presumably still better than "going dead").

We have treated ERPs as projects, with the assumption that someday the projects would end. But an enterprise system is not a project, it's a way of life. No organization that I've talked to – and I've talked to over a hundred on this subject – has yet to say, "We're finished." And few ever will. There will always be new modules and versions to install, acquired or divested business units to deal with and better fits to be achieved between business and system. Even if an organization could declare final victory on implementation of ERPs, many additional years could be spent in getting real business value from them.

The realization of a lifelong commitment has begun to dawn upon several companies. Some of the early adopters of SAP, for example, who implemented the R/2 mainframe version of the package, are now faced with an expensive, time-consuming conversion to R/3. One presumes that there will eventually be an R/4; then many more companies will be faced with the same prospect. Non-IT employees and managers who served as functional experts, or "super users," during implementation still can't return to their previous jobs because their help is needed in support roles. And companies that justified an ERP project on the basis of reduced IT head count are finding that they are unable to lay off anybody; people no longer needed for implementation are now needed for support and maintenance. The permanent nature of ERPs has numerous implications. Here are just a few:

Organizational structure

Most firms have created implementation project offices and appointed project managers with the assumption that the project will end and life will go back to normal. But it won't. So what they need is not a project office, but a new organizational structure that reflects the ongoing need for ERP-related activity. "Sponsorship" is one example of the need. Many companies appointed senior executive sponsors – often a CFO or COO – for implementation projects. Their expectations were probably that the CIO could own the systems after installation was "complete." But many companies are postponing business change until after they ram a basic system into place. Who's going to oversee those changes and ensure that they fit with the rest of the business? If the executive sponsor is temporary, who will ensure that the system and the business evolve hand in hand?

One response is to create a hybrid role that oversees change in processes, systems and information. There aren't many of these around, but they're not unprecedented. An organization I once worked with had a senior vice president of strategic change (we're not talking tactical change here, so you need an SVP to do the job). Another option is that CIOs can oversee long-term ERP change, but you'd better let everyone know before accepting the job that you're going to venture far beyond the realm of technology.

Of course, there are other organizational implications of these systems. A substantial support capability will have to be created, but that can probably just be glommed onto the existing IT support organization – though it will become a lot bigger. More important, the long-term use of ERP could change the broader organization in terms of its structure and function. It may be, for example, that there is less need for middle managers and that the organization can be a bit flatter. Maybe that's a responsibility for the "change czar."

Roles and skills

The post-ERP organization will need a different set of roles and skills than those with less integrated kinds of systems. At a minimum, everyone who uses these systems needs to be trained on how they work, how they relate to the business process and how a transaction ripples through the entire company whenever they press a key. And don't think that this training will ever end; new people will always be coming in, and new functionality will always be entering the organization.

Most companies use consultants to help with the implementation process. I'm hardly going to say this is a bad idea, as I get a monthly check from a consulting firm. But there is a big problem with how most companies use consultants in ERP implementations: They don't transfer knowledge from consultants to internal employees. If these systems will be around forever, it's important to have internal talent that knows as much as any consultant about how they work and how they can be configured to fit the organization. Make sure your consultants allow your people to work side by side with them on the implementation project, and before they leave tap the most knowledgeable consultants on long-term system evolution issues.

In every business function and department that's affected by ERP you'll need one or more people who know the system and its relationship to departmental processes. In the early days after you turn the system on, these people will save your bacon. They'll answer questions, find needed work-arounds and let you know what's working and what isn't. But, as I suggested earlier, the super user role is a job for life. You might as well put super users' responsibilities on paper and perhaps get them some sort of dual reporting relationship to the IT function and their department manager. It will also be useful to convene meetings of these hybrids every once in awhile so that they can share knowledge and group therapy.

Knowledge management

If you don't want to hire everyone in your standard metropolitan statistical area to help resolve ERP-related problems, you had better adopt a dose of knowledge management to leverage human support. Again, big companies like Johnson & Johnson have had knowledge networks and repositories to allow knowledge sharing during implementation, and this is a good idea. And if consultants have helped you implement, make sure that what you've learned about the system during that project is captured in a repository. But how about the post-implementation knowledge of how to use the system and related new business processes?

Most companies will benefit from a knowledge management initiative in which both ERP experts and garden-variety users can put what they learn about the system and processes into a knowledge base and then search it for what knowledge others have added. Since system and process knowledge will often be inextricably linked, it's important to capture both.

Application management

Further evidence that living with ERPs is an important issue is provided by several vendors that are bringing out ERP application management tools. Envive Corp. and BMG Entertainment have separately announced capabilities to monitor SAP systems and pass on any troubles they discover to humans or service management systems. And for a while now ServiceWare Inc. has offered prepackaged SAP support knowledge for help desks. It's all more grist for the mill that attention is shifting from putting ERPs in place to living with them comfortably for a long time.

Just as courtships and honeymoons are different from marriages, living with ERP systems will be different from installing them. Projects for implementing the systems get a lot of resources and attention, but I believe that how we live with ERPs will have more to do with the value we receive from them than the quick decisions made during installation.

POST-IMPLEMENTATION ISSUES
Partners for Change Ltd.

Introduction

A post-implementation review allows the programme team and operational units the opportunity to assess objectively the successful aspects of the implementation, and to learn – for enhancements to the new system, organisation and processes, and for future programmes. In addition it provides an opportunity to demonstrate to staff that the business 'listens' to their concerns. It can help build credibility in the organisation's capacity to undertake major programmes successfully. It also allows the development of a continuous learning environment within the business. It may also facilitate modified behaviour of individuals by, for example, linking continuing improved performance to personal development opportunities and other rewards. While a post-implementation review is sometimes required by an organisation as a part of its capital review process, a consistent finding of recent research on companies' experience of implementing ERP is that few post- 'go-live' reviews are carried out.

There is, of course, a cost attached to carrying out such a review, but without a formal audit senior management's impressions of the benefits brought about by the enterprise system and associated process changes are, at best, imprecise and may simply be anecdotal. Behaviour within the organisation may not be changing. Not all of the benefits expected at the outset may have been realised. There are several possible reasons why reviews are often not carried out, including:

- The focus after go-live is primarily on post-implementation support and on 'fire-fighting' problem solving;
- There may be no budget other than the operational budget after go-live;
- Any enhancements after go-live are achieved with limited, internal, resources only;
- Management believes that implementation is the end of the process, not the start of a period of continuous improvement and optimising the benefits realised;
- Other, new, initiatives within the business capture management's attention.

The nature of post-implementation reviews

A post-implementation review covers the activities that take place following the implementation of a programme or project in order to assess the success of the implementation and the benefits that were delivered. There are two main circumstances when an assessment of the implementation may be carried out. These are:

An assessment of the implementation. This typically involves identifying the issues that business units are facing, arising from the rollout of the ERP system. These are the unresolved, unforeseen or inadequately managed impacts of change. The assessment will include reviewing the benefits that were anticipated from the new system and processes, as documented in the business case, and comparing them with the tangible and intangible benefits achieved. Significant variations are analysed to establish the reason for their non-realisation. An action plan is then developed to address the shortcomings.

An evaluation of the design and the identification of further improvements that could still be made. These may be either improvements that were identified during design and development but which were outside the scope of the programme, and were therefore not addressed at the time; or lessons learned from the first-phase implementation that can, and should, be carried forward into a planned second phase. In the first situation, any proposals will need to be authorised in a similar manner to the original implementation, that is, they must be justified by an approved business case. Not all of the options for improvement are likely to be taken forward, and there is often a case for reviewing and prioritizing potential enhancements by a Continuous Improvement workshop of key staff. On occasions, where continuing enhancements are expected to be identified, a Continuous Improvement standing committee may be established. The second phase should, of course, also be supported by a positive business case.

Figure 1 illustrates the generic stages in a post-implementation review.

Figure 1: Steps in the post-implementation review

Assessing the implementation

During this phase feedback is sought from the system users, from users of the new business processes, and from those who are impacted by the system and processes. Information is normally gathered through a combination of interviews and workshops, and documented in a report. The input of customers is often particularly relevant. Where significant impact was foreseen at the outset, the implementation plan should include scheduled customer review sessions. The customer assessment may include interviews and reviews of customer documentation such as letters or comments recorded on feedback forms. These are then analysed and the reasons for the problems documented.

Assessing performance improvement

The business case and objectives for the programme should have included a description of tangible and intangible benefits. These need to be translated into key performance indicators that are measurable and clearly linked to the programme. Only in this way can the 'success' of the implementation be judged objectively. Performance indicators such as service levels and turnaround times that were set at the outset will need to be measured post-implementation. The results should be reviewed and analysed in order to establish performance against the baselines set, and to introduce improvements if the targets are not being met. This work should culminate in a statement of the benefits realised and concerns of the implementation, and actions proposed to rectify the problems identified. The following section provides some examples of possible remedial actions.

Instilling continuous improvement

The ability of an organisation to exploit its ERP investment to the full, from the opportunities presented by new system functionality and re-modelled business processes, will depend in part on its culture. Some companies are averse to rewarding improvement ideas by staff. Even where this is not the case, the pressure to 'move on' – to roll out the next phase, or to undertake new programmes elsewhere – often militates against full exploitation of the potential benefits. These situations present particular challenges to the team undertaking the impact of change review, if their recommendations are to be worth while. It is sometimes easier for a team that is external to the organisation to work closely with business-as-usual managers, to implement the improvements and encourage an attitude of supporting sustainable change.

Findings from post-implementation reviews

Why hasn't ERP always delivered the benefits?

Surveys suggest that the majority of companies that have implemented ERP in the first wave feel the benefits have been below expectation, and that the Return on Investment (RoI) has been inadequate. There are several possible causes, including:

- Aggressive implementation timescales, that often mean change issues became 'side-lined' in the race to implement the technical solution;
- Shortage of financial and human resources to tackle major business change on top of the investment in the enterprise system;
- Lack of the internal skills to implement the technology, or the process and organisation changes that went with it, and an over-reliance on external partners, who were not all of the first quality;
- An incomplete strategy, that did not allow for proper re-engineering of the business processes alongside the new technology;
- A poor business case, which did not articulate clearly the benefits that should accrue. Consequently, the business did not know whether it had 'arrived' at the intended destination;
- Redesigned business processes are not implemented as envisaged, or are applied inconsistently between sites;
- There is a lack of understanding of the context of processes across functions. There is a 'silo' effect;
- Documentation (particularly operating procedures) and operating practices do not reflect the business model as designed;
- Insufficient education and training was carried during implementation;
- There was inadequate preparation and resource for post-implementation training;
- Staff experience information retrieval difficulties;
- There are errors in data migration and inefficient data management.

Often, deficiencies in design or implementation lead to additional manual processes being developed (so-called 'workarounds'), or a return to earlier working practices. These usually adversely affect efficiency and cause an unplanned increase in workload. This in turn can badly affect staff morale and discredit the ERP system for future development.

Table 1: Addressing change management shortcomings

Change management deficiency	Proposals to rectify
New business processes not fully implemented	Next phase to plan adequate time to ensure fit-for-purpose processes and design.
Lack of cross-functional integration of system and processes	Agree responsibility for cross-functional integration. Design and implement education & training to explain the business context, at the affected sites. Develop operating procedures to cover cross-functional impact.
Operating procedures do not reflect the business model	Amend to ensure they reflect the business processes as well as the system transactions. Ensure training covers the business context.
Deficient education and training, before and after 'go-live'	Design and implement education & training across affected sites. Plan for next phase to include time to understand business needs. Ensure adequate training resources, post cut-over.
Information retrieval difficulties	Training to cover how to retrieve information and how to interpret reports. Managers and other non-ERP users to be trained in how to retrieve information.
Errors in data migration and inefficient data management	Review data collection processes, including paper-based processes. Ensure appropriate training of the data management administrator.

The business will need to assess and prioritise for rectification the findings of the impact of change review. Table 1 gives examples of some actions that might be appropriate to addressing the common findings identified above.

Sustaining change through continuous improvement

Continuous improvement activities are designed to ensure the programme has permanently implemented a change in the business, and has not temporarily altered the status quo, which will return to normal after the programme ends. Sustaining change activities are the responsibility of business-as-usual management, although the programme should leave in place the skills and environment that will foster the continuous improvement culture.There are a number of practical steps that can be taken to help instil a culture of evolutionary improvement in business performance, after implementation. These include:

- Translating the key performance indicators underpinning the business case benefits to the level of individual responsibility. In this way, individuals will understand explicitly what is expected of them, how it will be measured, and how it is reflected in the business's performance management system. It may be reflected in the organisation's performance and reward systems, so that on or above target levels of performance are incentivised appropriately;
- Providing refresher training, especially where the system is particularly complex, or where there is more sophisticated functionality available that requires users to become familiar with the base system first before they can progress to the other functionality;
- Introducing disincentives to continuing with the 'old' working practices. Remove access to redundant systems and manual practices. Withdraw transition support when the full user population has been trained and are capable of using the system and new processes;
- Measuring achieved benefits and costs regularly post-implementation, to illustrate progress towards achieving the business objectives as set out in the programme business case.

CONCLUSION

A common reason for implementing an ERP system is to gain a competitive advantage. ERP applications certainly have the potential to differentiate an organisation from its competitors. However, as the number of larger enterprises that have implemented ERP systems approaches saturation point (and the mid-market may follow), this reduces the competitive advantage that organisations achieve from such applications. They merely enable them to continue to compete. An organisation can look beyond the cost benefits to identify several soft benefits that can be achieved from implementing ERP systems. These benefits are intangible and usually difficult to quantify. Improved quality and timeliness of information is a major advantage. Better quality of management reporting, control and decision-making and improved drill-down facilities can drastically enhance the quality of decision support. Other examples include better forecasting, better inventory control, improved product delivery schedules, building better relationships with customers, etc.

A large number of organisations fail to realise the benefits offered by ERP solutions. A common cause for ERP systems failing to deliver anticipated benefits is the failure to redesign processes as part of the implementation. Streamlining and re-engineering business processes and improving the sharing of information are essential elements of any ERP implementation. A lack of standardised information across multiple sites or functions also prevents the advantage of integrated and consistent information from being exploited.

A sub-optimal system may also be caused by a number of IT issues. These include hardware, software and know-how factors. If a live system does not use the available functionality, this can result in parallel processes and systems-duplication and/or waste. Alternatively, functionality and features can be misapplied. Poor middle-ware, that is weakly integrated with other company systems, can also adversely affect performance and data quality.

A lack of appropriate technical skills and disciplines to support the implementation effort can have serious consequences. Meta Group predicts that the SAP skill shortage will continue for IT organisations and vendors alike. In many cases, experienced SAP experts either cannot be recruited or they cannot be retained.

Often the importance of organisational acceptance and change issues is not fully appreciated. The priorities in many implementations centre on more technical issues. However, the most perfect processes, system design, infrastructure and strategy alignment are useless if they are not accepted by the people in the organisation and not applied consistently when operating the system. It is a common problem that planned change often exceeds an organisation's capacity to change. Insufficient commitment from top management can result in inadequate resources being provided to successfully implement the system as well as ineffective authority or ability to implement change. Long implementation cycles can lead to team member burnout. The resulting loss of key people can pose serious problems in the project.

Other reasons beyond the areas of process, IT and organisational acceptance can also contribute to the disappointing results achieved from the ERP system implementation. An optimistic business case, which initially sets out unrealistic expectations, can be part of the problem. Indeed in many cases the lack of a detailed business case means that expected benefits were never outlined in the first place. Also, an over-ambitious implementation plan can reduce the probability that the anticipated results can ever be achieved.

All of the factors set out in this section contribute to the failure of ERP implementations to deliver the benefits that were expected of them. As a result firms struggle to achieve the target level of performance expected of the ERP systems. In the next chapter we will explore mechanisms for driving out the value identified in the business case and examine the techniques available for maximising the return on investment in ERP.

Chapter 3

ERP Benefits Realisation

INTRODUCTION

Davenport argues that enterprise resource planning (ERP) systems represents a new model of corporate computing that allow companies to replace their existing information systems (which are often incompatible with one another) with a single, integrated system. When implemented correctly, ERP systems have proved that they can achieve significant business benefits. A review of the recent literature however reveals that a large proportion of ERP implementations fail to provide the business benefits expected in the business case prepared at the outset of the project, and the expected return on investment is rarely realised.

The need for a benefits realisation programme arises primarily because of shortcomings in existing implementation methodologies and the way in which they are applied in practice. In the past these methodologies have tended to be excessively technology and process focussed and paid less attention to vital elements of the project such as cultural, organisational and benefits issues. This lack of emphasis on these areas is especially pronounced when time and budgetary constraints cause the project scope to be reduced.

Organisations are not as mechanistic as these methodologies suggest. On the contrary, they are highly systemic and react to all levers of change, e.g. people, products and services, customers and markets, etc. Implementation methodologies have not been adapted to meet the challenge of focussing efforts on driving out benefits from the new system. Because of the enormous complexity of configuring and implementing just the technological element of the system within budget, going live is seen as a major success in itself. Expectations often do not go beyond this result. In theory, the proprietary implementation methodologies proposed by vendors such as SAP cover all the elements of the organisation and the implementation project. In the case of SAP it covers strategy, planning, organisational dynamics and design, user procedures and training development and target gap analysis at early stages of the project. However, under the methodology many of these issues are not revisited from the design stage until the post-implementation review. The business case is not always developed in detail and where it is, it is often crafted for initial justification only and not revisited or revised throughout the project. In addition, it is frequently not clearly aligned with strategy and does not necessarily adapt to changes in strategic direction of the business, or a change in requirements and/or go-live date. It is common for operating targets not to be defined or benchmarked and no real assessment of potential benefits included.

Other shortcomings of ERP implementation methodologies identified include the lack of a feasibility/project initialisation phase and associated steps, and the absence of mechanisms for identifying, measuring and tracking benefits to be achieved by the live system. The primary focus (on processes and technological configuration) leads to a lack of emphasis on creating value. In addition an inappropriate project structure often means that the tasks to realise benefits are not integrated into an overall plan and reporting is abandoned. The project team may have limited authority to make organisation and process changes and, at crunch time, schedule and budget supersede benefits realisation.

In this chapter we will explore the nature of benefits realisation and the mechanism available to organisations to leverage their investment in ERP systems.

A SECOND WIND FOR ERP

Dorien James and Malcolm L. Wolf. This article was originally published in *The McKinsey Quarterly,* 2000, No. 2, and can be found on the publication's website, www.mckinseyquarterly.com © 2000 McKinsey & Company. All rights reserved. Reprinted by permission.

Throughout the 1990s, most large industrial companies installed enterprise resource planning (ERP) systems – that is, massive computer applications allowing a business to manage all of its operations (finance, requirements planning, human resources, and order fulfillment) on the basis of a single, integrated set of corporate data. ERP promised huge improvements in efficiency – for example, shorter intervals between orders and payments, lower back-office staff requirements, reduced inventory, and improved customer service. Encouraged by these possibilities, businesses around the world invested some $300 billion in ERP during the decade.

What most attracted many a chief information officer was the opportunity to replace a tangle of complete, disparate, and obsolescent applications with a single Y2K-compliant system from a reputable and stable vendor; one major oil company, for example, managed to switch off 350 old systems when ERP went live. By entering customer and sales data in an ERP system, a manufacturer can generate the net cycle's demand forecast, which in turn generates orders for raw materials, production schedules, timetables for shifts, and financial projections while keeping close track of inventory.

For many businesses, installing ERP was traumatic. Following long, painful, and expensive implementations, some companies had difficulty identifying any measurable benefits. Those companies that were able to point to them thought they could have been achieved without the help of the computer system. One chief information officer concluded that "80 per cent of the benefit that we get from our ERP system comes from changes, such as inventory optimization, which we could have achieved without making the IT investment." Today, as the information technology spotlight shifts to electronic business, where "nimbleness" and "Web speed" are the buzzwords, monolithic ERP systems look more and more like cumbersome relics of an older IT world.

Yet companies shouldn't bemoan the cost of their investment: the hard-won skills and capabilities they acquired during the ERP installation process will permit them to improve their ERP applications incrementally, and these improvements collectively add considerable value. ERP can also accommodate technologies that facilitate promising developments, such as electronic commerce and continuous-relationship marketing (CRM), that didn't exist when ERP systems were first installed.

Back-door gains

"What we bought was sustainability," said one ERP director. "Many of the benefits that we are able to achieve today could not have been predicted at the time that we started work on ERP." In fact, in hindsight it appears that much of the value of these large systems lay in the infrastructure foundation they created for future growth based on information technology.

The first element of this foundation is common data. To make an ERP system work in an enterprise or business unit, everyone must agree to enter information using the same vocabulary and format. This discipline renders the data both transparent and easy to compare, exposing anomalies – for instance, the use of different exchange rates to calculate the financial results of different plants – that must be resolved.

Standardized business processes are the second part of the foundation. ERP demands standardization to reduce the number of process variants that must be supported. Painful changes in even the best local traditions may be needed so that orders can be fulfilled consistently throughout a business. When customers demand consistent global quality, globally consistent processes become essential. At least the new processes resulting from ERP are a consequence of design rather than evolution.

The third and last part of the foundation is an organization that has been built to change continually. The implementation of ERP gives many people their first experience of an IT project that truly changes the way a business works. Companies learn – sometimes the hard way – the need for business leadership of IT initiatives and for operating in project rather than line structures. The ability to execute such business initiatives is a valuable asset at a time when fast and flexible IT deployment has become a major success factor in almost all industries.

Ascending the value staircase

For companies that already have ERP systems in place, the key problem is translating this infrastructure into bottom-line value. Think of such companies as standing at the foot of a "staircase of value" (Figure 1). In most cases, the initial implementation will have generated IT cost savings and process efficiencies. Ascending the lower steps of the staircase requires many small adjustments that will cut IT costs and improve business processes further. Reaching the summit means placing applications that can support new initiatives such as e-commerce and CRM on top of ERP.

The bottom steps

At the beginning of the ascent, you have to revisit the business case for ERP – or develop one for the first time – to see where further efficiencies and savings can be realized. You must also introduce a continuous-improvement mindset, which may not be popular with employees. One implementation consultant compared installing ERP to running a marathon; few teams that have flogged themselves to complete the initial systems, reengineering, and change management work on time and on budget are keen to revisit the course.

Still, the push to deliver the original implementation punctually is likely to have left value on the table, and that value can be captured through incremental initiatives.

The key to continued success is pushing responsibility for change outward by appointing a network of "initiative owners", from different functions and sites, who understand the ERP system. Their task should be to find the best ways to implement and sustain each of the improvements locally and to discover new opportunities for improvement.

Figure 1: Climbing the staircase of value

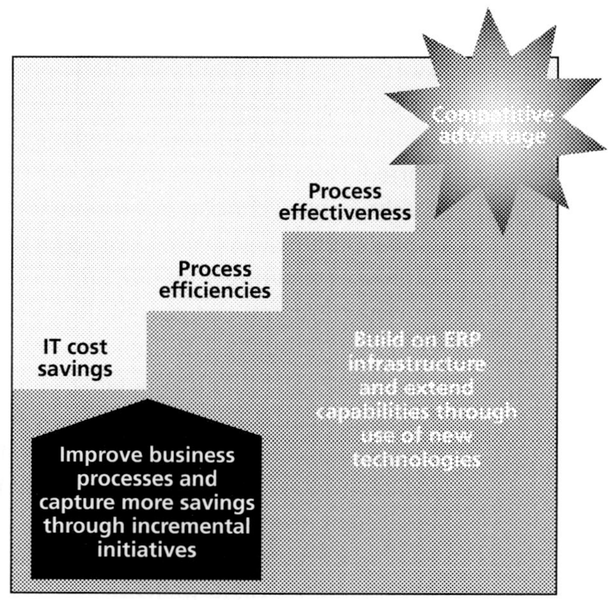

Refining the system. One such initiative involves refining the ERP system's technical and commercial operation in order to drive out costs. For example, service functions, such as accounts payable or IT operations, that are duplicated in different locations, can be consolidated.

"Nice-to-have" features. Deadline pressures probably forced the original ERP implementation team to jettison inessential but useful functions. Look for add-ons, such as electronic-ordering and -payment systems, whose payback times could be very short.

Captured data. ERP systems capture reams of information on customers, suppliers, and internal processes. By analyzing all this, businesses can find opportunities to sell more or spend less. Information from a payment data-base, for example, may show that a company buys comparable products from a number of suppliers. Placing orders with just a few could win a substantial discount.

Extending uniformity. Sometimes the desire to optimize local operations exacts a global price. One manufacturer, finding that its different distribution processes interfered with its ability to manage its stock-control system in a number of European countries, unified the distribution process. "It was obvious in hindsight," a manager said, but employees "needed the experience to understand why we all had to do it the same way."

The top steps

With these initiatives in hand, you can start mounting the top steps, which build on the ERP infrastructure, to achieve competitive advantage. A range of technologies, many of which emerged after ERP began to be implemented, can extend and enhance the capabilities of the original system. The four examples given here by no means exhaust the possibilities.

Sell-side e-commerce. It is easy to build a World Wide Web site to advertise products and accept credit card numbers. But to become an industrial-strength, high-volume on-line retailer, a company must have world-class order fulfillment and distribution – one of the biggest challenges for electronic retailers. Whatever advantages nimble new on-line entrants may enjoy, there is tremendous value in having a system that can handle not only order fulfillment but also returns, partial shipments, and refunds. Internet commerce applications such as BroadVision, INTERSHOP, and InterWorld can build on existing ERP systems to offer customers high-quality service through the Internet channel.

Electronic procurement. On the buy side, attaching an e-procurement module to an ERP system can restrict purchases to preferred suppliers and cut out maverick spending by employees who have too little time to go through required procedures. Say an accountant needs a new computer. An e-procurement module allows that person to choose "computer supplies" from the procurement folder appearing on everyone's desktop and to select the desired model from the company's preferred supplier. If the price exceeds the limit, the order automatically circulates to all designated approvers, and once they sign off, it goes to the supplier for fulfillment. The clincher is that the ERP system also receives and pays the invoice electronically, cutting out liaison with the accounts organization. E-procurement specialists such as Ariba and Commerce One have developed such systems, as have established ERP systems vendors, including SAP and Oracle.

Continuous-relationship marketing. Electronic orders yield far more information about customers than over-the-counter sales do – not only who those customers are, but also what else they looked at and even, if you care to track this, how much time they spent on each screen. An add-on application can combine customer data obtained from e-commerce with information in the existing ERP system, helping you cater to individual tastes and create lifelong relationships with customers. Such tools – supplied, for example, by the specialists Siebel Systems and Vantive, and by the major ERP vendors – make it possible to track customer interactions across all sales channels.

Supply chain optimization. Suppose that a toy manufacturer must buy lots of plastic. Applications from companies like i2 Technologies and SAP can take production schedules generated by the manufacturer's ERP system and compare them with information about current raw-materials costs. These applications can then automatically place orders with the supplier offering the best price in the right volume at the right time.

Roads to ERP

The vision of snapping leading-edge functions onto ERP like Lego bricks is seductive, but the reality is complex. Standard ERP systems use a single logical database shared by all ERP modules to provide a common view of an organization's data. In the early '90s, this was a farsighted way to overcome inconsistency and fragmentation; today it seems monolithic and inflexible. But a number of technologies, collectively known as middleware, are eliminating the requirement that all ERP modules share the same database.

Middleware allows application components to communicate through standardized messages, which simplify the coupling between systems. As a result, the integration of disparate applications becomes increasingly flexible and manageable; indeed, middleware can integrate applications running not only within but also beyond a company's boundaries, so it is particularly useful in fast-moving environments where alliances, mergers, and acquisitions are routine.

What next for the big vendors?

Unlike the early 1990s, when the use of ERP systems increased explosively, 1999 was a slow year for vendors (Figure 2). Saturation of these companies' core industrial-market sectors – consumer products, energy, manufacturing, and pharmaceuticals – as well as the reluctance of many of the companies to implement big systems before the start of the new millennium, put a crimp in sales. ERP vendors are now pursuing three major routes to renewed growth. The first is expansion into service-sector industries. Although the major vendors compete in all of the main branches of business, they have much more experience in heavy industry than in services. Because it is hard to find much similarity between a manufacturer's planning system and, say, that of a bank, expansion here may be difficult.

Figure 2: A slow year for enterprise resource planning (ERP)

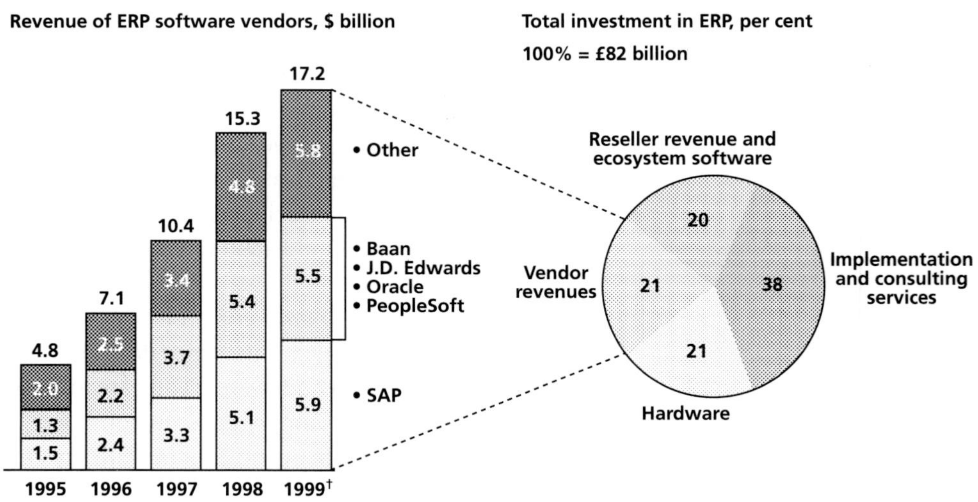

† Estimated
Source: AMR Research; Infact Research; McKinsey analysis

Expansion into new functional areas – such as sales-side electronic commerce, continuous-relationship marketing (CRM), and electronic procurement – is a second possible growth strategy for ERP vendors. Pursuing it would require them either to develop proprietary offerings or to acquire companies that have complementary products, much as the major vendor PeopleSoft did when it bought CRM specialist Vantive.

The third potential growth strategy is to address the needs of small to midsize businesses. The vendors could tackle this segment by serving as application service providers (ASPs), which offer companies (on a pay-per-use basis) ERP applications running on vendor-owned and vendor-maintained computer systems. Systems supplied by ASPs are particularly attractive to start-up companies that can't reliably predict their future business volumes, can't afford to pay for first-tier ERP systems, and don't want to be continually replacing cheaper, less capable systems as their businesses grow.

Such technical advances mean that companies enhancing their old ERP systems or buying new ones will gradually come to feel less need to get all of the elements from a single vendor (see previous section). Fast-changing businesses that use middleware to manage the integration of components are likely to choose different best-of-breed vendors for each of them (Figure 2).

But an organization that has already made a big commitment to a major ERP vendor should think hard before moving toward the best of breed. SAP, the ERP market leader, and Oracle, the number-two player, have consistently extended their product ranges to compete against emerging products in "hot" functional areas. Companies that build on existing ERP systems can stick with their original vendors, an approach that lowers their exposure to risk but leaves them lagging, to a certain extent, behind the state of the art.

Alternatively, they can use third-party products to extend their ERP systems, with the original vendors controlling the overall architecture. Or they can take the bull by the horns and combine products from a number of different vendors into a suite of heterogeneous applications linked by messaging middleware. Although the third approach frees a business from dependence on a single vendor, it is more expensive.

Figure 3: New technologies create new choices in enterprise resource planning

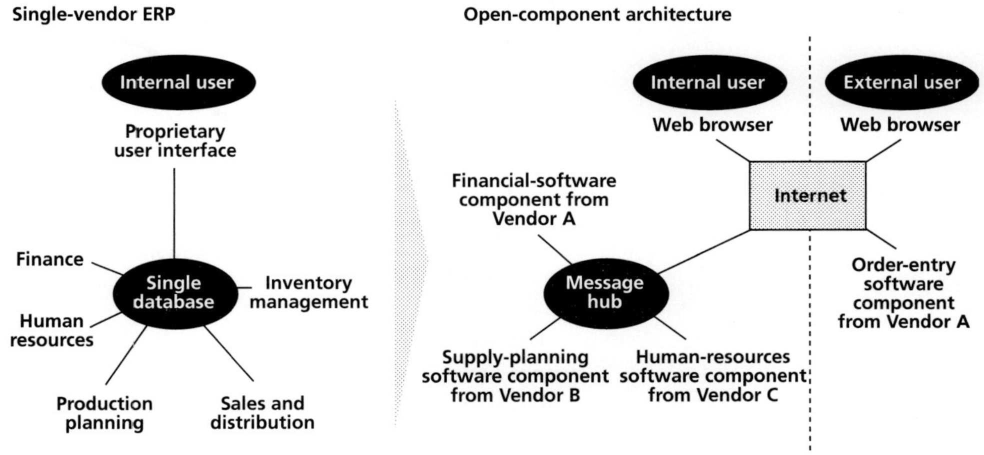

ERP systems may feel like an albatross to companies that have expensively and painfully installed them. Nonetheless, they constitute a valuable foundation for a wide range of new value-enhancing applications. And the emergence of middleware will give companies seeking distinctive solutions greater flexibility and choice.

ENTERPRISE RESOURCE PLANNING SYSTEMS (ERP):
A FRAMEWORK FOR BENEFITS REALISATION
Martin Fahy and Susan O'Connor

It has been shown that the significant benefits which ERP systems are capable of achieving are not currently being achieved in practice for many implementation projects. The long-term solution is to adapt the ERP implementation methodologies and the way in which they are employed in live projects. Making major changes to something as large and complicated as the ERP implementation methodology is not something that can be achieved in a short timeframe. It is also a solution that will not help organisations, which have already completed their implementation of ERP with disappointing results. The solution in the latter cases is the Benefits Realisation.

An ERP Benefits Realisation programme leverages the company's existing ERP system investment and capabilities to significantly increase the return on the ERP investment with a relatively small incremental investment. It provides the opportunity to realise many tangible and intangible benefits that the ERP investment can enable which were never realised, or envisioned, during the initial implementation. A Benefits Realisation project establishes the ongoing processes which deliver continuous shareholder value for the company in a 'low risk/high reward' scenario. It integrates performance goals with all project initiatives. The approach should be highly interactive with continuous client involvement ensuring skill transfer and development of the new process 'champions'. It should promote the use of benchmarking and 'best practices' concepts to facilitate continuous change within the organisation and challenge the organisation to look at information technology as an investment, not an expense, therefore using its power to gain competitive advantage.

Figure 1: Performance without a Benefits Realisation programme

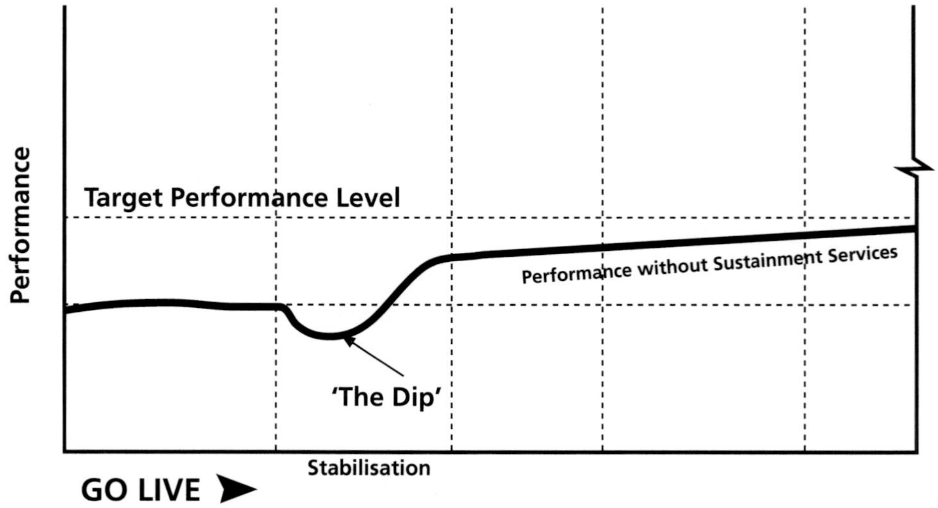

The whole concept of a Benefits Realisation centres around the fact that the ERP system life cycle does not end after the go-live date. If the extent of the organisation's activities after the go-live date are limited to stabilisation activities, research has shown that most organisations do not achieve their expected performance level once it has been fully implemented. In fact, the performance level may even decline after stabilisation as the system is gradually reconfigured back to the old one.

In such a scenario, the level of investment in ERP may be reduced (i.e.: IT, change management and business process reengineering are materially cut back, as demonstrated by Figure 2) but total investment to date has not achieved an acceptable return.

Figure 2: Total investment in ERP without sustainment services

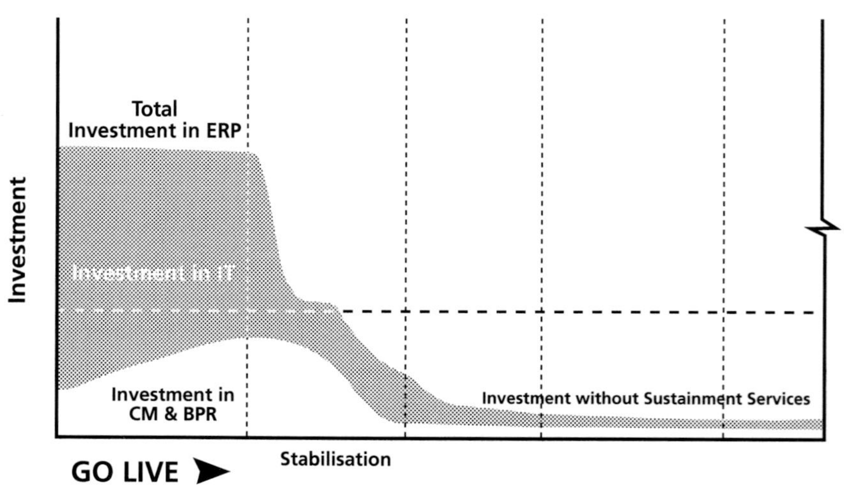

The ERP Benefits Realisation approach is focussed on driving out value. It provides significant improvements in performance through completion of high value and high impact programs that have been proposed in the final deliverable of the Benefits Realisation project.

This performance improvement is achieved by a relatively small incremental investment. A large proportion of the incremental investment is directed at change management and process improvement, especially when compared to the split of the implementation investment (between IT and change management and business process reengineering, etc.).

The Benefits Realisation should be very focussed on maximising the return on investment. This can be seen when the performance improvement achieved is compared to the incremental investment made during the implementation project and during the Benefits Realisation project. This ROI is significantly higher than that achieved by the original implementation project.

Figure 3: Performance with ERP sustainment services

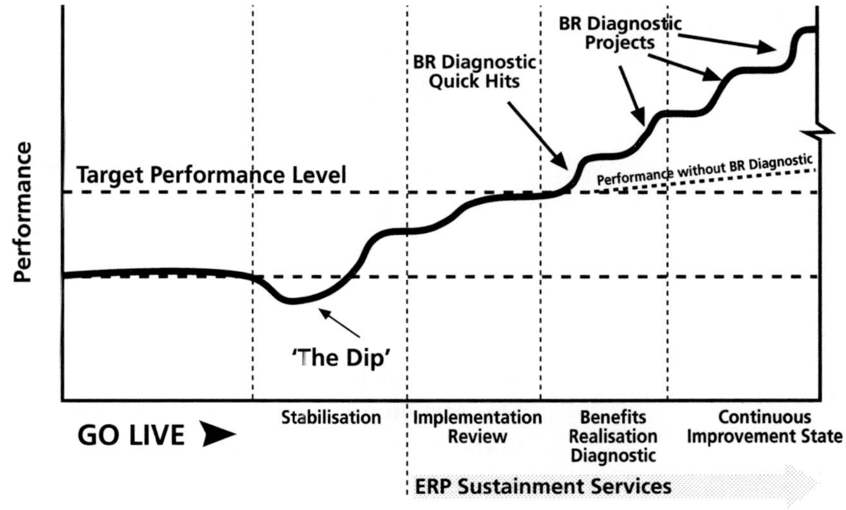

Figure 4: Total investment with sustainment services

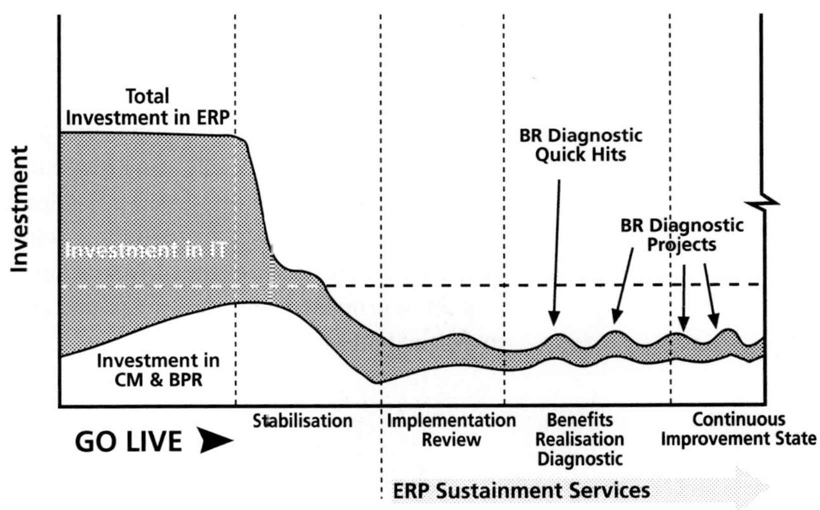

Figure 5: Total investment and performance improvement with sustainment services

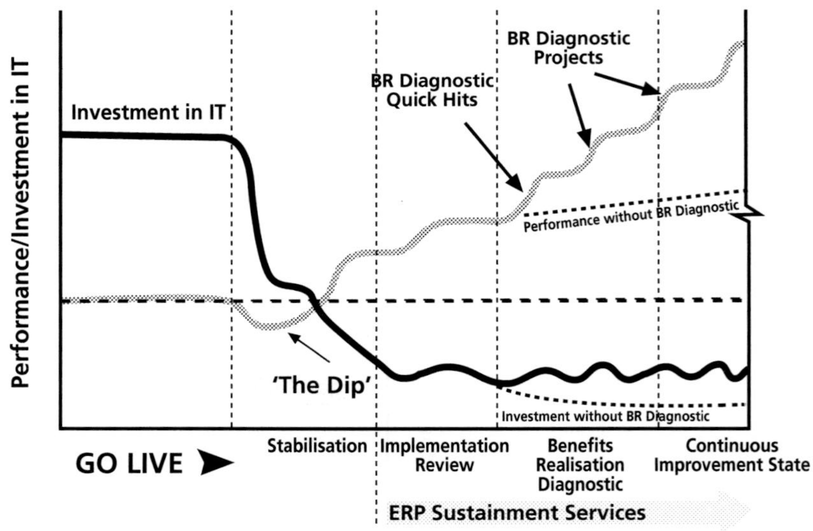

A framework for Benefits Realisation

This section presents a framework for Benefits Realisation in ERP environments. The purpose of the framework is to support the development of a realistic agenda of improvement opportunities which will create the most value for the enterprise and its shareholders. The framework is designed to enable practitioners to provide a rapid assessment of how effectively the organisation is applying its ERP system along several key dimensions. It seeks to integrate the overall corporate strategy, information technology, business processes and organisational change aspects of the enterprise. The overall aim is to maximise the level of business value derived from the ERP system and its environment.

The framework has four phases. Within each phase are a number of tasks. Each task requires a number of steps to be carried out. To carry out all of these steps, practitioners will require additional information such as methodologies and benchmarking information. A variety of inputs will be involved to achieve several deliverables for each of the four phases. These inputs include senior management interviews, surveys, process walkthroughs and industry experts. Deliverables include work products such as a description of relative position, a list of key opportunity areas, summary of the potential impact of proposed solutions and value chain process analysis, all of which contribute to the next phase.

Figure 6: The Benefits Realisation framework

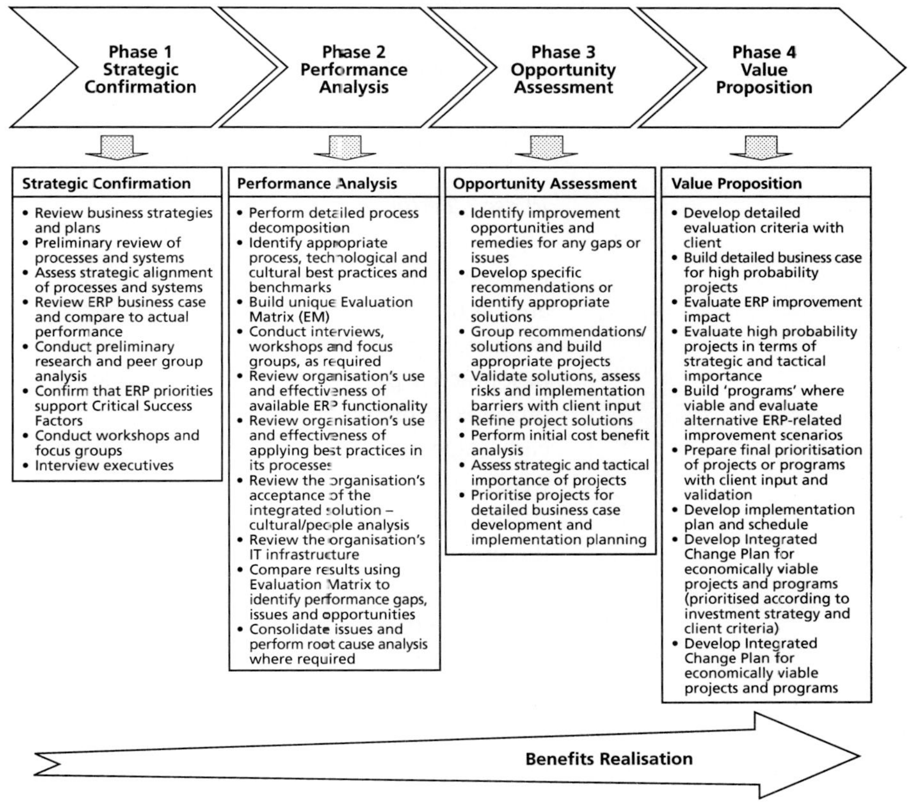

Phase 1. Strategic confirmation:

The primary aim of this phase is to confirm that the organisation's current systems and processes support its overall corporate strategy. This phase involves a high level review of strategies, processes and systems to identify key opportunity areas and material misalignments between strategies and the supporting environment. This will determine the focus for efforts in later phases when more detailed assessments will be carried out. The intention is that this phase will be relatively brief (one to four weeks, depending on the size of the organisation). The overall aim of this phase is to confirm the alignment of the organisation's IT and corporate goals. To do so will involve some or all of the following tasks:

- Review business strategies and plans;
- Preliminary review of processes and systems;
- Assess strategic alignment of processes and systems;
- Review ERP business case and compare to actual performance;
- Conduct preliminary research and peer group analysis;
- Confirm that ERP priorities support Critical Success Factors;
- Conduct workshops and focus groups;
- Interview executives.

Inputs in the strategic confirmation phase include strategies, plans, business case(s), senior management interviews, publications, industry experts, etc. Additional information that would be relevant to carrying out this strategic confirmation includes checklists, interview guides, analysis tools and publications. This opening exercise yields a number of valuable deliverables. The practitioner gains an understanding of the organisations mission, strategies, business environment, key products, markets and systems. The tactical support of processes and systems is confirmed, or conflicts between processes, systems and strategies are identified. A preliminary list of key opportunity areas and risks is created and owners may even be assigned to these at this stage. Also, initial baseline data for later comparisons and benchmarking is established. Finally, this phase provides the opportunity to establish and manage client expectations and determines the emphasis for the remainder of the project. These deliverables are used in the next phase for more detailed analysis or to adapt the focus of efforts in that phase.

Phase 2. Performance analysis

The primary purpose of the performance analysis phase is to gauge the current position of the enterprise relative to benchmarks and best practices. The organisation is evaluated at the detailed process level. Key performance indicators (KPIs) are identified and measured, processes and other factors are reviewed in detail, benchmark values and best practice processes are determined and a comparison is made. The intention of this phase is to highlight areas where the current performance is particularly weak at an early stage in the Benefits Realisation project. This will enable efforts to be focussed on weaker areas where the potential improvements and returns are greatest.

In applying the benchmarking and best practices methodology, the performance of the organisation is assessed from four integrated perspectives – process, ERP software, cultural and IT infrastructure. The use of the ERP system and all of its functionality will be examined to determine its effectiveness. The processes being applied by users will be reviewed and critically assessed and the activities and acceptance of users will be considered. Finally, the technical infrastructure will be looked at to determine possible performance and capability improvements that may be made. As a result of this detailed comparison of the organisation to best practices, several performance gaps and issues are identified. In some cases, these issues may be consolidated and the causes of these issues determined.

This is the most detailed phase of the framework and the one where most knowledge and experience is required on the part of the consultants. The tasks to be undertaken in the performance analysis phase are:

- Perform detailed process decomposition;
- Identify appropriate process, technological and cultural best practices and benchmarks;
- Build unique Evaluation Matrix;
- Conduct interviews, workshops and focus groups, as required;
- Review organisation's use and effectiveness of available ERP functionality;
- Review organisation's use and effectiveness of applying best practices in its processes;
- Review the organisation's acceptance of the integrated solution – cultural/people analysis;
- Review the organisation's IT infrastructure;
- Compare results using Evaluation Matrix to identify performance gaps, issues and opportunities;
- Consolidate issues and perform root cause analysis where required.

The Evaluation Matrix will be tailored to each organisation and its design will require several interviews with users and management, plant tours, observations and a review of available documentation to determine how different areas conduct business and how well the ERP system supports that business. Workshops and focus groups may also be appropriate. This task will involve comparing processes and uses of system functionality in different areas to "best practice". The ultimate goal is to develop recommendations that can be applied to a number of areas. These will aim to optimise the ERP system functionality to the internal practices within the organisation or world class best practice processes (depending on the best practices used). Alternatively, if the comparisons are made against industry benchmarks, the end result sought would be optimising system functionality to industry best practices.

The exact details of the matrix will depend on the client organisation, its industry and the scope of the Benefits Realisation engagement. The main deliverables of the performance assessment phase are an ERP and technology analysis, an organisational acceptance analysis and a value chain process analysis. These may be summarised for each area where an evaluation matrix questionnaire was completed or consolidated across all areas. Finally, the causes of these gaps should have been identified, whether these were determined during the review tasks or by means of a separate root cause analysis exercise. These gaps and causes are fed to the next phase to identify opportunities and develop recommendations to overcome them.

Phase 3. Opportunity assessment

The opportunity assessment will involve an examination of the issues and gaps highlighted by the performance analysis phase. Process, technological and people issues are considered. Improvement opportunities are identified. Recommendations and solutions are proposed, considered and grouped together into viable projects. The associated risks and implementation barriers are assessed and the solutions are validated with the client. Preliminary cost-benefit analyses are carried out where appropriate and the strategic and tactical importance of projects is assessed.

The tasks to be carried out in phase three include:

- Identify improvement opportunities and remedies for any gaps or issues;
- Develop specific recommendations or identify appropriate solutions;
- Group recommendations/solutions and build appropriate projects;
- Validate solutions, assess risks and implementation barriers with client input;
- Refine project solutions;
- Perform initial cost-benefit analysis;
- Assess strategic and tactical importance of projects ;
- Prioritise projects for detailed business case development and implementation planning.

Several deliverables are created in this opportunity assessment phase. Improvement opportunities are quantified in terms of cost and estimated return and a list of general and specific recommendations and benefits is produced. Evaluation matrices are completed at the detailed sub-process level identifying recommendations for each location assessed or consolidated recommendations for the organisation as a whole. The main work product that is used in the final phase is the refined list of potential projects, for which initial prioritisation and draft charters for high priority projects has been completed.

Phase 4. Value proposition

Proposed projects that appear to be viable following phase 3 are then evaluated and prioritised according to the client's investment strategies and other relevant criteria. The client may require assistance in determining these evaluation criteria. A business case is developed for high priority projects. The impact of the expected improvements and strategic and tactical importance of each project is considered. The priority of projects is revised, where appropriate.

Programs of improvement projects may be built involving different combinations of viable projects. Each scenario is evaluated and the final prioritisation of projects or programs agreed with the client. An implementation plan and schedule are developed for each project or program and an overall integrated change plan for a portfolio of viable projects or programs is developed as a final deliverable of the project.

The value proposition phase involves the following tasks:

- Develop detailed evaluation criteria with client;
- Build detailed business case for high probability projects;
- Evaluate ERP improvement impact;
- Evaluate high probability projects in terms of strategic and tactical importance;
- Build "programs" where viable and evaluate alternative ERP related improvement scenarios;
- Prepare final prioritisation of projects or programs with client input and validation;
- Develop implementation plan and schedule;
- Develop Integrated Change Plan for economically viable projects and programs (prioritised according to investment strategy and client criteria).

These implementation plans are integrated to produce an overall plan for projects to be undertaken following the completion of the Benefits Realisation project. Where more than one project or program is involved, they are prioritised according to investment strategy and client criteria. This plan will consider possible overlaps of scope, resources and other factors.

The final deliverables of this value proposition phase and the Benefits Realisation project as a whole include a portfolio of prioritised projects and/or programs and a value proposition business case for each high probability project. A final action program and individual project charters are also produced, as are implementation plans and schedules and an overall integrated change plan.

The value added by the Benefits Realisation framework

The Benefits Realisation framework integrates four core capabilities to maximise the potential for driving out value from a number of perspectives. This is the key strength of the framework. It combines detailed ERP-specific "know-how" and experience with process, change management and infrastructure expertise to drive the maximum value from the entire system.

As seen below, the reasons that benefits are not realised from ERP implementations are primarily as a result of process, organisational acceptance and change and IT issues. The proposed framework addresses these reasons under similar categories. Skills from each of these perspectives are integrated in the Benefits Realisation approach. The "other issues" identified are addressed using management, organisation, risk management, planning and other project experience to improve the performance of the organisation as a whole. Figure 7 summarises the four perspectives used to identify improvement opportunities in the organisation's ERP environment and a number of the tools applied in each case. The authors believe that the framework is unique because of a number of its features. The proposed reviews integrate four different areas, each approaching the problem from a different perspective. Value is driven from the total ERP environment by projects that address people and cultural, process, ERP and technical and organisational issues. The assessments are also very detailed, whether it is down through several levels of sub-processes, specific ERP product configuration design and extensive functionality in use, server and network performance or enterprise-wide organisational and change strategy issues. The best-practices approach is also a key feature. The benefits being sought go beyond those that were identified in the business case

Figure 7: Core capabilities for the framework

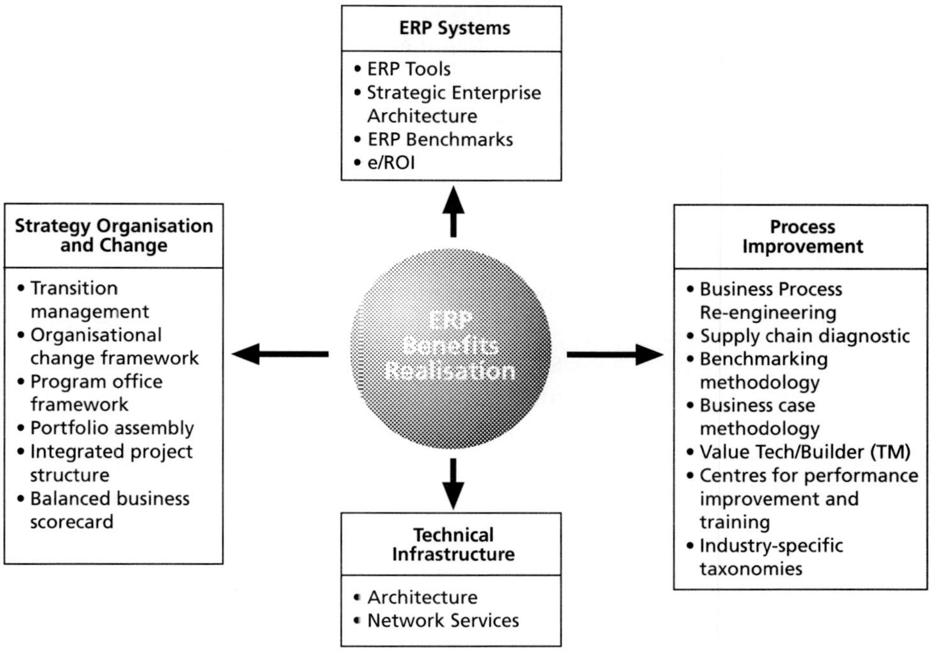

or reaching predefined benchmarks. The approach is intended to identify the performance gap between the organisation's current performance and the moving target of best practices and introduce the processes that will enable it to reach those performance levels on an ongoing basis. It is tailored to the organisation, provides a basis for a continuous improvement model and is a baseline by which all future performance can be measured. In addition, it is a repeatable process and provides a blueprint to implement industry-best practices and move to a best-in-class organisation.

There is a strong emphasis on driving shareholder value and maximising return on investment (i.e. the Benefits Realisation investment and also the return on the entire ERP investment to date). The benefits and projects identified by a Benefits Realisation project are suggested after their contribution to shareholder value has been assessed in detail. This value focus changes how success is measured. In the past, companies were measured by profit and loss (a somewhat subjective value), and earnings per share. In the future, value based management will become more of the norm for measuring their success or failure. Shareholder value and cash flow (where cash is more factual and involves less judgement) will be key measurements. Currently, projects have a significant IT focus and are often considered a success if the system is implemented on time and within budget. In contrast, the proposed framework's emphasis is on business, the return on system investment and delivering a value proposition. This focus on Shareholder Value Added (SVA) is a key feature of the methodology.

The Benefits Realisation framework is scalable across facilities, processes or functional areas. It effectively applies a breadth and depth of ERP, process improvement, change management and IT expertise. Also, it includes high levels of user/client involvement ensuring significant transfer of skills. It provides a low risk with high reward potential and attempts to achieve full cost recovery within a relatively short period of initiating "quick win" projects. The ERP Benefits Realisation framework leverages the company's existing ERP system investment and capabilities to significantly increase the return on the ERP investment with a relatively small incremental investment. It provides the opportunity to realise many tangible and intangible benefits that the ERP investment can enable which were never realised, or envisioned, during the initial implementation. A Benefits Realisation project establishes the ongoing processes which deliver continuous shareholder value for the company. It integrates performance goals with all project initiatives. It promotes the use of benchmarking and "best practices" concepts to facilitate continuous change within the organisation and challenges the organisation to look at information technology as an investment, not an expense, therefore using its power to gain competitive advantage. Finally, it is a process for establishing ownership and accountability for achieving benefits and an ongoing tracking and measuring of benefits. It aims to operationalise Benefits Realisation processes to become an integral part of the organisational activities that remain in place after the Benefits Realisation project.

The ERP Benefits Realisation approach is focussed on driving out value. It provides significant improvements in performance through completion of high value and high impact programs that have been proposed in the final deliverable of the Benefits Realisation project. This performance improvement is achieved by a relatively small incremental investment. A large proportion of the incremental investment is directed at change management and process improvement, especially when compared to the split of the implementation investment (between IT and change management and business process reengineering, etc.). The Benefits Realisation service is very focussed on maximising the return on investment. This can be seen when the performance improvement achieved is compared to the incremental investment made during the implementation project and during the Benefits Realisation project. This ROI is significantly higher than that achieved by the original implementation project.

MAKING ERP SUCCEED: TURNING FEAR INTO PROMISE

Scott Buckhout, Edward Frey and Joseph Nemec Jr.

***strategy + business*, 1999 Second Quarter**

Reprinted with permission from *strategy + business*, a quarterly management magazine published by Booz•Allen & Hamilton.

The FoxMeyer Corporation used to be one of the largest wholesale drug distribution companies in the United States, with more than $5 billion in annual revenues. Attempting to improve its competitive position and prepare for growth, the company decided to use a popular enterprise resource planning (ERP) system, a group of software programs designed to tie together disparate company functions to create more efficient operations in areas such as the assembly or delivery of products.

FoxMeyer became an early believer in the potential merits of ERP systems and installed one with the help of one of the most reputable system integrators. Yet, by 1997, after FoxMeyer had invested two and a half years of effort and more than $100 million, the company could only process 2.4 per cent of the overnight orders that it had with ancient legacy systems – and even that small percentage suffered from information errors. The company fell into bankruptcy and was acquired for a mere $80 million. Its trustees are now suing its system suppliers, blaming the ERP implementation for its business failure.

Is this an extreme case? Clearly. Is this unusual? Sadly, no.

Implementations of ERP systems are struggling throughout the world. They take too long, cost too much and fail to deliver the promised benefits of competitive advantage and cost reduction. Despite the promise and the high investment required to implement ERP systems, statistics show that more than 70 per cent of ERP implementations, whether self-created or designed by established ERP software vendors, fail to achieve their corporate goals.

In a landmark study, the Standish Group, a market research company specializing in software and electronic commerce, looked at implementations in companies with more than $500 million in revenues. The study found that the average cost overrun was 178 per cent; the average schedule overrun was 230 per cent of original expectations, and the average slide in functional improvements was an astonishing 59 per cent deficit (see Figure 1).

Figure 1: Few ERP implementations hit targets

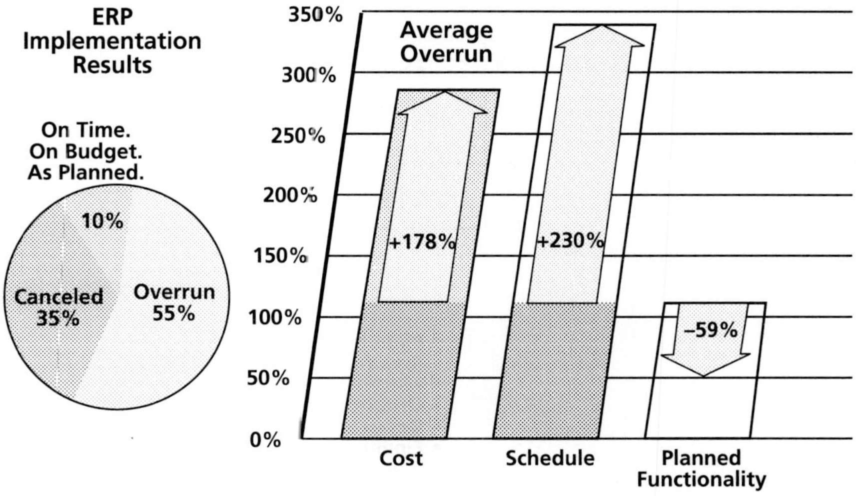

Source: Booz-Allen & Hamilton

Still, such aggregate statistics hide real, and specific, horror stories about companies such as FoxMeyer Drug and the Dell Computer Corporation that have tried the systems. Dell publicly canceled its ERP system after two gruelling years and an expenditure that exceeded $200 million. The company could tell it would not get the results for which it had paid so dearly and switched to a combined system/process solution that has redefined the industry.

Despite the horror stories, more than 20,000 companies worldwide paid in excess of $10 billion to adopt ERP systems in 1997 alone. Why do companies persist in trying? Some believe ERP systems will reduce the complexity inherent with using multiple data sources and systems that plague growth in global enterprises. Others hope ERP systems will solve the problem of legacy systems that inhibit re-engineering projects or the unknown difficulties that will arrive on Jan.1, 2000. Still others consider ERP systems the strategic weapons of the 21st century.

In fact, ERP systems have delivered for some companies. For example, use of such a system helped the Chevron Corporation cut purchasing costs by 15 per cent and promises an additional 10 per cent in the near future. International Business Machines Storage Products reduced the time required to update pricing data from as much as 80 days to five minutes. AutoDesk Inc. saved enough from inventory reductions alone to pay for the entire implementation.

So what is the problem with ERP systems? Is it a question, as some academic observers suggest, of poor corporate organization? Or is it, as some technicians believe, due to a real corporate inability to make the tough decisions necessary for a profitable implementation?

After more than five years of helping chief executive officers and general managers implement ERP systems, we believe neither of these reasons explains the gap between corporate expectations and results. Our experience shows ERP difficulties stem from two issues:

- The company has not made the strategic choices needed to configure the systems and processes;
- The implementation process spins out of business control naturally. This is inherent in the ERP implementation process.

Figure 2: A product-aligned process flow lowers system requirements

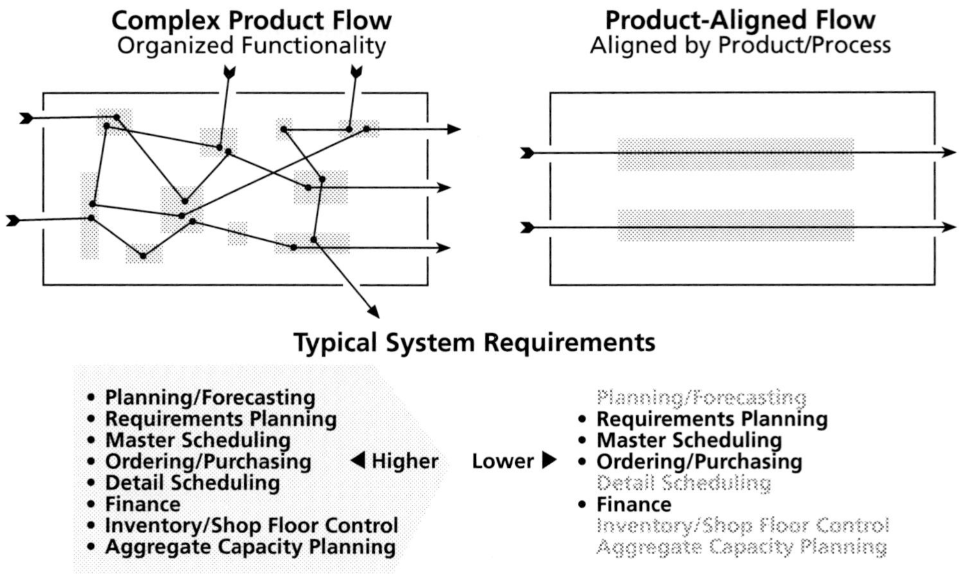

Source: Booz-Allen & Hamilton

ISSUE NO. 1: Getting strategic choices made

ERP systems integrate key data and communications on planning, scheduling, purchasing, forecasting and finance for companies across regions, products, divisions and functions. Popular extensions can broaden this reach to sales, marketing, human resources and other functions. Many of the examples we will use will draw from the core ERP functionality, but the issue of strategic choices becomes even more important for a more comprehensive system. The system can provide management detailed insight into the operations of the business. For example, for a manufacturing company, an ERP system can show how much raw-material inventory is on hand, how much it costs to manufacture each product, and where each order is on the shop floor.

While an ERP system can provide this information, the key question is, Should it?

Stepping back from the ERP system – looking at the information, communication and control functions it can provide – it becomes clear that the amount of control over a company's operations that needs to be provided by the ERP system depends on the design of the flow of products and services in the company.

A complex flow requires much system control. A well-designed value chain (e.g. "Product-Aligned Flow," in which the product flows using visual signals and well-defined routes) can embed many of the controls and other functions in the business process simply and far less expensively than the ERP system possibly could (see Figure 2).

The legacy processes that are being replaced, by necessity, embedded much of the communication and control in the business processes, and years of learning made this set of business processes very efficient and effective. Most implementations do not recognize and therefore do not capture this organizational efficiency.

Another celebrated version of the information, communications and control choices that companies miss is exemplified by the famous Japanese lean production systems. In these, much of the communication and control are designed right into the production system – and the computer has a very small role. (A Japanese visitor, after thoroughly examining a new ERP system in a United States automobile company, said, "This is a very impressive system. Of course, we'd have one too if we needed one.")

Lean production systems deliver low cost, low overhead, highly effective communication and control. How? For example, when a production process using Japanese kanban visual signals needs more raw material from a supplier, production workers pull a card and send it to the supplier. No computers, no orders, no overhead needed. The communication and control are built into the process design. Yet United States companies that are implementing ERP and lean production techniques often put a firewall between the two, not recognizing that this undermines both. The right answer is to recognize the decision the company is facing and make the decision explicit for all the company's efforts.

What can go wrong? At one company, the implementation team installed the detailed capacity-planning module of the ERP system, assuming that the company needed to understand and control capacity in detail (for example, per shift). In the legacy environment, detailed capacity planning had not been an option because the system was incapable of delivering it, so shop management got by with aggregate capacity planning as needed for staffing and capital decisions (which were made annually or quarterly). When implemented, the detailed capacity planning processes added overhead costs to do work no one had needed before. Tragically, the level of granularity required in the data (e.g. detailed, accurate setup and run times, scrap factors, machine downtimes) to develop the detailed capacity estimates accurately was impossible to achieve, so the capacity profiles created were useless. Nobody bothered to ask if the company in fact needed detailed capacity planning, and senior management saw the decision only when it was too late.

Judy Johnson, program director for the Integrated Systems Solutions Company, a subsidiary of the International Business Machines Corporation, put it this way: "This [is] not a decision to simply buy an I.T. tool – it [is] a decision on how to shape [the] business."

The reality is that an ERP system locks in the operating principles and processes for the corporation. Once the ERP system is installed, the odds of being able or willing to pay for modifications are close to zero. The cost, complexity, investment of time and staff, and implications and politics of untangling such an expensive investment, prohibit most companies from tackling this issue. Consequently, it is important that ERP systems be implemented in a business-driven, cost-effective fashion from the start.

Management needs to translate the business strategy/key future competitive advantages into factors for the implementation. This often requires non-system actions to develop the physical or business resources to support the simpler system needs. For example, in a manufacturing company, lean manufacturing or alternative supplier relationship initiatives may be needed to eliminate the system-ordering functionality that adds so much cost and complexity. The result, of course, is a more efficient overall delivery process as the production or other delivery process embeds low cost communication and control.

Fortunately, only a limited number of critical business decisions require continuing top-management ownership. For example, in a manufacturing environment, senior management only has to focus on eight key areas to determine what actions should be inside or outside the system. (see Figure 3).

ERP systems often provide a backbone of information, communication and control for a company, but managers seldom ask: "Which information? What communication? Where should control reside?" Even if they do ask and answer these questions, it is sometimes difficult to keep the decisions intact because the implementation process takes over and the decisions get recast on the basis of the system, not the business.

Figure 3: Focus on key business decisions

Typical ERP approach	Business-critical ERP decisions Critical business issue	Alternative
• Frequently run Manufacturing Resource Planning (MRP) to generate planned production orders – Explode multiple layers in the Bill of Material – Schedule with detailed multistep routings for end part number	• How will we know which parts to build and when?	• Build to rate for basic and stable parts • Cycle schedule for 'Option' oriented parts
• Print work instructions every time an order is produced	• How will the mechanics know how to build each part?	• Use resident work instructions that leverage process stability in part families
• Run Capacity Requirement Planning module to build up capacity for each machine based on individual part set-up and run time	• How will capacity requirements be estimated?	• Estimate capactiy requirements based on aggregate demand on the bottleneck machine
• 'Wand' each operation 'complete' in the system for every order as it is moved between machines on the shop floor – indicating the exact location of every order	• How will we know the location of each order on the shop floor?	• Co-locate machines in cells; minimise work in progress; track orders with visual controls
• Run MRP system to generate start time for every operation on every order • Sort through queue in front of each machine to find next 'hottest' job	• How will each mechanic know which order to work next?	• Work orders on a 'first in–first worked' basis – no system information required
• 'Wand' orders into system, which generates specific location in warehouse for every order received • Use system to allocate raw material to specific production orders and 'debit' from available stock	• How will we know where to store raw material and how much is available?	• Store inventory in a dedicated 'static' location • Replenish inventory when level reaches visual reorder point (based on required lead time)
• Run MRP to generate purchase orders based on reorder lead times • Create individual purchase orders for every required shipment for raw material • Close every purchase order for each shipment received and pay upon delivery	• How will we know when to order raw material when it has been received?	• 'Blanket' purchase orders that cover multiple shipments • Base shipments on cycle schedules or production rate • Base periodic payment on production rates (payment adjusted for exceptions)
• Use system to build up overall cost from each order: (1) Set up and run time for each required operation (2) Actual material consumption based on inventory allocations to each production order	• How will we compute product costs?	• Periodically compute costs based on aggregate prodcution (by part family) and aggregate resources consumed
Defaults to 'just-in-case' most complex solution	**Focuses on business needs**	**Opens up simpler alternatives**

Source: Booz-Allen & Hamilton

ISSUE NO. 2: How to keep the implementation process from spinning out of control – put the C.E.O. in charge

The new ERP commandment for senior management is "Put the chief executive officer in charge." We hasten to add that we are not referring to the usual "first commandment" of getting support from the top. Putting the chief executive officer in charge defines a different level of involvement in the implementation process.

The business case for implementing an ERP system is invariably built around significant cost reductions and improved capabilities. The cost savings are based on reduced legacy information technology costs as well as decreased indirect labor, direct labor and inventory costs. Improved capabilities often include world-class processes, tighter control and reduced cycle time.

Once the business case is closed, companies often focus on software and not business objectives – with an implicit assumption that the benefits will follow. At this time, senior executives typically relegate too much responsibility to technical experts. They mistakenly view the endeavor as an information-technology project, not a business project. Once management abdicates its responsibility for control, the working team is forced to make critical decisions by default.

Under this scenario, it is not long before the implementation begins to go off track. Well-intentioned people add "nice to have" functionality that can exponentially increase the level of complexity. Just getting to system cutover is a major accomplishment. Further complications are inevitable; it is common for an implementation to extend months beyond cutover because of unexpected problems such as missing data, slow response times or poorly trained staff. Jim Johnson, chairman of the Standish Group, estimates that at least 90 per cent of ERP implementations end up late, over budget or both. "Once you hit $10 million, the chances of a project coming in on time and on budget are statistically zero."

Project managers sensing that budgets and schedules will soon far exceed original estimates try to get back on track by eliminating the redesign of certain business and physical processes. Implementation teams frantically tailor the new software to fit existing business practices. This rarely works.

As a result, the organization, having lost sight of any business objective, implements a crippled system, or one that is overloaded with unnecessary functionality. Whether the ERP system does not have enough capability or has too much, the company now has a system that needs to be fixed. The process of upgrading or reworking is not only expensive; it is also almost too complicated to implement.

Given the investment required to implement ERP systems, why are senior managers not more involved? Our experience suggests that chief executive officers and top managers are simply unsure of the role they should play. Top executives and senior managers focus on objectives and issues, while systems experts focus on processes. Neither side can ask the right questions of the other.

On a typical job, the chief executive might say, "ERP costs me half a billion dollars – give me some status, some sense of the results." The experts, always beyond budget and behind schedule, overwhelm senior managers with technical detail. Senior executives realize they cannot manage what they do not really understand and/or cannot translate into outcomes. As a result, they withdraw into pre-project boundaries, announcing that – despite the experience with systems implementation over the past 20 years – they will control the ERP installation with budgets and schedules.

Only when management realizes that an ERP implementation is a complex undertaking can management set out to make the right choices about what the company's ERP system should do and what it should not. Then, it can create a process of planning and implementation that will be effective. When the technologists make the technological decisions and senior management makes the strategic and business ones, the implementation meets its objectives, budgets and schedules.

Involvement by the chief executive officer on a small set of issues will greatly improve the likelihood of an implementation that is on budget and on schedule and that has the capabilities that support the corporate vision. The chief executive should get involved in three ways: by clearly outlining the organization's strategic priorities; by involving the organization at the appropriate level, and by linking management controls and incentives to project success.

C.E.O. ACTION ITEM NO. 1: Outline strategic priorities

The C.E.O. must take charge of the planning step for the ERP system. It becomes the most important and the most neglected step in making sure that the ERP system does what it is supposed to do. Without a strategic connection, the ERP system does what the technicians believe it should do – and not what is necessarily best for the company.

The key is to translate the company's vision, and the strategy that results from that vision, into concrete priorities, and then decide exactly how the ERP implementation will help the company deliver some, but not all, of these priorities.

What are the top priorities? How do they fit in with the industry's evolution? How do they resolve competitive issues? Which measures of operating performance are expected to improve and at what rate?

This front-end process is time-consuming, and, in some respects, irritating to most managers who want to get on with the implementation. Yet, without it, no ERP system will work. Some senior executives counter this argument by saying, "We did articulate strategic goals, yet the ERP implementation is still a nightmare." When questioned more closely, we find that these goals, such as "improve customer service" or "standardize our processes," are too generic. With such objectives, middle management and staff do not have a framework for making decisions, and they generally allow the technologists to make them. As a result, system priorities remain out of line with corporate vision and senior managers complain that their ERP system has unnecessary capabilities, locked-in complexity and no strategic value. In a very successful ERP implementation, Bay Networks developed four strategic objectives to communicate to its organization and implementation team:

- Growth: Future business growth will not be hindered by information-system capacity;
- Global Order Administration: Accept customer orders from any location into one system; assign shipment dates to available products in real time; schedule future ship dates for products not in stock, and check order status at any time;
- Financial Reporting: Have the ability to run profit and loss queries at any time on any day;
- Process Redesign: Focus re-engineering efforts on processes in which Bay derives its competitive advantage. The key here is to focus on priorities.

In two other very successful ERP implementations (at Owens Corning and the Compaq Computer Corporation) senior managers made the decision to modify the basic ERP software to match strategic goals. Both companies devoted significant time and expense to embed in the software key capabilities that were considered competitive advantages. Owens Corning, for example, needed to incorporate individualized distribution costs in their quotes. Compaq changed its manufacturing strategy from "build-to-stock", which calls for manufacturing to keep warehouses full, to "build-to-order", which runs plants only to fill consumers' orders. Compaq adapted its production processes and modified the generic ERP software to make that shift happen.

By creating this framework of strategic priorities, the chief executive focuses the implementation on exactly what is critical to the company's vision. In essence, this narrows the scope and prioritizes the business objectives within that scope; it creates absolute necessities. This alone simplifies the implementation and increases the likelihood of success. The chief executive, who has the required strategic insight and vision, is the only person who can take control at this level. Chief executives understand the industry's evolution, the company's competitive position and the next levers for growth.

C.E.O. ACTION ITEM NO. 2: Get the organization involved

Certainly, no one expects a chief executive to design data entry screens, or a software developer to determine how the company should face the market. Yet, in a way, most companies' current approach to ERP implementation seems to require both. Companies need to establish guidelines for involvement – or "rules of engagement" for different levels in the organization – so team members understand how and where their skills will be utilized and, more importantly, what issues they should resolve and what issues they need to raise to the next level of management. In most ERP implementations, these rules are not clearly defined. As a result, key strategic decisions are often made by the implementation team, those least equipped to make business decisions. A well-constructed implementation allows the people who best understand the issue to make the decision.

The chief executive manages the inevitable trade-offs among strategic priorities. Top operating management is accountable for the operational/tactical trade-offs. The first-line managers and implementation teams make the detailed design and execution trade-offs.

In one company with multiple divisions making different airplane subsystems, a corporate growth strategy was to extend past the traditional, original equipment manufacturer customers and serve new markets in service and maintenance. This would require that the divisions work together in new ways to provide one face to the new airline customer. The ERP "go" decision had been a division-level call, but the chief executive recognized that local division ERP implementations would complicate the servicing of new markets. He mandated that ERP implementation for these aviation subsystem divisions be done in concert with the new service strategy. This left the top operating management to make operational/tactical trade-offs and the implementation teams to focus on designing screens, data structures and detail steps.

In our approach, various levels of the organization engage in a series of dialogues, which help move the process along while aligning it with key strategic and operating priorities. The company translates the various choices that must be made during the implementation into the right language so dialogue can occur throughout the organization. Fortunately, setting up the process of dialogue is not difficult. Unfortunately, most ERP methodologies never mention it.

A meaningful series of ongoing discussions has to start at the top, with the chief executive and top management. The conversation should focus on implementation issues that affect the achievement of strategic goals. The chief executive always keeps in mind the alignment between the implementation and the strategic vision, making certain that the top management team understands the strategic priorities in a very concrete way. They discuss the short- and long-term impact of each trade-off, and continually monitor how each will affect the way the company meets its priorities. This will only include the small set of critical issues.

Armed with a better understanding of the company's vision, top operating management then makes the tactical and operating decisions that will align the processes and the ERP system with these goals. In the same way operating management has an ongoing dialogue with the chief executive, it conducts discussions with the implementation teams, focusing on operational and tactical alternatives. The goal is to balance physical and business processes, as well as system roles. These decisions often drive where a new process or control will reside – inside or outside the system.

For example, the management of raw-material inventory can either be embedded in processes or designed into the system. If it is embedded in the physical process, visual cues such as empty bins can signal a need for more material. If it is controlled by ERP, the system tracks total available inventory. When the inventory levels reach the reorder point in the system, a purchase order is generated. The first alternative provides lower cost with control at an aggregate level, while the second provides detailed control, albeit at higher cost.

The pros and cons of each alternative must be weighed against the priorities of the business, and top managers are best informed to make these trade-offs. They understand both the operational details of a particular business unit, and the strategic priorities of the business. For example, if minimizing raw-material inventory is a strategic priority or if inventory costs must be tightly monitored because of fluctuating commodity prices, then the detailed control may be worth the higher cost. The cost/benefit trade is made specifically by those best qualified to make the decision, not by low-level systems implementers.

Within this overarching framework, the implementation teams and technologists make the detailed design decisions. Because they understand the system's technical aspects in great detail, as well as each unit's operating characteristics, they can design an optimal system. In a recent ERP implementation at Autodesk, for example, senior management decided that a rapidly changing business environment could make some of the ERP benefits disappear. As a result, management made speedy implementation a top priority. Aware of this goal, the implementation team focused solely on the core functionality the company needed, ignoring other "nice to have" features. The result was an implementation completed in just six months at the same time the company re-engineered 25 of its 40 business processes.

C.E.O. ACTION ITEM NO. 3: Link management controls, incentives to project success
The chief executive can control the implementation by expressly linking key controls systems, performance measures and incentives to strategic priorities. In this way, the company:

- Prevents false declarations of success (the specific criteria are set up in advance);
- Helps implementation teams resist "scope creep" and focus on delivering results;
- Balances systems against business and physical processes, helping the company optimize overall business performance;
- Following the successful Autodesk implementation, for example, Bill Kredel, the company's chief information officer, said, "Developing specific metrics to gauge project success and then tying those metrics directly to each executive's compensation played a major role in our success. Ten per cent of the executive management's bonus and 20 per cent of the implementation team's salary was tied to the success of the project." In a different approach, Bay Networks formed a risk-sharing partnership with the systems integrator, paying the integrator on the basis of the system's success.

HOW TO KNOW IF YOU ARE ON TRACK
Once a company commits to an ERP investment, it spends a great deal of time and effort determining if the implementation is working. We have found that, even with our approach, a large-scale implementation has to take some senior management attention away from the business for a time. Problems always arise and organizational infighting can get out of hand.

Keeping the following in mind can assist in determining whether the implementation will succeed:

- Does top management understand the connection between the system implementation and the achievement of strategic goals well enough to describe the system's priorities in strategic terms?
- Is the implementation plan coherent, comprehensive and linked to corporate objectives and non-system-related capabilities?
- Does the process include dialogue and discussion about the hard choices necessary between the systems and other sources of control?
- Does the company buzz indicate the organization buys into the link between strategy and system implementation?

These are key indicators that will help determine whether an ERP system will create a delivery system that runs like a dream, or a nightmare such as that faced by FoxMeyer.

Next steps for ERP
The fundamental issue facing senior management is to insure that high – and in certain

cases, very high – ERP investments generate full business benefits. The promise of the first wave of ERP installations has largely not been fulfilled. This is due not only to the problems in implementation described in this article, but also to the fact that many ERP installations were driven by the need to solve "year 2000" (or Y2K) compliance problems and/or were focused on fundamental financial applications.

Both of these areas of focus are by definition not going to generate major business benefits. One of the drivers of ERP investments has been the necessity to modernize systems due to Y2K. Obviously, the Y2K problem will either be resolved or systems will crash soon after Jan. 1, 2000. Thus, many installations were pressed by the Y2K schedule, and priorities were as simple as possible: a Y2K fix without the time to fundamentally rethink business processes to achieve step changes.

In the case of the financially focused applications, the installation of an ERP does not by itself generate much business value. Business value in financial areas is generated mainly by moving to shared server operations, which have been shown to generate savings of 30 per cent to 40 per cent.

So what is the next ERP opportunity? Simply stated, it lies in fundamental change in business operations focused on the "guts" of an enterprise: channel management, supply chain optimization, demand forecasting and other operations that can maximize customer service levels, minimize inventory levels and control other costs. These "guts" applications can be dramatically changed by examining overall business processes: Rethink organizational authority and responsibilities, and select and implement appropriate ERP applications to focus on these areas.

The challenges facing senior management are concentrated in the development of the strategic vision, say for the supply chain of an aerospace component subsystem supplier serving multiple end-users (original equipment manufacturers, repair depots, airlines, etc.) from decentralized profit-and-loss-based business units where the supply chain must be managed above the P.&L. sites. This example illustrates the key business decisions and change issues. Once the business vision has been developed and agreed to, the next challenge is to select the most appropriate ERP modules and/or best of breed bolt-on applications (e.g. for supply-chain management or decision support).

When these decisions have been made, the challenges of ERP implementation remain. The approaches described in the article apply.

The end result of successful next-step ERP applications in the "guts" of a business have been shown to generate very significant benefits, such as a 40 per cent reduction in inventory with a 30 per cent improvement in customer service levels.

These central or "gut" ERP applications represent the real business value yet to be realized from the larger ERP system investments.

CONCLUSION

The Benefits Realisation market arises because of shortcomings in existing implementation methodologies and the way in which they are applied in practice. They tend to be very technologically and process-focussed and pay less attention to vital elements of the project such as cultural, organisational and benefits issues. This lack of emphasis on these areas is especially pronounced when time and budgetary constraints cause the project scope to be reduced. In their favour, implementation methodologies typically cover strategy, planning, organisational dynamics and design, user procedures and training development and target gap analysis at early stages of the project. However, many of these issues are not revisited from the design stage until the post-implementation review. The business case is not always developed in detail and where it is, it is often crafted for initial justification only and not revisited or revised throughout the project. In addition, it is frequently not clearly aligned with strategy and does not necessarily adapt to changes in strategic direction of the business, or a change in requirements and/or go-live date. It is common for operating targets not to be defined or benchmarked and no real assessment of potential benefits included.

In addition to these inherent shortcomings of the implementation methodology, many more problems arise when it is applied in practice. These may arise as a result of the methodology or of the project itself that the methodology does not help to avoid.

During the assimilation stage, there is often an assumption that everyone is at the same level of readiness. This is rarely the case and the change management and planning elements of the project should adjust accordingly. There is also the danger that generic changes can be made without tailoring them to fit site needs and the ERP functionality may not be adequate for business needs throughout the organisation. Inconsistencies across the enterprise must be taken into account throughout the project. The effort required to sustain behavioural change is underestimated and under-funded and expectations are not managed aggressively.

When it comes to execution, the resources required to "scale-up" or rollout the organisation and process changes are underestimated and contingency plans are not fully developed and/or budgeted. Legacy systems and processes may be allowed to remain 'on-line' through the migration period, thereby facilitating any lack of acceptance of the new system and increasing the level of resources required. Resistance to change also increases because of poor project processes.

An inappropriate project structure often means that the tasks to realise benefits are not integrated into overall plan and reporting is abandoned. The project team may have limited authority to make organisation and process changes and at crunch time, schedule and budget supersede benefits realisation.

Companies rarely formally identify, measure and track benefits during the life of the implementation project. When the stage of the project is reached where results are expected to be realised, a lack of follow-up, ownership and measurement of these results contributes to the failure to achieve them. An inability to articulate 'cause and effect', *vis-à-vis* other initiatives adds to the problem that the benefits achieved by the ERP implementation are unknown. Furthermore, operating assumptions should be actively maintained during extended life cycle as unanticipated implementation issues arise. Results achieved should be well marketed throughout the organisation to gain recognition for any successes achieved by the system and the individuals who contributed to this success.

In addition, the methodology and project plans currently do not emphasise the importance of benefits ownership. Where this is the case, executive ownership is often limited and managers are not held responsible for delivering business benefits. No direct links from benefits to rewards are set and accountability processes are lacking.

In many projects, the post-implementation effort consists purely of stabilisation efforts for the period immediately after the go-live date. ERP implementation is a golden opportunity to create sustainable shareholder value. Unfortunately many of the systems implemented to date have failed to recognise the multi-dimensional nature of ERP projects and the need for a holistic approach to change management.

The next chapter explores the approaches available to organisations to help them move beyond the existing narrow technology-based approaches to change and to look at mechanism for bringing about more effective change management.

Chapter 4

ERP and Change Management

INTRODUCTION

The management of ERP implementations in organisations is intrinsically bound up with change. There is a widespread view that there is more change and greater pressure for quick change than ever before. Whether we think of continuous improvement of existing products, the pressures to bring new products to market, or the shift towards more customer-centred practices, staying competitive today means being prepared to change fast and frequently.

The technology literature abounds with examples of change projects that have gone wrong, some disastrously so. If we look back at the introduction of new technology in the 1980s, when information technology was coming into its own, we discover that the failure rate of new technology projects was between 40 and 70 per cent. In the case of TQM, reports say that over 90 per cent of initiatives in the US failed while, in Europe, research indicated around 80 per cent failed. BPR, being newer, has less extensive research, but the indications are that it has typically achieved much less than promised. In the case of ERP there is evidence to suggest that a vast number of projects fail to deliver the expected benefits.

Failure rates such as these are sobering. In individual cases people put the blame on personalities or poor workplace relations, if change is not going well. However, a failure rate of 70 per cent suggests it would be better to look hard at how well we understand the change business and how well we are managing it. There are three kinds of things we can do to make the implementation of ERP systems work better:

- Understand the context of change;
- Understand the management of change;
- Acquire some knowledge of change management techniques and frameworks.

Effective change management lies at the heart of successful ERP deployment. However, effective change management is not easy and demands a substantial organisational commitment and top mangement support. It means helping the organisation get information on its current position. It means helping it make sense of what success means for it and putting this into a new framework. This involves bringing together the change concept and the current organisational context and asking hard questions as to why the one should work for the other. It means creating a structure to manage the transition between the existing situation and the new situation and setting up that structure in a way that maximises its chance of success. Skilful steering of the process is required, including knowing how to manage resistance to change in an appropriate way. In this chapter we grappled with the these issues and the actual management of the change arising from ERP implementations.

THE NATURE OF CHANGE IN ERP ENVIRONMENTS
Partners for Change Ltd.

Most organisations that participated in the 'first wave' of ERP implementations recognise that enterprise systems had a positive impact on their business. Many enterprises successfully re-engineered their processes using ERP as the enabler. In areas such as inventory reduction, personnel shrinkage, cost of IT and cash management, ERP has delivered benefits although, as shown in a recent study, these improvements were often lower than expected. Sometimes, however, other benefits that were identified in the original business case were not realised at all.

Some of the organisations that failed to realise the full benefits of their initial investment in ERP exhibit a degree of scepticism about investing further in their enterprise system. The scepticism is understandable but, as this section aims to show, failures to capitalise fully on the investment was predictable given the organisations' attitudes to people-related impacts of change.

The experience of 'first wave' implementations now shows that the failure of organisations to capitalise fully on the benefits of ERP was often not due to weaknesses in the technological solution. Rather, it was in the barrier to full transformation presented by changes to their organisation and processes. Further, change management was often viewed in many implementations as a discretionary cost and therefore dispensable as cost pressure increased. The reality is that this was a false economy. Poor change management often resulted in longer programmes, higher implementation costs and extended periods of stabilisation after go-live, as the 'people' issues ignored during the implementation emerged later.

As a result, there is a growing acknowledgement of the need to address human resource issues as an integral part of programmes to implement enterprise systems and, in particular, the need to manage change effectively.

The early expectations of ERP

The first wave of ERP implementations were justified by a number of key benefits, including:

- Integration of systems, eliminating the transfer of data (often manually) from one system to another, removing barriers to process improvement;
- Consistency of data, enabling better management decisions;
- Consistency of processes, based on best practice;
- Standardisation of technology platforms;
- Improved access to information;
- Improved productivity and time to market;
- Service level improvement to customers;
- Reduced staff cost from process improvement and the elimination of non-value-added activity;
- Reduced purchase costs arising from improvement in procurement activity;
- Reduced stock costs arising from improved management of the supply chain;
- Improved accounting and cash management.

A quick glance at some of these factors hints at the importance of human – as well as technological – influences on the outcome of the completed programme. For example, the elimination of manual processes means that the staff affected will be displaced from familiar roles. In cases where manual intervention is reduced but not eliminated, some employees will be trained to use new technology, whilst others have to relinquish part of their role and learn new skills. Similarly, in other areas, improved access to information will only lead to better performance if the recipients are trained to use it and disposed to do so.

The benefits identified above, which were usually incorporated with greater or lesser efficiency in a business case, related to expectations of improved performance at the conclusion of the implementation programme. They were the expected outcome of applying the new technological solution – sometimes allied to process and organisational changes – by system users and their managers. However, the success of the ERP implementation is not only dependent on the original business justification, but on the effectiveness of the programme team that implemented it. In other words, the extent to which benefits were realised also depended on the quality and quantity of internal staff and external resource chosen to implement the programme.

(For clarification, most 'people' benefits are usually classified as 'intangible' in a business case; that is, benefits that cannot be measured directly in monetary terms or are quantifiable in another way. They are benefits for which a project can be seen to make a contribution, but for which a reliable measure of that contribution cannot easily be derived – for example, improvements in staff morale.)

The dawning reality of 'first wave' implementations

A number of factors acted, often in concert, to reduce the benefits achieved – particularly the intangible, people benefits – below initial expectations:

ERP can be expensive: It can cost £5–10 million and take at least 12 months to implement. Many multi-nationals have rolling programmes of projects extending beyond £100 million and taking many years. The heavy expense of ERP led many businesses to seek ways of reducing the cost of implementation and ownership: the additional cost to re-engineer processes and to manage change were often seen as discretionary and were consequently cut out. The sheer scale of most ERP implementations meant that there was little time, money or energy left for radical business change.

In the first wave, many organisations allowed technology to drive the programme: IT management took the lead, especially where ERP was just a technical solution (to Year 2000 compliance, for example). Technical delivery of the programme, rather than running the business and satisfying customers, became the priority. Poor relationships between IT and the business were common. End users and their managers were often insufficiently involved in scoping, planning and running the programme. It was only after tackling ERP as a software implementation programme that most organisations realise that there was more to change than just technology.

Many systems' implementations were driven to very tight deadlines. Where organisations lacked the capability to implement the technology or the changes that went with it, there was insufficient time to build an effective internal team. Sometimes, programmes were led and staffed by new entrants to the market, who lacked the necessary experience to understand the implications of the technology on processes and people.

Weak business cases: The bandwagon effect meant that organisations decided to implement ERP because their competitors were, without looking closely at their own business case. As a result insufficient attention was paid to managing projects towards the delivery of benefits. Consequently, the opportunities to use the standardisation and best practice processes delivered with the systems were not taken up. Instead, companies misused the flexibility of the systems to accommodate existing processes and practices that might be far from best practice and far from standard.

Incomplete strategy: Many companies aimed to implement the ERP system quickly against existing working practices and then start process improvements that delivered benefits over time. The initial implementation tended to be faster and less disruptive than attempting to re-engineer the business as part of the initial implementation. The benefits are delivered later, but it was perceived to be a less risky approach. In practice, many companies failed to establish the process improvement programme that delivered the benefits, usually for reasons of cost or time pressure.

Effects of competing change programmes

In most businesses, the number of systems programmes and other change initiatives has increased substantially in recent years.

Management overload: The combination of ERP with other concurrent change initiatives can result in 'overload' on senior management, as their number and complexity increase, and managers attempt to balance competing calls on their attention. Communications often break down, in turn resulting in poor decision-making, internal conflict and confusion. In addition, senior managers often spend inordinate amounts of time resolving inter-programme conflicts and issues at an unnecessary level of detail. This can result in failure to make important decisions and a failure to keep the programme aligned with strategic changes in the enterprise or the external environment.

Stakeholders: Senior management overload resulting from the multiplicity of initiatives often also means that the most important stakeholders are insufficiently involved in scoping and planning the programme. Their full commitment is not engendered, and even when it is, their attention is often later redirected to other initiatives. As a result, no single view exists of the programme and project load on the enterprise, leading to the risk of duplicated effort by other initiatives, omissions or resource conflicts.

Inadequate resources and skills: Multiple change initiatives invariably compete for resources from a finite internal pool. Funding may not be available to bring in sufficient temporary, external support. This is often compounded by managers' reluctance to dedicate full time resources from the line to support programmes and projects that are not considered to be 'real' work. The outcome is often a shortage of programme resource, discontinuity of staff availability, or poor quality personnel.

Last, even when the ERP projects were initiated with proper reference to a business need, they may 'grow old' and lose relevance as new initiatives take precedence. This often leads to a loss of sponsorship at a senior level and a reduction in the motivation of project staff.

Other change issues

The recent survey of companies which have implemented ERP, referred to in the Introduction, saw people issues as the major obstacles to success up until now. Respondents highlighted the following people issues as obstacles during implementation and going forward:

- Change management;
- Internal staff adequacy;
- Programme team;
- Training;
- Resource prioritisation and allocation;
- Top management support;
- Consultants;
- Ownership (of benefits and other issues);
- Discipline.

The potential impact of many of these have been alluded to in the previous sections. The comments below relate to the remaining influences. They also expand and add emphasis to some of the earlier, critical, factors.

First, *internal staff adequacy:* Business managers do not always have the skills and experience to drive programmes. Many early ERP programmes were led by the internal managers who could be spared from running the business, sometimes irrespective of their experience or interest in programme and project management. The results were, as could be expected, 'patchy'. Elsewhere, external consultants, suppliers and contractors were brought in. Most were unfamiliar with the culture and practices of the company they were engaged to support and, in some cases, with the industry they operated in. Pressure from competitors who were also implementing ERP often outweighed the desirability of effective programme planning and resourcing.

Second, *training:* many ERP programmes slip their planned dates in the course of implementation. User training, most of which is normally carried out in the latter stages, is therefore vulnerable to the 'squeeze' between late-running development and test activities, and the need to 'go live' on time. Even where time is not the issue, there is often pressure on costs, for which a reduction in training resource is often seen as an easy option. It is almost always a false economy.

Third, *top management support, and ownership of benefits and other issues:* Significant ERP programmes affect the whole company. In these cases, where all functions are affected, the CEO should be the ultimate sponsor. Changes in individual functions will need to be sponsored in turn by the functional heads. Sponsorship skills need to be developed, and support needs to be provided to help sponsors fulfil these vital and often underestimated tasks. Too often, sponsorship is delegated to too junior a level. Even when the appropriate director or manager is appointed, interest often wanes over time as new initiatives and priorities appear.

Owners should be identified for all benefits, risks and issues. Again, the owner should be sufficiently senior to be affected by the benefit or issue, and be able to influence the outcomes. They should regularly review target benefits and be prepared to modify their plans when necessary.

Finally, the *cost-benefit analysis* embodied in many business cases misses out the internal implementation costs associated with the participation of the business in the programme, and omits the critical 'buy-in' process by the programme sponsor, owners, and other participants.

Future trends

During the first wave of ERP programmes, relatively few stakeholders were affected due to the emphasis on back-office functions. Nowadays, e-commence solutions have a much wider impact on a greater number of communities, both inside and outside the company.

As the world becomes increasingly electronically linked, ERP is itself undergoing a transformation. The emphasis is shifting from internal processes to customer and supplier transactions and to the achievement of greater connectivity and integration. Consequently, the range of available ERP products has grown – for CRM, e-procurement, data-warehousing and so on. The scope for impact of ERP on processes and people is therefore increasing, at a time when some clients have failed to realise the full benefits of their initial investment in ERP.

The implementation of new solutions will also always have some impact on the existing ERP system and, more frequently, on the 'soft', human, aspects of the enterprise. For example, an e-commerce solution may remove the need for the customer services function, by allowing customers to tap in directly to the company's system. Similarly, a pharmaceutical development company which recently extended their ERP implementation to include a fully integrated e-procurement solution found that, as fewer staff were needed in procurement, there was an opportunity to reallocate resources upwards to more strategic areas. The human resource implications of these two examples will need to be handled effectively.

Key lessons going forward

First, intangible, 'people-related' benefits will need to have a higher profile in the business cases for 'second wave' ERP implementations, especially those that relate to global electronic connectivity such as e-procurement and CRM. Where there are implications for people that should properly be regarded as costs rather than benefits (for example displacements and redundancy), they will need to be handled in an equally effective manner.

Second, the business case needs to have a contribution from the people who will be accountable for implementation and delivery of the benefits, and for the administration of 'people-related' costs. Buy-in from the key stakeholders in each affected group is essential. At the end of the programme these people will be accountable for achieving the department's objectives. Having made people accountable it is important to get them involved in the programme in a meaningful way so that they can influence it. The consequences of failing to get this buy-in will result in longer implementations and potential failure to deliver the benefits.

Third, the ERP programme team should be led by a sponsor of sufficient seniority – if appropriate, by the CEO.

Finally, *all* communities affected by the change are stakeholders. A communication strategy and plan must be developed, so that messages are developed and communicated that meet the needs of each constituent, in a timely and appropriate manner. Also, management reporting should occur on a timely basis and in the appropriate level of detail, so management has the true picture of the programme status.

Reference

1. "ERP's Second Wave: Maximising the Value of Enterprise Applications and Processes", Deloitte Consulting LLC, 1999.

WANTED ERPEOPLE SKILLS

Polly Schneider, *CIO Magazine,* 1 March 1999. Reprinted through the courtesy of CIO.

As anyone who has ever survived the implementation of an enterprise resource planning (ERP) system can tell you, it's not about the technology, it's about reinventing the business. And, although your company may pay tremendous lip service to people and cultural issues, when it comes to a major ERP initiative you ignore them at your peril.

In its brief history, ERP is more often identified with out-of-control budgets and questionable returns than with business transformation. Replacing dozens of legacy systems with a single integrated one for managing operations across every discipline – finance, human resources, procurement, materials management, sales and distribution, production, order management – is challenging even for companies with generous IS budgets and a hefty staff. Equally daunting, because ERP is so intertwined with business processes, is the task of effectively changing the daily activities and behaviors of many of your employees. For instance, a warehouse worker managing inventory spreadsheets pre-ERP could be forecasting customer demand and making critical business decisions after ERP. Are you confident your workforce is ready for those kinds of changes?

From an organizational viewpoint, ERP concepts are especially tricky because they go against the mantra of decentralization, which many companies adopted in the '70s and '80s to spur innovation among business units. These sophisticated enterprise systems require a switch from a functional to a process orientation because modules often cut across traditional departmental lines. That's tough for companies with myriad independent business units that are unaccustomed to sharing information or coordinating with other divisions.

Finally, the spate of mergers and acquisitions in many industries over the last decade has made the integration problem more vexing. Taking a hard look at your company's unique culture – before you choose a system – is the first step toward preventing resistance in the ranks.

Time to talk

Unfortunately, many companies have paid the price for ignoring corporate culture in a mad rush to slam-dunk the system. Take Westinghouse Electric Corp. (now CBS Corp.), which began an SAP/R3 finance and purchasing installation encompassing six business units in 1994. During the recession of the early '90s, Westinghouse was forced to write off $5 billion in bad loans – approximately one-third of its revenues – from its financial services unit, according to Don Janson, former SAP project manager at Westinghouse, now director of financial process improvements at Ingersoll-Rand Co. in Woodcliff Lake, N.J. When a new chairman was hired to lead a turnaround strategy that included cutting costs through standardization, the IS department had just over a year to get the system up and running.

Westinghouse had been organized in a highly decentralized fashion since the 1970s, with each business unit controlling its own finances and resources. The project team did not spend much time educating the businesses that moving to a centralized, shared environment would help Westinghouse become more efficient, and it met resistance as a result. Faced with a loss of autonomy, managers from various divisions haggled over the new reporting structures, standards for coding systems and other common processes. Further, they were slow to provide information the project team needed for the implementation. Finally, says Janson, "senior management had to come in and lay down the law." The project team extended the deadline by three months to work through the problems, costing Westinghouse an added $3 million to $4 million. Janson says the company learned the value of educating all stakeholders, not just the end users. In his new position at Ingersoll-Rand, Janson predicts he will soon head another ERP project. His first step will be to hire a consultant to help assess the culture. "Most companies don't have good change management resources, and sometimes it's better to get an outside view." Second, he plans to hire a change management director, who he believes should report not to the CIO but to a general manager or other cross-functional title.

Learn new roles

In some cases, the challenge of ERP is not so much gaining buy-in but helping employees cope with fundamental job makeovers. And if ever there was a company in need of a face lift, it would be The Boeing Co. The embattled aviation giant has been struggling for 20 years to shed its 1940s approach to building planes. Since World War II, Boeing's commercial airline division has built up an amazing conglomeration of legacy systems, including the 450 that feed data into the production process and that are being replaced through Boeing's business process and systems improvement plan. At last count, there were 14 bill-of-material systems and 30 shop floor control systems. With every change to an order, parts data must be manually updated in all systems and then triple-checked for accuracy. Still, there have been embarrassing and costly gaffes. In 1997 the company had to shut down the 747 production line for 20 days after a series of mishaps resulted in missing parts and delayed schedules. Boeing's announcement in late 1998 that layoffs planned for the next two years had risen to 48,000 is a further indication of the company's production ills. Publicly, the company blames the layoffs on canceled orders from Asia, yet spokesperson Vicki Ray freely admits, "Our planes cost too much to make."

In 1994 Boeing devised a business process improvement plan, of which ERP is just one piece, with the arrival of new management. The cost of the plan was a reported $500 million, although Boeing would not comment. The new ERP system, based on Baan IV finance, manufacturing and distribution modules, an Oracle database and process planning software from Cimlinc Inc. in Itasca, Ill., is up and running in all 19 parts plants across 18,000 users. The engineering area will follow this year. The company is now working from a single source of product data, departments are communicating better and one plant has already shown an 80 per cent reduction in the cycle time for a part to flow through the manufacturing process, according to Martin Ritchie, director of Boeing's ERP Competence Center. Boeing is pinning its future on these systems – up to 2,000 people are working on the overall reengineering project implementation, from developing the processes and system to preparing their areas for implementation, at any given time.

While Ritchie says that many of Boeing's workers are glad to see the changes, the company's culture of independence formed a barrier to introducing common processes. Each department had free rein to make decisions and set procedures. "This culture can lead to one in which 100,000 people are going out and taking charge," he admits.

The ERP project team encouraged flexibility and user involvement in decisions whenever possible. In manufacturing, for instance, plants can choose to install one of four different MRP modules. In areas like materials planning, change was dramatic. Previously, roughly 300 materials planners (under different job titles) worked as expediters, hunting down parts on the shop floor. Now they work as buyers, ordering raw materials from suppliers and letting the system track parts. Individuals who used to work as buyers are now contract administrators.

To ease anxiety and help employees learn their new roles, Dave Clark, Boeing's director of knowledge transfer, introduced a "proof of concept" exercise, an eight-week knowledge transfer course on the system that involves users and managers from every department in the plant. During the course, employees work together on a problem, such as how to handle an emergency order or a last-minute design change. Cross-functional training has torn down walls between previously isolated areas like finance and engineering and helped everyone understand the impact one change to the system has on the entire operation, according to Clark.

The first course had 300 participants but no managers, a mistake the company paid for after the system went live. Managers continued to work off the old "hot lists" for parts requests and began to reshuffle work rather than follow instructions in the system. That caused further parts shortages and general chaos until the managers came up to speed on the new process, Clark recalls. Now managers attend the training, and, says Clark, "life is good in the parts plants."

Before you begin

A few things to ponder when planning for ERP

- Which processes are most important now and why?
- Does this sytem meet our needs or go beyond them?
- Who will be the change champion(s)?
- Who are the stakeholders?
- What is the business culture at our company and what are its strengths?
- What subcultures do we have and what are their strengths?
- How can we apply those strengths to business change?
- What cultural attributes are weak or will interfere with the change?
- What will be the toughest changes, and how will we address them?
- Who will be responsible for change management?

Clark knew the exercise was a success when he learned that a manager in one of the divisions called the accounting department to report that an error he made in the system might affect a customer's invoice. "Now people at the plants have an understanding of finance. That's a real powerful thing," he says. Clark hopes the massive reengineering program will catapult the world's largest exporter out of the Dark Ages. Early results show the company is headed in the right direction: the machine fabrication plant in Auburn, Wash., has met its 25 per cent cost reduction goal and is delivering sales orders on or ahead of schedule 85 per cent to 90 per cent of the time, as opposed to 65 per cent to 75 per cent of the time under the old processes. Casual surveys also suggest that employees have better control of their work and higher job satisfaction. Boasts Clark: "We have replaced the informal knowledge sources with people who are pretty savvy with how the enterprise works."

Going global think local

Introducing ERP across a complex production process is an ongoing communications struggle. Imagine the rise in complexity once the project crosses U.S. borders. As AlliedSignal Inc. learned, the people you choose to lead the effort make all the difference. A $14.5 billion manufacturer of aircraft and automotive components, chemicals, fiber and other advanced materials, AlliedSignal's turbocharging systems division is in the middle of an SAP/R3 project spanning 11 countries, 18 sites and 9 languages. The company developed an enterprise systems strategy in 1996 to help improve productivity in logistics and supply chain management, beginning with its turbocharging systems division, which makes turbochargers for cars, trucks and airplanes.

In the last two years, Jeff Smith, CIO of the turbocharging systems division, has spent 28 weeks in Europe, Asia and South America and could probably write a book on the subtleties of international business culture. Despite the cross-culture challenges, Smith decided that a big-bang approach of launching all nine SAP modules at once at each site would help the division meet Allied's broader corporate goals for common global processes and would also eliminate Y2K costs. With a time frame of roughly seven months to implement new processes, data standards and systems in each country, the pressure was intense, Smith admits.

Cultural hot spots

Tips for handling ERP's cultural issues

- **View ERP implementation as a business initiative, not an IS initiative**. Educate and engage senior management as early as possible.
- **Don't let technical problems dominate the project's time**. Create a dedicated staff position for change management. Use your best and brightest people on the change team.
- **Articulate expectations before implementation**. What will the project's stakeholders say are the attributes of the new environment in a year? Where are the gaps in the plan? What conflicts of opinion exist today?
- **Avoid political infighting between previously isolated divisions**. Managers from the various business units must have a clear understanding of the reasons behind the change. What's in it for them? Write a change management document that includes the communication strategy and core business principles of the company.
- **Encourage users to change their job roles.** If employees are already overworked, eliminate any nonessential tasks the system may require. Develop incentive programs to motivate change and incorporate them into performance reviews.
- **Don't change too much at once**. Major change requires an evolutionary approach. Don't overwhelm your organization with a system that has more functionality than you absolutely need. Consider a phased rollout and shoot for short wins to generate momentum during the project.

Given the cultural and political differences between nationalities, Smith realized that people would resist the new business model unless there were local representatives on the project team. He attributes the project's success largely to the global team, whose 15 members represented all 11 countries. "It never would have worked if they were all Americans," he says. Each member of the global team brought expertise in one of the SAP modules and worked with the local teams as consultants during the implementation, defining requirements, assisting with training and ensuring design consistency around the world. The global team also facilitated and approved requests for customization, which, if deemed appropriate, were copied around the world. Smith says conflicts over standards lessened with time as people learned of progress at the early project sites. Smith calls the global team "the fabric that held all the decisions together."

A major roadblock was overcoming skills gaps between the plants. In some countries, workers were using paper or, at best, spreadsheets to manage the production schedule. In France, workers had no concept of modern production principles such as planning ahead for customer demand. With the help of in-house trainers and experts from Buker Inc., an Illinois consulting firm, every user attended functional training in ERP manufacturing disciplines, along with SAP technical training.

At the national level, the local business culture dictated the training method. The French, for instance, tended to segment workers into narrow, vertical job roles and required heavy documentation, while the Irish, who have broader responsibilities, needed more general training across several disciplines. "We wanted to make sure that when SAP turned on, we had the right people in the right positions, ready to execute the job," Smith explains.

While Smith says many low-skill jobs at the plants were eliminated with the new system, company growth has allowed the displaced workers to find other factory positions. Smith proudly reports that the turbocharging division is now managing customers and suppliers from a central database, and on-time product delivery rates have jumped from 65 per cent to 92 per cent. He says the hardest part of the project has not been resistance but a lack of readiness in countries where ERP processes were brand new. He adds that prioritizing requests across several countries at once became "a very draining process."

Keep to the basics

Spend a few minutes with ERP warrior Jorge Taborga, vice president and CIO of networking company Bay Networks Inc., who took his company through a kamikaze nine-month implementation from October 1995 to July 1996, and you'll get a little different perspective from Smith's. "It was a blast," he says. Not one to mince words, Taborga's overall message is to think simple. Resist customizing the software or including optional features and promise only what can be delivered in the time frame. "The objective should always be to aim high enough to make a difference, but not so high that the target will be missed," he says.

Since the Silicon Valley networking company replaced a patchwork enterprise system based on software from Ask (now a Computer Associates division) with SAP/R3 financial, distribution and manufacturing modules, the company has realized a $20 million return on investment from a number of improvements, including better inventory turns and on-time delivery. Formed from a 1994 merger of SynOptics Communications Inc. and Wellfleet Communications Inc., Bay Networks (now owned by Nortel Networks Ltd) was struggling to keep up not only with its hotshot competitor Cisco Systems Inc. but also with 35 per cent growth rates in the networking industry. The company needed an integrated system that wouldn't take two years to install. Taborga focused on three principles to ensure success: scope management, speed and "constant care," his term for a stable, ongoing support team. The trick was to convince stakeholders that a slimmed-down system would help the company achieve its goals more quickly – and avoid the typical burnout of ERP project teams. As the SAP project director, Taborga was the disciplinarian. He issued business managers IOUs for functionality that would not be included in the nine-month project scope and instituted a 70 per cent accuracy rule for rapid decision-making that allowed the project team to make decisions based on incomplete information. Taborga says speed was a major factor in managing the change. "It eliminated a lot of the 'why' and 'how' arguments," he says. Taborga spent most of his energy selling the project to top executives in each department, who were then charged with the task of carrying the message to their staffs. Taborga also worked to minimize job changes. New jobs were not created to match the system as in some ERP projects. Aside from basic SAP training, the project team worked individually with users to explain the added responsibilities they would have and designated "power users" in each area who serve as both ongoing training resources and IS liaisons. The project team then ran SAP workshops so that managers could learn the system's impact on daily operations. If he could do it again, Taborga says he would have included more business simulation sessions. He worries about the ramifications of giving users such power at the desktop. "SAP is like a jet fighter, capable of destroying cities. If a mistake is made [in the system], it can affect product availability, which, if it were to happen at the end of the quarter, would be fatal."

Taborga believes the experience has created a "good change culture" (which he defines as the ability to adapt to change and embrace teamwork) at Bay Networks and is proud to report that the IS department has not missed a deadline for an SAP implementation in the four years since the project began. The company even created a new service offering to help its customers better manage their SAP projects. In ERP initiatives, Taborga believes the CIO's most important task is developing relationships with the business and ensuring constant support. "If the CIO does not take this active role, the project is not going anywhere," he says.

Find a champion of change

Communicate with stakeholders, develop relationships, foster collaboration, strive for simplicity. Sounds pretty basic, right? Not really. ERP is a long-term commitment that requires long-term support. Training and education shouldn't end after the system has gone live. While there is no "right" way to implement ERP, the core ingredient of every project – and the toughest to do well – is active and engaged leadership. Someone from the top – whether it's the CIO, COO, CFO or CEO – must own the role of "change champion" for the life of the project. As the companies above demonstrate, the most important step you can take as the leader of an ERP project is to plan for culture change well before the implementation begins. The second step is to act on those plans with a dedicated change management program.

Consultants believe that evolutionary change in business from ERP will not occur until organizations begin to reorganize their businesses around processes, which means pitching the old organization chart and starting anew. Ideally, says Ingersoll-Rand's Janson, companies should create employee support departments for HR and payroll, vendor support for purchasing and a customer department for sales, marketing, manufacturing and scheduling. But remember, there are people behind that org chart. As one CIO joked about the challenge of converting a paper-based manufacturing plant to the company's new ERP system: "It's much easier to reprogram a robotic piece of equipment. It's not going to talk back to you."

A FRAMEWORK FOR CHANGE MANAGEMENT

Partners for Change Ltd.

In its broadest sense, change management refers to all the non-technological activities that are required during and after the ERP implementation to achieve the desired business benefits. They include: stakeholder management; communications; education and training; benefits management (particularly of the 'intangible', non-quantifiable benefits); culture and organisational change; and resource management.

The following sections highlight some of the key factors to be recognised in each of these areas, and suggest some ways of avoiding the 'people' related failures that have bedevilled some earlier ERP-supported change programmes and led to lower than anticipated benefits being realised.

The list below provides some examples of change management risks and issues that have been observed in previous implementations, and serves to illustrate the range of possible pitfalls:

- A lack of consistent understanding of the objectives of the business change programme, that could undermine 'buy in' and active support;
- A failure to fully support and commit to the programme by the most senior managers;
- A difference in the levels of commitment between UK-based managers and those in other countries;
- A possible change in corporate direction that could reduce senior management support or weaken day-to-day programme management activities;
- Perceived weakness in project management skills in some functions;
- Reduction in the time or resources made available for user training in the new ERP system.

The list is clearly illustrative rather than exhaustive. It is good practice at the inception of a programme to carry out an examination of the change management and human resource risks and issues, often through a structured workshop. A stakeholder management plan, communications strategy and plan, and other plans should be developed that address the risks and issues deemed to have unacceptable impact on the achievement of the programme goals.

What is a stakeholder, and why is stakeholder management important?

At its simplest, a stakeholder may be defined as: 'anyone impacted by the solution'. This definition is broad enough to include a great number of constituents: direct users of the new systems and processes; managers who are accountable for improved service levels accruing from the enterprise solution; other people in the organisation who are impacted by the rollout; and external parties such as suppliers and customers.

Effective stakeholder management of these constituencies will allow:

- Their commitment, or 'buy in', to the programme objectives and benefits;
- A clear view of who is impacted by the implementation, and the issues concerning them;
- Visibility of 'who is responsible for what', during the ERP programme;
- Strong project governance, through the allocation of accountabilities for benefits achievement;
- Third parties' interests taken into account, and management of external dependencies.

Classes of stakeholder

Sponsors and internal stakeholders

The importance of appointing the programme sponsor at the right level of seniority cannot be overstated. If the whole company is affected then it must be the CEO who sponsors the programme. The CEO should be the champion at board level. Changes in individual functions will need to be sponsored in turn by the functional heads. Members of this group will normally constitute the programme board and steering group, together with other key personnel such as the programme manager.

At the outset of the programme there is a need to map the stakeholder territory, that is, to ascertain who will be affected and to what extent. In addition to the senior programme participants, there will be other stakeholders who are 'internal' to the programme. These include: project managers and project teams; members of the programme office; and employees who will be users of the new ERP system and business processes.

All the stakeholders need to be identified and managed throughout the programme. For stakeholders who are board- or steering-group members, or other senior members of the programme team, the best way to engage them is to give them clear accountability for project delivery and meaningful roles in the programme.

The sponsor and programme stakeholders need to understand what influence they have, how to exert it and how to get involved. In reality, the sponsors and programme stakeholders will have many priorities. They will buy into the programme at the outset, but there is a risk they will get distracted, resulting in inconsistent messages being given out. Employees get the impression they can drop the project as it is not a priority.

Sponsorship skills need to be developed and sustained and support needs to be provided to help people fulfil these difficult and often underestimated roles.

External stakeholders

During the first wave of ERP programmes, relatively few external stakeholders were affected due to the emphasis on back-office functions. Nowadays, e-commerce solutions have a much wider impact on a greater number of communities, not all of which are inside the company. Suppliers and customers will increasingly become key communities that need to be involved in projects. Other parties may have a legitimate interest in the programme; for example, regulatory authorities. This adds a new level of complexity to ERP programmes.

There will also be other groups of stakeholders who are 'external' to the programme but who work within the organisation. These may include, for example:

- senior business managers, who are not involved in the day-to-day progression of the business change programme, but who are nevertheless affected by the programme outcomes and benefits;
- other employees, not directly affected by the implementation;
- trades unions and works councils.

These stakeholders' expectations, too, will need to be managed through the lifetime of the programme. For all stakeholders – both 'internal' and 'external' – a communications strategy and communications plan will be required.

Stakeholder management activities

Figure 1 illustrates the main activities involved in stakeholder management during the programme life cycle.

Figure 1

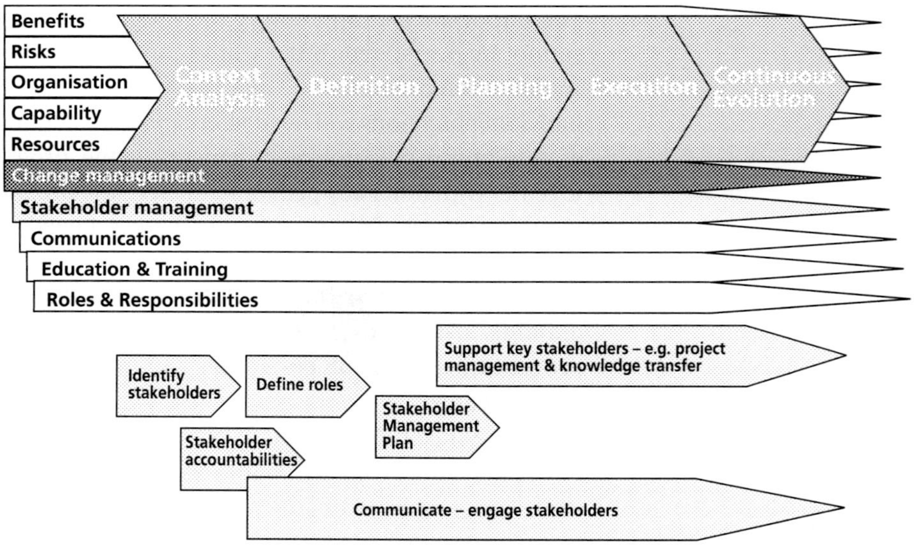

Communication management
The fundamental objectives of programme communications management are to:

- Ensure that sufficient information is available to allow effective decision-making;
- Maximise commitment to the programme from stakeholders, and involve them as required;
- Provide inspiration within the programme;
- Inform stakeholders on progress.

It follows that the risks of poor communication include:

- Managers being unprepared to deal with internal and external discussions, or the unexpected;
- Work is duplicated or omitted;
- Interdependencies within the programme or with other business initiatives are not identified, resulting in waste and delay;
- Programme leaders are unaware of risks or issues.

Figure 2 illustrates the main steps in developing and implementing a communications strategy.

Figure 2

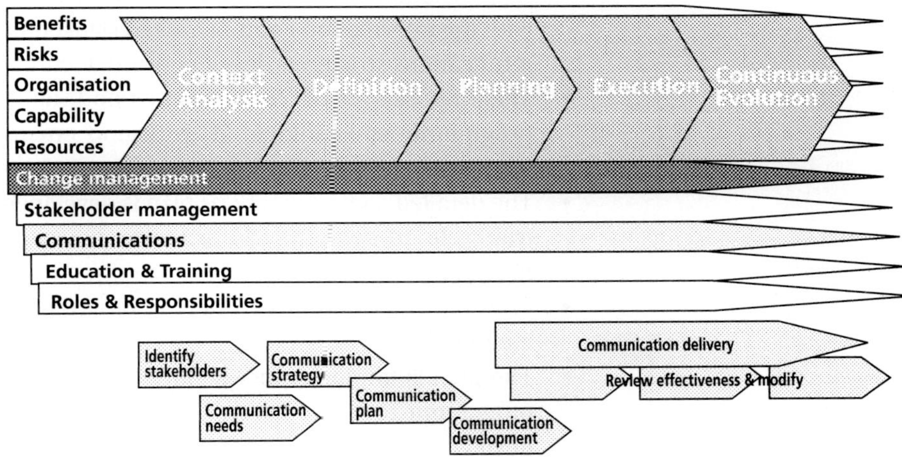

The following main steps need to be followed:

- **Analyse** the audience for programme communications – identify the constituencies, their personal objectives, information requirements, and how they will use the information;
- **Develop** an appropriate level of detail, format, content and frequency for communications;
- **Document** the findings, in the programme communications strategy and plan. Incorporate the details in the programme plan and programme handbook;
- **Implement**, assigning responsibilities for the communication flows. For each stakeholder group, the information should be:
  - consistent;
  - relevant and to right level of detail;
  - concise;
  - factual, and of appropriate quality.

The information content and format should be customised to the organisation's culture.

On many significant ERP change programmes, the human resources director or equivalent will lead the development and implementation of the communications strategy. In most cases, a programme office will also have been established, with a role that includes providing support in implementing effective communications with the stakeholders.

In outline, the following steps will normally be covered:

- A list of principal stakeholders will be developed, together with a statement of purpose of communication for each stakeholder group;
- An appreciation of existing communications activities is carried out (including status reporting mechanisms), and an initial assessment of programme communications requirements is made. This is often achieved by means of workshops and interviews, which allows stakeholders to become engaged in defining the programme and to gain their commitment and understanding. The output will be the documented shared understanding off the programme's goal, scope and content;
- At the same time, an assessment can be made of existing capability within the programme team, highlighting any requirements for additional resources, training, briefing, or cultural realignment;
- A provisional selection of appropriate communication media is proposed, together with the information content for each stakeholder constituency. The proposed communications strategy is developed and documented;
- The proposals are developed further and validated in consultation with the relevant programme stakeholders. A workshop environment may also be an aid to this process;
- The detailed communications plan is developed and published. It will include a control cycle, to define the information flows, periodicity of reports and key review meetings;
- The communication plan is incorporated in the programme plan and programme handbook;
- The plan is implemented. Reports are prepared to communicate the status of the programme to stakeholders;
- Reviews are held, to assess the effectiveness of the strategy and plan and to take account of changing circumstances and potential new requirements. Any revised plans will reflect changes in the key objectives for communicating with the various stakeholders.

Table 1 provides some examples of the purpose of communication for some typical stakeholder groups in an ERP programme.

Table 1: Purpose of communication by stakeholder group

	INTERNAL STAKEHOLDERS
Programme Steering Group	To seek approval for project- and programme business cases, and authorisation to commit funds. Provide the necessary information for decision-making – to initiate and terminate projects; to agree programme priorities and any changes to scope; to resolve programme-level issues. For endorsement of programme- and project plans. To inform the group of the programme's contributions to expected business benefits and give an overview of the progress of the projects.
Project Sponsors	To establish their support. To inform them of the progress of projects in the portfolio and any inter-project issues involving their project (particularly resource constraints). To inform them of gaps in the programme portfolio to enable them to propose a project to fill the gap.
Project Managers	To provide feedback from Steering Group meetings, including decisions on project priorities and interdependency issues. To provide support to them in setting up and managing their projects (including the co-ordination of any training requirements). To identify programme risks and issues; to establish the risk/issue owner. To advise progress of dependent projects.
	EXTERNAL STAKEHOLDERS
Functional Managers	To establish business function support. To keep informed on the projects' contributions to the business's goals, including the delivery of expected benefits. To help resolve business issues that impact on the programme.
Employees	To inform them of the purpose and composition of the change programme. To give them confidence that the company is co-ordinating the large number of ongoing change projects in a professional manner. Provide progress reports on the change projects. Provide opportunities for questions and comments.

Communication media usually fall into two categories: direct media, e.g. briefing documents, status reports, company newspapers, team briefings, notice board bulletins, surveys and questionnaires, and technology-enabled media, e.g. company intranet; voicemail and telephone conferencing facilities; Internet e-mail; in-house systems, including e-mail and shared areas on the computer network; software applications such Microsoft Office products for word processing, spreadsheets, graphics, and projects planning; and electronic team rooms, e.g. Lotus' Electronic Project Notebook (EPN). The type of communications medium will vary over time and by stakeholder group. It is often helpful to vary the method of communications over time, as particular media can become 'stale' and are overlooked.

Strategies for benefits realisation

Historically, organisations that have invested in ERP have been motivated by either operational or technological reasons. Operational drivers for ERP include better time to market, more efficient inventory management, better control of costs and margin, reduced headcount and more effective balancing of demand and supply dynamics. The restructuring of organisations due to mergers, acquisitions and divestments is playing an increasing role, together with the globalisation of markets and creation of shared service capabilities.

Technological drivers for ERP have primarily been Year 2000 and the limitations of legacy systems in enabling the integration of information and rapid response to changing market conditions.

Many organisations are now employing a structured approach to identifying exploitation opportunities. Regardless of their motivation, organisations are now focusing their attention on extracting return on investment (ROI) from their initial investment. They want to exploit their ERP system and maximise the benefit it brings. This often implies revisiting the original ERP business case and checking if it is still valid.

ERP benefits realisation needs to be done in a careful and systematic way and it is important that ERP development programmes reference the strategic direction of the business to ensure that the ERP system continually supports the business objectives.

Organisations need to adopt a structured approach and ask some basic questions:

- What was the initial business case and did we deliver the expected benefit?
- Was our business case as it could have been, given the potential of the technology?
- How can we leverage the infrastructure we have established to deliver more benefits?

A range of opportunities will emerge from the answers to these questions that will tend to fall into three main categories:

Quick wins: these are benefits that are readily available from the current ERP system, but are not yet realised. Normally these benefits can be achieved relatively easily with minimal effort. Their value is partly in allowing the organisation to start to recoup some of the programme cost fairly soon after the start. Perhaps more important, however, is that the gains should help to build credibility in the programme and perhaps bolster the case for continued investment.

Medium-term wins: these are benefits that are available from changes to current ERP configurations, but are not yet realised. The difference from the quick wins is that these would require investment in time and resource, with benefits being delivered through small/medium-sized projects.

New benefits: these are the benefits that would add value to the organisation, but are available only through additional investment in more functionality and/or complementary software/packages, to provide capability in CRM, e-commerce, HR or data warehousing, for example. Large or complex projects may be necessary to deliver these additional benefits.

Benefits identified should be measurable and quantifiable so that organisations have a basis for prioritisation. Opportunities for benefit need to be filtered to determine where the best value can be obtained. Business cases need to be articulated for every benefit opportunity, identifying whether they are strategic or tactical, quantifiable or intangible, and the logical timescale for implementation.

The planning and launch of benefit realisation projects needs to be just as carefully managed as the original ERP implementation. The establishment of a formal benefit delivery process is probably the most important factor in successfully extracting benefit from ERP investments.

Becoming more disciplined about the delivery of real benefits also enables ERP sponsors to build credibility into their programmes. This is important as the range of opportunities available from ERP broadens and the competition for internal capital increases.

Benefits management and the business case

The success of any ERP-enabled change programme will be measured by its ability to deliver significant business benefit to the organisation. The full benefits will arise as a result of redesigned business processes and organisation that are enabled by the functionality of the ERP system.

The costs incurred in delivering the programme and realising the benefits will also need to be measured. This will allow a cost/benefit comparison to be made, so that the value that the company realises from the programme may be measured.

The cumulative benefits and costs will be documented in a programme-level business case, which will be approved and baselined. Proposed changes to the baseline should be approved before the baseline business case (and target benefits and costs) is changed.

A benefits management process is needed to keep all those in the programme focused on delivering the identified business benefits. Benefits that are not tracked are less likely to be realised. It is often a key role of the programme office to introduce a 'good practice' approach to benefits management for individual projects.

Benefits will need to be reported at a programme level, to highlight the total contribution that the individual change projects within the programme are making to delivery of business objectives. It will also point to where resource should be directed within the organisation to maximise potential business benefit.

Benefits management in detail

The benefits management process has five main steps, which are illustrated in Figure 3:

- benefits profile development;
- business case development;
- benefits management planning;
- benefits review;
- realisation management.

Figure 3

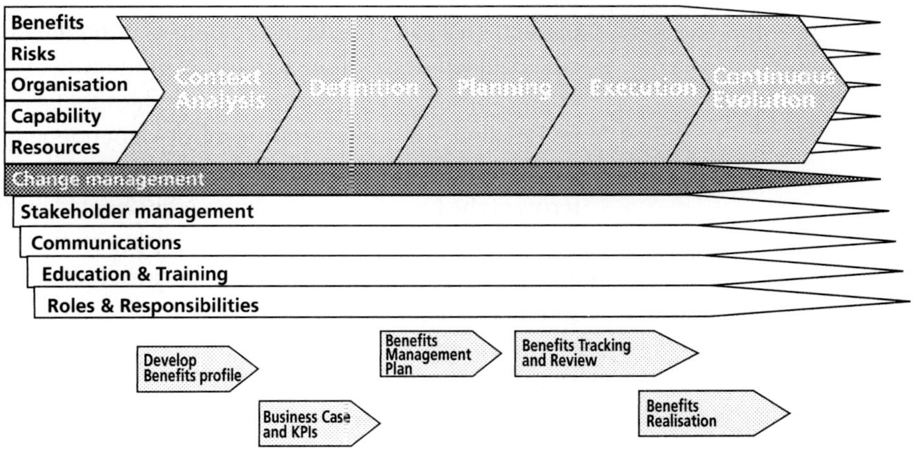

Development of the benefits profile

The benefits profile development is undertaken by each project as part of the project business case development. Once the business case is approved, the current projected benefit levels and timings are included within the programme plan. This will produce an initial view of the expected benefits for planning purposes. Benefits will be managed as a part of each project with reporting to programme level, where a central co-ordinating function will take place. It is essential that key internal stakeholders, such as the project sponsor, project manager and the end users work together to develop the benefits profile for each project. The purpose of this part of the process is to determine the nature of the business benefits flowing from the features provided by each project and to consider mechanisms for measuring achievements. This activity should take place with the project manager and business users, to identify and agree specifically the project features that will provide the business with enhanced capabilities.

Business case development

The next step is to identify the business benefits available as a consequence of the project features identified. The benefits profile is a key component of the business case for the project. Once completed, each project business case should be reviewed by the steering group to determine whether the project should proceed. Where appropriate, the business case for each project and for the overall change programme may also be reviewed and approved by the company board before execution. At this point it should be possible to quantify each benefit identified using the following measures:

- Financial (those that can be measured in terms of increased revenue streams or cost savings achieved by the business). These include benefits that can be converted to financial measures, e.g. headcount reductions;
- Other quantifiable (those that can be measured in terms other than cash, for example, improved response times to customer complaints);
- Intangible (those to which the project in question can be seen to make a contribution, but for which a reliable measure of that contribution cannot be derived, for example, improvements in staff morale).

Following identification of each benefit a date should be identified at which point the benefit is expected to have been realised. If, for example, some cost savings are to be realised in advance of the final benefits delivery date, then this should be reflected in the benefits profile.

As noted above, the sponsor for the project has overall responsibility for the realisation of business benefits. It is also important to identify the dependencies between each project. This will include dependencies upon the delivery of other project features. Specific detailed description is required of the way in which the benefits are dependent on other projects, stating specific deliverables that need to be in place for dependencies to be satisfied. An understanding of the dependencies between projects helps to identify whether particular project deliverables or features are 'must haves' or 'nice to haves' in terms of the benefits. In developing the benefits profile and ultimately the business case, assumptions are made about the inputs to the project, the environment and other events. Where an assumption has a causal effect on the delivery of a benefit then this should be stated explicitly.

Benefits management planning

Once each project is approved there will be a phase of scoping and planning where the project is defined in greater detail. The project manager should also prepare a benefits management plan, often with guidance from the programme office. The purpose of the benefits management plan is to record the baseline or original plan for benefits and to support the monitoring and review of benefits delivery or realisation as the project progresses. The benefits management document sets out: the objectives (features) which the project will deliver; the measures for delivery of the project objectives; the benefits which flow from the delivery of the project features; when the benefits will be realised, as stated in the benefits profile; specific actions needed to be taken for the benefits to be realised; the measures which will be used to monitor realisation of each benefit. The benefits management plan should form an integral part of the project planning exercise, with milestones for the realisation of benefits (or key dependencies and events) incorporated within the project plan.

Benefits reviews
Benefits reviews should take place at regular intervals, where possible allied to strategic points in the life of the project such as the completion of a pilot or following a major milestone. These reviews will involve the programme manager, the project sponsor and the project manager. During each review the assumptions behind the original benefits case should be re-evaluated and amended or confirmed as appropriate. The levels of benefit predicted for the project may change over time. In order to take account of these changes, and to manage the expectations of the end users for the project, it will be important to review benefit projections at regular intervals. It is recommended that two sets of reviews should take place:

- A brief analysis should be conducted at quarterly intervals to ensure that changes in project scope and any external factors are reflected in the understanding of the benefits to be delivered;
- A full benefits review should be conducted at the conclusion of each key phase of the project, to ensure that the projected benefits still represent a comprehensive picture. This should aim to identify previously unrecognised benefits as well as reflecting any changes to the existing benefits profile.

The output from each benefits review will be a revised benefits profile, management plan and statement of assumptions, as appropriate.

Benefits realisation
This is essentially a process of monitoring achievement and, where the targets for benefits are not being met, determining the reason for any shortfall. Where there is a shortfall identified in the benefits achieved it will be necessary to take corrective action, the nature of which will be dependent on the benefit in question and the problems encountered in its realisation. Where the difficulty is outside the control of the project team it will be necessary to escalate the requirement for action. Where the cause of the problem is outside the control of the business (for example regulatory requirements) it may be that the only action available is to modify the benefits target or the timescale for achieving it. Any decision to relax the target should only be taken after thorough analysis of the options and in consultation with the programme manager and, if necessary, the programme steering group.

Roles within the benefits management process
There are a number of key roles involved in the benefits identification and realisation process. They must work together as a team for the process to be efficient and effective. The main responsibilities of some of the key participants are described briefly below:

Project sponsor
The sponsor for the project has overall responsibility for the definition and realisation of the business benefits. While the benefits planning and management activities may be delegated to the project manager, ultimate ownership of the business benefits remains with the sponsor.

Project manager

The project manager will have worked with the project sponsor in producing the project business case submission and will therefore have had a key role in defining the business benefits to be delivered by the project. He or she works closely with the project sponsor to ensure that the target benefits are properly understood and can be realised.

End user

The end user is the person or persons who will use the outputs from the project, whether these are new business processes or the ERP system, and are therefore key in realising the benefits from the project. It is essential that they understand, and buy into, the benefits expected from the new business processes and system.

Programme manager

The programme manager is responsible for ensuring that the programme is focused on the realisation of benefits, and that the projects within the programme enable the benefits as planned. He or she also ensures that any deviations from target benefits are identified, and corrective actions are put in place and executed. The programme manager also presents regular progress reports on benefits to the steering group and other stakeholders.

Programme office

The programme office will normally be responsible for the measurement and monitoring of benefits throughout the life of the programme. The programme office is also responsible for preparing progress reports relating to the definition, measurement, tracking and realisation of benefits.

Target benefits will be documented in the programme business case. Changes will only be made to the business case once the necessary approvals have been gained (normally from the programme steering group).

Managing the change process – skills, processes and structures

It is now recognised that most businesses experience a 'dip' in performance immediately after go-live. Change management processes during and after rollout and cutover has a key role to play in minimising this 'dip', by:

- engendering a smooth 'go-live';
- minimising the effect on normal business operations;
- achieving rapid stabilisation after 'go-live'.

There are a series of key components to the change management stream in an ERP programme, as shown in Figure 4.

Figure 4

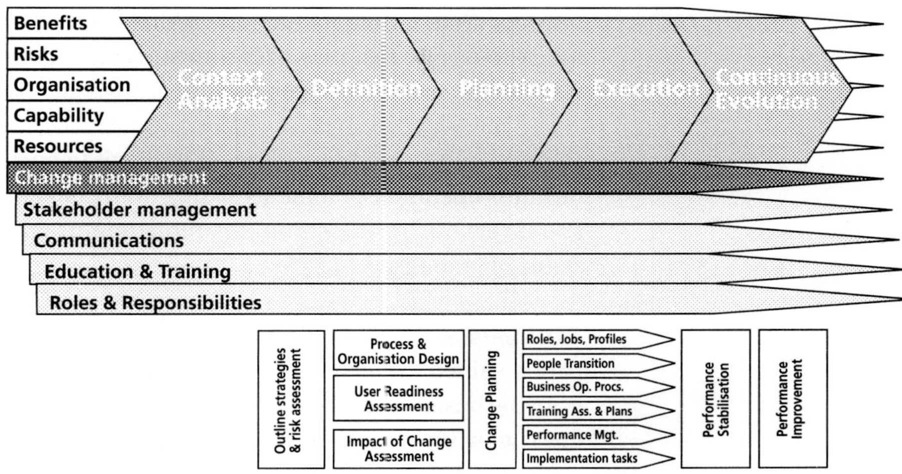

The most critical of these are addressed below:

Readiness assessments: these should be used to understand the programme 'terrain' before embarking on any change management work. Other initiatives, the history of change and the change skills already present in the organisation will influence the capacity of the business to implement ERP-related change.

Impact of change assessments: these will identify exactly what will be different as a result of the ERP implementation. Focusing on the big changes and on those business communities with the most change to manage will help direct resources to where they are most needed.

Change planning: this will bring together the readiness and impact assessments for each affected community and determine the appropriate package of interventions needed to get the business ready for the system.

Interventions for each affected business community vary from some training and development for those experiencing little impact to extensive business participation and involvement for those fundamentally affected. There is a need for particular focus on those who are key to the success of the programme.

The change management plan would normally consist of a package of interventions including education, communication, training, business operating procedures, definition of roles and responsibilities, skills assessments and detailed transition planning for individuals. The whole transition will be much easier to manage if the business case and the impact of change are clearly communicated at the outset.

Business implementation: ensuring effective business participation in certain stages of the implementation will make a significant difference to the quality and acceptability of the system and new processes. This will complement the change management activity described above. In particular:

User acceptance testing: – this should be led by the business and be focused on ensuring that the system and processes work in an environment as close to real life as possible.

Data management: – this should not only address the process for getting quality data into the system, but should also address the processes and organisation required in future to ensure that new data standards are followed and that weak disciplines do not result in the system being undermined.

Cutover: – this should be planned in detail to ensure that there is no discontinuity in business operations. Problems arising from poor cutover often take a long time to rectify and divert the business from the more important task of getting the business back to stable operations.

Participation: one of the key components of well-managed change is the level of participation gained through implementation. When there has been inadequate participation from the business, the quality of the solution is often poor. It is usually too theoretical and does not work in practice, causing people to work 'around' the system rather than with it.

In order to get people to take ownership of the solution it is important to get the right people from the business involved from the start. If they have an input to the design, development and testing, they will be more supportive post go-live, thus reducing the dip in productivity. If they are not involved, there may be a prolonged period of reduced productivity with detrimental effects on the business.

There is a need to decide who will be involved and how to structure the programme. There may be a need to take some people out of their line roles completely in order to work on the programme. Others will remain in their posts and contribute to the programme on a part-time basis. The business will need to be stabilised and positions backfilled with appropriately skilled temporary staff.

Resource management and capability transfer

As part of the programme planning process, resource skill requirements should be defined, current capabilities assessed, gaps identified, and training provided. Where resource shortages are identified – both within the programme team and in the staff required to support the completed ERP system and processes – plans will need to be constructed to bridge the gaps. Formal plans should also be established and managed to transfer key skills from any external resources to the organisation's employees.

In many instances, particularly in large enterprises, the ERP programme will be just one of a number of concurrent initiatives. In this situation, there will be a need to prioritise all the programmes and initiatives to ensure that resources are deployed in the most effective way. Again, shortfalls will need to be identified and plans developed for resolving the shortages. Early planning will enable adequate sourcing of resources. There will need to be clear and specific allocation of resources to projects and tasks to ensure that the resources are used effectively across programmes and projects.

The following sequence of activities will normally be followed:

- *Analysis:* interview potential programme staff, functional heads and other stakeholders; assess the impact of culture of the organisation and the personalities – their power and influence, ability to adapt to change, and motivations; review the company organisation diagrams and role descriptions; undertake capability gap analysis to identify skill and resource shortages;

- *Development of proposed programme organisational framework:* determine the proposed programme participants and organisation; identify relationships between the participants; establish the programme director, programme manager and steering group;
- *Detailed planning:* refine and agree the programme organisation; develop role descriptions and responsibilities; agree the transition- and recruitment plans; populate the organisation framework; develop the capability transfer plan (from external resource to the company's staff); document the arrangements within the overall programme plan;
- *Implementation:* monitor the effectiveness of the plans and revise as external circumstances change; monitor against evolving business requirements; maintain leadership alignment; implement the capability transfer plan.

A word on coping with culture and distance

This section is concerned with the performance of teams, and on the effects of different cultures and disparate locations. Differences will arise both between organisations – for example, between the companies participating in the ERP implementation – and within the host organisation, particularly where the rollout affects operations in several countries.

Some of the factors to be considered are:

- *Task versus team focus:* organisations do not all strike the same balance between task-orientated behaviour and the social and emotional factors that affect individual performance. This may be reflected in different performance appraisal and reward arrangements within the companies.
- *Consensual versus authoritarian management styles:* these vary widely between individuals. However, there are also patterns of acceptable behaviour that are embedded in countries' cultures. For example, a directive, authoritarian style of management is likely to be far more acceptable to most American employees than to Japanese ones.
- *Risk-taking or risk-averse behaviour:* managers in some countries are more likely to make decisions without reference to higher authority, and to accept the consequences of those decisions. In Japan, consensus is the aim.
- *Social proprieties:* in some countries and cultures it is easy to inadvertently give offence to the host. For example, in some cultures, it is considered abrupt to raise the business purpose at the first meeting: welcomes and social exchanges, only, are expected. The consequence, clearly, is that the pace of conducting business can be much slower.
- *When 'yes' means 'no' or 'perhaps not':* it is not acceptable in some cultures to be put in the position of admitting a failure – failure to understand; to have authority to make a decision; to be able to carry forward an action.

There are also some guiding principles for effective team behaviour that extend beyond cultural or physical boundaries, these include: mutual respect for team members' cultures and working practices; a focus on solutions rather than problems and no recriminations ('finger pointing') when things go wrong. While a detailed discussion of these issues is beyond the scope of this section, it is clear that ERP implementation requires a wider understanding of change management and cultural issues than many practitioners have demonstrated to date.

CONCLUSION

To date, many ERP implementations have been treated as technology projects and not business-driven transformations. Approaching the implementation from an IS perspective often leads to attempts to try to tie down all of the major requirements at an early stage, with large disincentives for changing these at a later stage. As a result many firms have found themselves trapped in a technological straitjacket solution which ignores the dynamic, evolutionary nature of ERP implementations and the business environment. An ERP system needs to be implemented in a business-driven, cost-effective fashion, where the focus is on driven-out real long-term benefits in pursuit of shareholder value. If long-term competitive advantage from ERP systems is to be achieved it requires the ongoing commitment of senior executives to the project. The failure of senior project sponsors to remain involved in a project will result in the project team losing sight of the business nature of the implementation and allow it to become an IT project. Project sponsors/champions must not only provide the resources for the implementation but they must also take an active role in leading change. In particular they must create the emotional climate for change and be proactive in building co-operation among the diverse groups on the implementation team and throughout the organisation, often across national boundaries.

Chapter 5

ERP and Management Accounting

INTRODUCTION

The past decade has been a period of dramatic change in management accounting. Indeed at first glance the management accounting literature in the past ten years seems to have been a succession of latest 'hot topics' and firms struggling to come to terms with yet another 'silver bullet' change programme or strategic initiative. ABC, ABM, balanced scorecards, BPR, and the more recently conceived shareholder value management, have led to a plethora of management seminars and books on how to survive in the turbulent environment of the new century. Few corporations have failed to escape from the army of consultants and management gurus offering attractively packaged 'solutions'. One of the most resource-intensive initiatives of the past ten years for the finance function has been the introduction of enterprise resource planning (ERP) systems.

ERPs change the relationship between accountancy systems and other management information systems. Previously, accountancy systems were the main focus of corporate information systems with supplementary systems added when necessary (Scapens, 1998). ERP integrates the accounting modules directly to the main information system with the common database ensuring consistent information for all purposes. This chapter examines the impact of ERP systems on organisations and in particular on the management accounting function of organisations. It looks at the challenges facing the finance function and the role that ERP systems can play in meeting those challenges. In particular the chapter examines the following issues: (1) the role of management accountants in ERP projects, (2) the impact of ERP systems on management accountants and management accounting activities particularly with respect to product costing, and performance measurement, and (3) the issues which management accountants must address if they are to realise the full potential of their organisation's ERP investment.

ERP RESPONDING TO THE CHALLENGES IN THE FINANCE FUNCTION AND MANAGEMENT ACCOUNTING

Davenport (1998) predicted a number of benefits for management accounting and control from the implementation of ERP systems. In particular it was suggested that ERP systems would provide the following:

- Support for strategic planning and organisational change in the form of tighter integration of functions to support management by process. Multiple sites could be managed as a single entity using proven processes;
- Enterprise-wide integration of systems and information through standardisation yielding improvements in data integrity and site headquarter reporting;

- Cost reduction and revenue enhancements from improvements in management reporting and control as well as improved efficiency and more timely access to accurate information;
- Data rationalisation through the use of universal transaction codes, and consolidation procedures;
- Improved forecasting for production, distribution and other purposes based on real-time integration with suppliers and customers;
- Improvement in transaction processing in the form of better cash flow control, payables accounting, etc.

The finance function in many organisations is undergoing significant change. This change is been driven by the need for accountants to make the transition from a score-keeping role to one in which they actively drive and support the value-creation activities in the firm. While technologies such as ERP, data warehousing and budgeting/planning software have brought greater efficiency to the management accountant's role, the promise of technology remains largely unfulfilled. In the coming years accountants will face a variety of challenges, some of which are discussed below.

The pressure for continuous process improvement in the finance function. In common with other functional areas the finance function is under pressure to improve performance in the key areas of process cost, cycle times and quality. In particular the relatively high cost of European accounting operations compared with their North American counterparts had led to calls for greater efficiency and in some cases the establishment of shared service centres in an attempt to drive down the cost of the finance function. ERP technologies have a key role to play in improving process quality and costs by removing the costly integration and duplication associated with incompatible systems. Research shows that the implementation of ERP systems can help to eliminate costly manual reconciliations and improve reporting times significantly.

The need to operate at a pan-European or regional level. While globalisation is the buzzword of the moment, in practice most large multinational corporations organise their operations on a regional basis. A typical MNC will normally have three regions EMEA (Europe, Middle East and Africa), the Americas and Asia Pacific. In the European context the advent of the euro and the move towards more market-driven organisation structures has led to attempts by the finance function to operate at a pan-European level. This reflects the need to align finance with the firms' operating structures that are usually product or market driven. Increasingly firms are attempting to standardise and integrate the finance processes across Europe. In particular, firms are simplifying their statutory structures to allow them to roll out US or UK GAAP accounting standards across multiple sites while retaining the ability to report in local GAAP for compliance and regulatory purposes. Firms expect to be able to 'slice and dice' their profit and loss and balance sheets by country, by legal entity, by market and by product line. In the past such reporting involved a large amount of scrubbing of data from diverse legacy systems and spreadsheet-based reporting. With the complex and very comprehensive transaction coding capabilities of most ERP systems, firms are in a position to report multi-views of performance with relatively little effort. Statutory and inter-group adjustments as well as local GAAP adjustments which previously delayed monthly and quarterly reporting can be made more efficient and less time consuming. As a result a regional perspective on firm performance is available to business unit and product line managers.

Improve reporting cycle times and reduce the burden of ad hoc reporting. In the past, management accountants spent a large amount of time extracting information from different legacy systems and using spreadsheets to summarise and present the information to senior executives. As Figure 1 illustrates, these difficulties arise primarily because of the diverse systems that were supporting the firms' operational activities. A typical firm might be running its accounting systems on an AS400 while its manufacturing operations ran on a separate HP or DEC platform. In some cases each functional area and indeed each operating site had different IT architectures. As a result a large amount of effort and resources was spent trying to extract and reconcile information from the diverse systems. Consequently the management accounting function at corporate or business unit level spent a large part of the monthly close-out manually scrubbing the data from different operating sites and systems. This information was then supplemented with information from external sources and with forecast data. Tight deadlines for reporting typically led to a situation where there was very little time for value added analysis of the firms' performance. The problem was exacerbated when the executive committee requested once-off or ad hoc analysis of a particular issue such as declining sales in a particular market. This inevitably led to additional extract programmes and spreadsheet analysis. As a result management accounting staff in such decision support roles often complained about the burden which incompatible systems placed on them. With well-designed and implemented ERP systems management accounting staff are freed from the drudgery of wading through large amounts of data from legacy systems and the manual consolidation of data in spreadsheets. Instead ERP systems allow greater focus on value added analysis and commentary. Thus the executive committee is presented with more informed views on performance and a more responsive reporting system.

Figure 1: Traditional management reporting systems

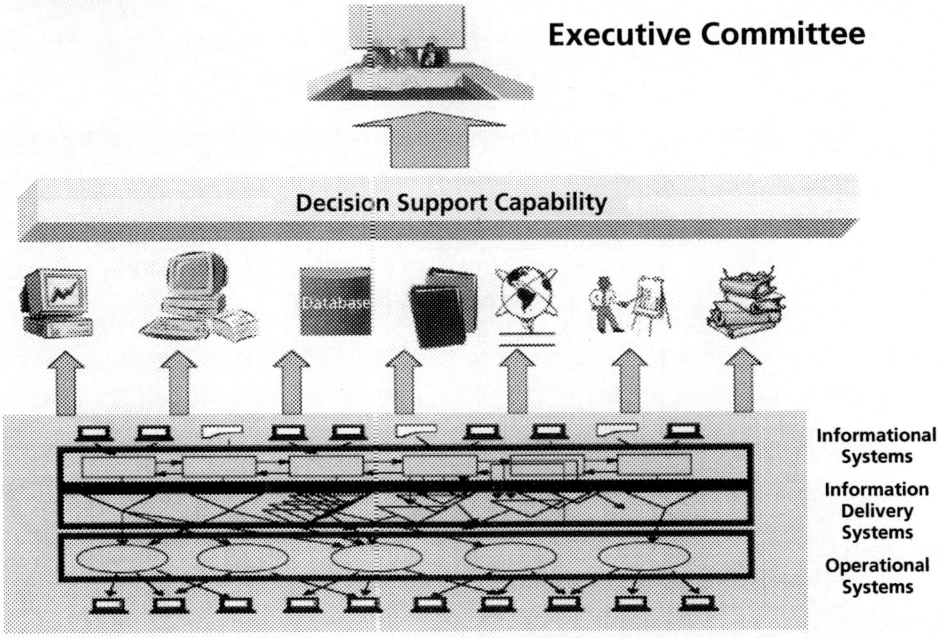

Addressing the shortcomings of traditional management reporting systems. Traditional management accounting systems have a large number of shortcomings. Management accounting researchers have identified the following:

- A lack of strategic focus on competitors, customers and products and the failure to address the information needs of the wider stakeholder groups;
- The absence of the 'balanced scorecard' approach and the focus on mainly financial historical measures of performance;
- Reporting under traditional legacy systems is cyclical in nature and often restricted to batch and month end reporting;
- In many cases IT is a constraint on the firm's ability to implement new reporting processes and measures;
- Important business knowledge and understanding of the underlying processes is often embedded in poorly documented spreadsheets;
- With business models and corporate strategies continually changing, many firms find that their reporting systems do not reflect the changing corporate strategy;
- Lack of support for flexible organisational structures and multi-dimensional reporting;
- Poor support for planning, direction setting and forecasting and too much focus on information for tracking and control purposes;
- The strong financial accounting bias in many management reporting systems often leads to a lack of focus on the drivers of performance and in particular the customer facing revenue-creation processes. Management accountants continue to focus on the manufacturing and cost of sales elements despite the fact that in many industries sales and marketing and other brand-building activities constitute the biggest element of product costs;
- While traditional management accounting systems were effective in identifying where costs were incurred, they failed to provide support for cost reduction programmes;
- Finally the excessive tracking and control focus of management reporting often led to a neglect of and a lack of decision support for the important areas of business problem-solving, business intelligence and direction setting.

Figure 2: ERP allows management accounting to be more strategic

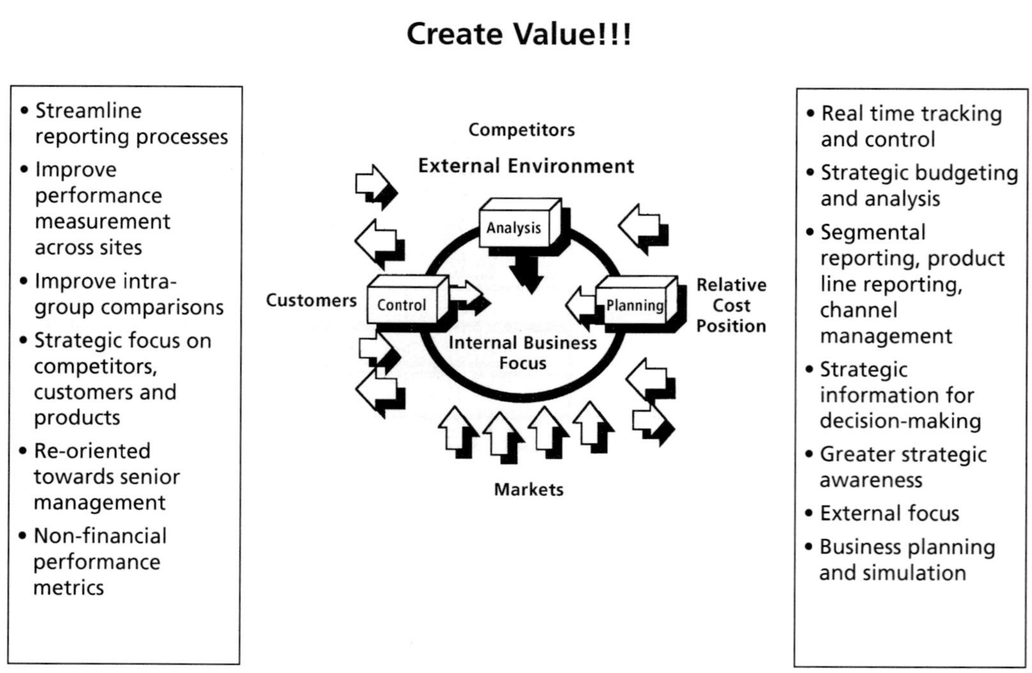

While ERP is not a panacea for all of these problems or shortcomings it does provide a framework and the data access to allow management accountants to fundamentally alter the orientation of their reporting systems away from cyclical routine reporting of historical financial performance to a more strategic and value added focus, as outlined in Figure 2. In particular, ERP systems provide the flexible data access to allow management accountants to gain the richer cross-functional process insights into performance which senior managers typically require.

The failure to institutionalise many of the performance improvement techniques and technologies. The last fifteen years has seen a succession of techniques and technologies aimed at improving management accounting and reporting. ABC/ABM, balanced scorecards, shareholder value management are all recognised as having the potential to bring significant improvements in operations. Many firms have however failed to get beyond the prototype stage with these initiatives. One of the reasons for this was the difficulty in tying what were often stand-alone techniques back to the data sources, which were incompatible legacy systems. A similar experience resulted from technologies such as EIS, data warehousing and so-called 'dashboard' software. While the underlying concept was fundamentally sound the technologies themselves lacked scalability and robustness. For a number of years ERP vendors have been criticised for the inadequacy of the DSS capability within their systems. Trends such as EIS, data warehousing, balanced score cards, etc., have prompted vendors such as SAP to focus on analytical applications including GIS which are designed to support top managers in their decision-making. The strategic enterprise management tool developed jointly by PWC and SAP is an example of this shift to supporting the more strategic management problems facing managers.

With the expanding functionality of ERP systems, firms can now get ABC/M and BSC functionality as part of the ERP as outlined in Figure 3. This resolves many of the integration issues that plagued earlier efforts. Similarly the incorporation of data warehousing and EIS capability into ERP has allowed management accountants to move beyond mere prototype applications to fuller business unit applications.

Figure 3: The expanding funtionality of ERP

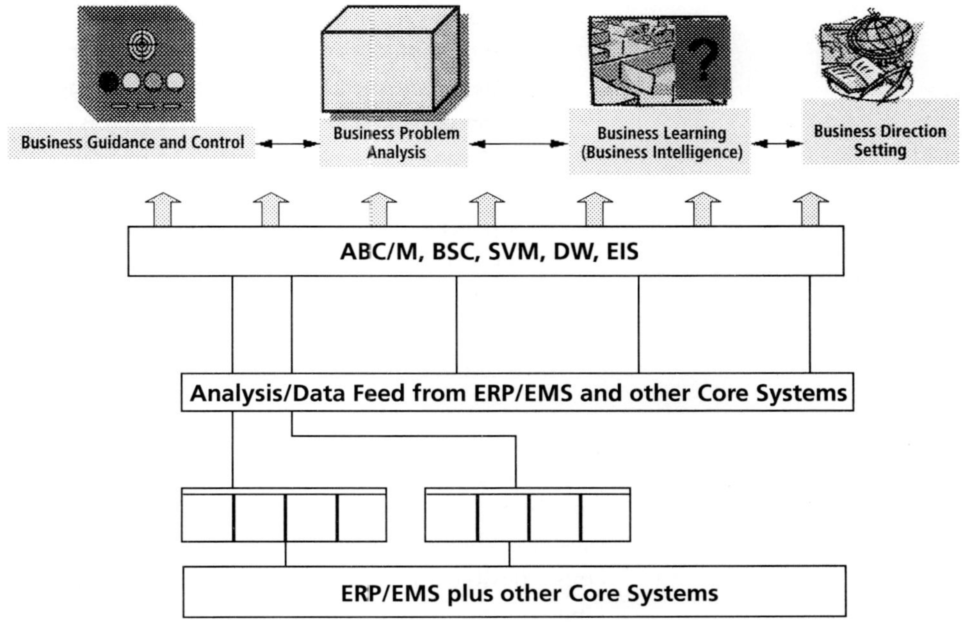

Table 1: Impact of ERP systems on management reporting and information processing

Single worldwide data repository
Improved performance measurement and control processes across the sites
Improved intra-group co-ordination of production and supply chain management
Replaced non-Y2K compliant legacy systems
Provided EMU convergence
Reduced lead time, improved response time to *ad hoc* requests for analysis and DSS
Improved tracking and control at operational control level
Inventory cost control, job costing,
Reduced clerical and re-keying errors
Time and resource savings reported
Reporting cycle times cut
Better budgetary control and variance analysis
Reduced accounting costs through shared service centres
Better segmental reporting and product line peporting
Reduced use of spreadsheets
Reduced reliance on extraction programmes and report generation capabilities

It would be wrong to think that ERP systems have only had a positive impact on the work of management accountants. Research results indicate that while ERP systems improve the supply of transaction data for strategic management accounting activities they typically cause significant damage to the existing decision support capability of the firm. In particular the introduction of ERP systems will lead to the elimination of many of the existing approaches to management reporting. The increased operational control achieved through the introduction of ERP systems may inhibit the strategic learning which is a hallmark of management accounting decision support activity and may lead in the long term to a loss of strategic thinking and problem-solving capacity at the local operating site level. Table 2 summarises these and other difficulties encountered by management accountants as a result of ERP implementations.

Table 2: Difficulties arising for management accountants from ERP implementations

- Information overload
- Monthly reporting poorer initially
- Short-term damage to management accountants' decision support capability
- Steep learning curve for the new technology
- Loss or removal of traditional data sources and associated business knowledge
- Management accountants more strategically aware but not acting strategically in information reporting
- The elusive external focus is still missing for many firms
- Easier access to non-financial measures but not getting cross-functional integration of these
- The ongoing need for spreadsheets
- Loss of organisational knowledge in legacy systems

In addition to having important strategic implications, enterprise systems also have a direct, and often paradoxical, impact on a company's organisation and culture. On the one hand, by providing universal, real-time access to operating and financial data, the systems allow companies to streamline their management structures, creating flatter, more flexible and more democratic organisations. On the other hand, they also involve the centralisation of control over information and the standardisation of processes, which are qualities more consistent with hierarchical, command-and-control organisations with uniform cultures. ERP systems offered an escape from legacy systems and their associated Y2K problems to a more integrated system based on a single data repository that supports data mining and other data warehousing derivatives. In particular, ERP systems promised to eliminate the need for spreadsheets, shadow systems and expensive manual integration of data from different legacy systems (Korzeniowski, 1998).

Scapens (1998) argues that with modern database technology it is quite feasible to have a single system of data capture for both management accounting and external reporting, with data selected, analysed, aggregated and reported in different ways for different purposes. He goes on to suggest that the increasing availability of computer technology at all levels in the firms studied and the integration of operating control systems with management information systems mean that managers can have on-line access to the information they need to control all aspects, including the costs, of their operations. Scapens (1998) contends that the dispersion of computer competence around the firms means that all managers, and indeed supervisors and operators, are able to access computer software both to input data and to obtain information on their current performance. The dispersion of computer competence and the widespread availability of information technology mean that a great deal of information is available for both decision support and control. Rather than waiting for formalised periodic reports, managers and other personnel can access the information they need directly.

Cooper (1998) suggests that the cost of data collection and manipulation is falling, so a new approach to cost information can be considered. In this approach, the users collect all of the cost information that they require and use it to help them improve their performance. This detailed information can then be forwarded to accounting where it can be aggregated for financial reporting purposes. Cooper (1998) also points out that there is one significant implication to letting the SBUs collect their own data, namely that cost information will become more widely available in the firm. In many firms today, cost information is considered strategically sensitive and is available to senior managers only. In contrast, in the new approach the workforce will have access to the cost information that they need to help them improve their performance.

Scapens (1998) found evidence to suggest that while systems such as SAP integrate separate functions and business processes in one system for the whole company, such centralisation can lead to a loss of control at the local level. In particular they found that management accountants in subsidiaries of overseas multinationals had to rely increasingly on the company-wide system as the basis for information they provide to their managers. In some cases control over the delivery of local management accounting information had diminished and this could lead to a lack of locally relevant information or a return of supplementary local information systems.

CASE STUDY

Thermo King (Ingersoll-Rand) manufactures transport temperature control units for truck trailers, small trucks and seagoing containers and air conditioning for buses. Its main customers include transporters and distributors of temperature-sensitive products, such as perishable food, pharmaceuticals, paints and photographic films. It has manufacturing locations in the USA, Puerto Rico, Ireland, Spain, Denmark, Germany, Brazil, the Czech Republic and China. The company has its headquarters in Minneapolis USA. The Irish operations, which employ close to 1,000 people, concentrate on the refrigerated trailer and truck units for long-haul delivering of perishable and non-perishable foods and products. There are three sites in Ireland, Dublin, Shannon and Galway. Galway is the main branch office for the European division and it also acts as the shared service centre with responsibility for financial reporting for all of Ireland and most of the European operations. The combined turnover of the Irish operations last year was in excess of $350 million.

The ERP implementation in Thermo King originally began while the firm was part of the Westinghouse group. Implementation and prototyping originally took place in Pittsburgh with representatives from the Galway site being sent for training on implementation issues. In 1998 the firm was sold to Ingersoll-Rand. The Irish sites went live in January 1997 using SAP R/3 with a subsequent upgrade to SAP R/4 in late 1999. In common with the other two firms examined, TKE implemented all the main ERP modules except HRM. While external consultants were used at the headquarters none were involved in the Irish implementation. However the approach to the implementation was heavily dictated by the staff in the USA. The principal motivation for implementing the system was to 'streamline the organisation to further its competitive advantage'. In addition the firm's legacy systems were revealing problems with respect to multi-currencies and YK2. The implementation was carried out in two stages. Firstly a prototype was developed in Pittsburgh and run parallel to the legacy systems for a period of 3 months. Four members of the Galway site were involved in the development of the prototype; these included three management accountants and one distribution manager. These managers were trained in using the system and returned to form the core of the implementation group on site. After the SAP system was run in parallel for a number of months it went live in June 1996 for the headquarters in Pittsburgh, PA. The second stage was going live for the Galway site in January 1997. Backed by the team members who had been in Pittsburgh, general ledger and payables were among the first modules to be implemented.

The total costs of the ERP rollout to the TK group were approximately $14 million involving sites in the USA, Spain, Germany and Ireland. The main benefits of ERP to the firm included streamlining the financial processes of the organisation, and in particular removing the inefficiencies associated with extracting information from the diverse legacy systems. For example after the ERP implementation it was possible to have a complete profit and loss account for the European section of the organisation in just three working days, compared with a week prior to the new system. Other reports, which had to be requested by the accounting department and often took hours to be completed even though they had priority, could be provided in a matter of minutes. In addition the new system brought significant cost reductions in IT and software. Unlike many other organisations TKE chose not to dramatically redesign its business processes as part of the implementation. Instead processes are slowly changing as users come to realise the potential available with the SAP system. Staff in the management accounting area continue to use spreadsheets in conjunction with the SAP system. Typically staff use spreadsheets in areas where SAP is weak. In most cases these spreadsheet systems are used until changes can be made to the SAP system. Overall the management accounting staff feel that the usefulness and contribution of spreadsheet systems has improved as a result of the SAP implementation. Information is of better quality and is taken from fewer sources. In addition to streamlined financial reporting processes in the organisation, the ERP implementation has reacquainted managers with the other processes of the organisation.

In terms of performance monitoring SAP allowed the firm to consolidate financial reporting for Europe, at the Galway site. This in turn gave management accountants there the ability to carry out intra-group comparisons by site, market segment and product line at the touch of a button. In addition the drilldown capability of the SAP database allows managers to request reports at varying levels of detail. The single biggest improvement was in the area of information for cost management. The ERP system allows the firm to report actuals against budget and projected outturns at the most detailed level of product sub-assemblies or manufacturing cells. Overall the firm had achieved improvements in the areas of monthly consolidation and forecasting. While SAP has replaced all the legacy financial systems, the firm still makes extensive use of spreadsheets for presentation and modelling. The data extraction and reporting capabilities within SAP have allowed the management accountants to export raw data to spreadsheet models.

With the exception of a move to a single consolidation of all European sites into one set of financial statements, the introduction of SAP led to very little change in the institutionalised or routine management accounting reports. In particular there was no move to strategic management accounting techniques such as product line profitability analysis, segmental reporting or customer profitability analysis. All of the major improvements achieved were in the areas of ad hoc reporting. As one member of the management accounting group pointed out, 'The drilldown feature of SAP gives immediate access to detailed level of information and gave rise to increased opportunities for data manipulation. In particular, exporting information to Excel or another spreadsheet application allows the user to perform further analysis. Data which previously took several hours to extract from legacy systems was now available in a matter of minutes'.

The firm's use of spreadsheet or local MIS changed significantly. More time was spent on analysis of the results rather than on the extraction and construction of the data sets. As ad hoc reports become more institutionalised the management accounting function is continually striving to migrate them to the SAP system and retire the spreadsheets. Management accounting staff reported that their understanding of the 'big picture' had improved and that they were more aware of the firm's strategic posture and the changes that were taking place at the firm-wide level.

In general the firm has yet to introduce a significant number of newer performance metrics as a result of the ERP system. While the ERP system has resulted in significant improvements in data gathering and the mechanics of information processing, it is not clear that the system has impacted at the more strategic level in terms of improved decision support for senior managers.

ABC AND ERP: PARTNERS AT LAST?

***Management Accounting,* November 1998**
Shaw Russell, Volume LXXX No. 5, pp 56–58. Reprinted with permission from the Institute of Management Accountants, Montvale, NJ, USA. Website: www.imanet.org

One of the biggest recent challenges to ABC/M adoption has been the increase in Enterprise Resource Planning (ERP) implementations. Installations of this software that runs all the operations of a company have diverted attention and resources away from "change enablers" like ABC/M and toward infrastructure applications such as financials, human resources, and manufacturing/logistics. ERP implementations also have caused organizations to question the ability of ABC/M systems to complement the multimillion-dollar ERP architectures being installed across the enterprise. Afraid of clashing with these powerful ERP implementations (usually executive driven), many of those in charge of ABC/M implementations have delayed or even abandoned their projects.

Now the road may get smoother. In September, 1998, ERP vendor SAP AG performed a strategic move into the ABC/M marketplace by making a substantial equity investment in ABC Technologies, developer and producer of Windows-based ABC/M applications. "These two companies are market leaders in their respective industries, and this partnership not only establishes the blueprint for cooperation but also promises to transform the cost management industry worldwide. Arthur Andersen is excited about the benefits this alliance will provide our clients," Steve Player, partner and firm wide director of advanced cost management at Arthur Andersen, said.

Is this the start of a new phenomenon? ERP titans like SAP, Oracle, and PeopleSoft have only recently been mentioned in the same breath as ABC, yet it has been a decade since ABC software hit the market. (Other enterprise vendors created their own ABC applications as part of their systems.) Even though enterprise application companies have acknowledged that ABC is strategic to their product portfolios, both groups had remained separate until now.

Why is this significant? For starters, ABC now has a greater chance of getting onto an executive's radar screen because of some recent partnerships. SAP, PeopleSoft, and Oracle recently announced their foray into the ABC space. Oracle purchased Activa (an ABC/M tool developed by Price Waterhouse LLP – now PricewaterhouseCoopers – for its consulting business), and PeopleSoft has partnered with KPMG to develop its activity accounting module. Given the amount of business generated from these three enterprise applications vendors, almost 50 per cent of all large companies are directly affected by alliances in the ABC/M arena.

I believe these developments are positive news for the management accounting and financial management community because: now that powerful, very visible ERP players have blessed it, ABC/M has been validated in a new way as an accepted cost measurement approach. This development could give management accountants and financial managers an additional avenue into the senior executive suite. The combination of analytic ABC/M applications and operational ABC/M allows management accountants and financial managers to play the role of proactive business strategist rather than reactive, "retrospective reporter." As connections between ABC and organizational initiatives like Economic Value Added (EVA) and performance measurement have solidified, management accountants and financial managers have sought software that could help them implement the principles. Now that market has grown.

In late 1997, consumer goods manufacturers indicated that ABC will be the hottest IT application area for them for the next 18 months to three years. In a 1998 survey, "Technology Issues for Financial Executives," conducted by the Financial Executives Institute (FEI) and Computer Sciences Corporation (CSC), financial professionals indicated that measuring product and customer profitability and reducing operating costs (both key outputs of ABC) were by far the most important issues they needed to focus on. So what was missing?

Like a lot of things in this world, if you can't define it, you tend to ignore it. Admittedly, ABC had been looking for a home. Organizations could not decide whether it was an initiative that was part of a business process reengineering (BPR) exercise, just another costing mechanism, or a disposable acronym that would disappear in a few years. Also, best-of-breed applications – such as commercial ABC/M software systems – have been separate applications. Because they have not been integrated into enterprise-wide operations software, users have struggled to gain access to the raw data contained in the larger transaction-intensive systems.

Now one of the world's leading analyst firms, International Data Corporation (IDC), has reported that activity-based costing is firmly placed in one of the fastest growing segments in the marketplace – analytic applications. "In the future, the strategic use of information will be the key to competitive advantage," says Henry Morris, director of the Data Warehousing and Information Access practice of IDC. "This trend positions the market for analytic applications as a growth market. IDC forecasts that the market for analytic applications will grow from approximately $1 billion in 1997 to over $2.6 billion by 2001." No wonder the ERP players are noticing ABC/M.

Now let's talk about analytic applications. First, I'll define them, and then I'll explore their benefits to companies that use them. Analytic applications are packaged software products that provide value by: structuring and automating a group of tasks pertaining to the review and optimization of business operations. Software for ABC can automate the processes for developing, maintaining, and applying activity models.

Functioning independently from an organization's core transactional applications, yet still dependent on such applications for data, they are capable of sending results back to these applications. For example, a popular output of ABC/M software is the activity driver cost rates that serve as inputs to customer quotation systems.

When summarizing how activity-based costing impacts the market for analytic applications, Henry Morris stated IDC's opinion in an August 1998 IDC Bulletin (#16838):

"Activity-Based Costing (ABC) is now recognized as a fundamental business methodology for enabling business improvement. ABC Technologies, a pioneer in packaged software for ABC, helped shape this recognition and, in turn, benefited from increased business investment in activity-based management projects. Now a new market for analytic applications is emerging, and activity-based management will be incorporated into a range of systems, from budgeting and planning to sales and profitability analysis and optimization. This new market is attracting the attention of major enterprise application players that represent potentially strong competition for ABC Technologies' core business. This challenge is also an opportunity for an agile ABC Technologies to leverage its experience and market leadership in ABC by partnering with application and ERP vendors to ABC enable a broad range of analytic applications."

A few months after IDC offered its opinion, ABC Technologies and SAP partnered. Woody Noxon, president of the Consortium for Advanced Manufacturing – International (CAM-I), said, "This partnership should benefit the entire cost management industry and that, by working together, ABC Technologies and SAP are charting a new direction for the industry."

The ABC technologies and SAP combination

The combination of ABC Technologies' Oros application and SAP's R/3 CO-ABC demonstrates a model of how an enterprise-wide ABC/M environment can be constructed effectively. Oros is an analytic ABC/M application. Per the earlier definition, these applications should be separate and apart from an ERP system yet remain dependent upon the data resident in the ERP system and other systems.

R/3 CO-ABC is an operational ABC/M application that requires an offline modeling and prototyping environment, like Oros, in order to build the ABC/M models but requires an online environment to use the activity rates in managerial exercises like formulating (rational) pricing proposals for clients.

So, envision an environment where ABC models can be built fluidly and then loaded into the operational system for use on a production level. Because modeling is offline, there's no reason to be concerned that data integrity will be compromised. This means that organizations can answer the question, "What do I do with my ABC/M system when my ERP system comes online?" Now the possibility exists for ERP operational systems to live in harmony with best-of-breed analytic systems such as ABC. The bridge that SAP and ABC Technologies are building between their respective products is testament to this. It means that a company can go ahead with an ABC implementation while it is considering ERP implementations.

Another important implication is that ABC does not have to be relegated to an offline system that is used merely to "spit out" updated results every quarter – or semi-annually – only to have the results distributed to a select few people in the organization who merely glance at the report. The recent partnerships between ABC and ERP mean that the ever-elusive operational managers (the ultimate target for ABC outputs) will have access to ABC data through their ERP system with "real-time" ABC data contained in the system. That should make it a lot easier for the ABC champions in a company to bring operational managers on board with their ABC efforts.

Another benefit that derives from the coexistence of analytic ABC/M applications and ERP systems is that the operational system can be separated from the offline analysis and simulation system. Translation: Management accountants and financial managers can conduct "what-if analysis" business simulations in an offline application ensuring that the data integrity of the operational system can be maintained.

To date, this has been a major issue facing corporate ABC champions – how could they gain access to the ERP system when the keepers of the implementation were concerned about compromising the data structures they worked so hard to establish? The data integrity issues no longer will be a barrier.

The future of the partnerships

The attention placed on ABC by SAP, PeopleSoft, and Oracle (whose installations are multimillion-dollar undertakings for an organization and therefore visible at the executive level) inevitably will raise executive awareness of ABC. In addition, the ability of companies such as ABC Technologies and SAP to provide a rational technology and methodology bridge between their products further eases any concerns related to integration and data integrity.

Financial managers and management accountants seek business benefits through the increased alignment of technology and strategy and want their role to be enhanced from record keeper to strategic advisor. The connection between the key enabler of managerial decision making (ABC) and the core enabler of information and data flow in an organization (ERP) makes this seem more within reach than ever before.

ERP IMPLEMENTATIONS – ROLES AND CHALLENGES FOR THE FINANCE FUNCTION

A pertinent question for all management accountants is, 'What is my role in ERP implementations?' In practice, accountants will encounter ERP in a number of roles. The purpose of this section is to explore the responsibilities that they typically have in ERP projects and the challenges facing them in the future.

ERP projects and accountants

The ERP initiator and executive sponsor: Many ERP projects are driven at the board level by the CFO or director of finance. In many ERP implementations the CFO is the person responsible for starting the ERP project. As a senior executive the CFO is ideally placed to spur along the ERP development. In the role of executive sponsor the CFO is normally responsible for bringing the project to the attention of other executives and for securing funding for the development effort. In addition he/she will have an important role in acting as a link between the project team and senior executives at board level and helping overcome problems that arise with regard to organisational politics, resistance from senior managers, etc. It is important that as an executive sponsor the CFO does not become embroiled in the day-to-day detailed management of the ERP project. The CFO will make his/her most valuable contribution by maintaining their executive-level objectivity and should not be tempted to drive the project forward from the perspective of a single functional area.

The operating sponsor manages the project effort on a day-to-day basis and works with executives, IS staff, functional area personnel, consultants and vendors. This is a key role and in a large multi-site implementation make last for several years. The key contribution of the operating sponsor is to leverage the influence of the executive sponsor and to ensure that the strategic objectives of the original ERP business case are not lost sight of. As such the operating sponsor carries day-to-day responsibility for ensuring that the implementation meets its objectives. This is a highly demanding role that may not suit everyone. While many accountants may feel they have the detailed process knowledge to manage the ERP project, the reality is that an effective operating sponsor must have a very broad range of skills and ideally have undertaken at least one other ERP project. The skills which the operating sponsor will need will include: a detailed understanding of ERP architecture and technologies, experience of large-scale change management (ideally in a BPR setting), an ability to empathise with senior managers in different functional areas, and finally strong interpersonal and communication skills. Many organisations will not have such a person available in-house and he/she will normally be headhunted to the project. This presents its own difficulties since someone new to the firm may lack the detailed industry/organisational knowledge. In the past, accountants would have been temperamentally unsuited for the role of operating sponsor, but increasingly a small number of talented management accountants have shown that they have the necessary skills.

The project steering group is responsible for a number of important tasks as part of the project – the responsibility for the overall ERP planning and the control of the ERP deployment with the steering group. This is normally a high-level senior management team that is responsible for ensuring that the master plan that has been created for the ERP is in fact implemented. This senior management committee initiates the first stage in a project by launching a feasibility study. The functions of the steering group include: approving feasibility studies on systems, and approving the initiation of implementation/development of information systems based on a feasibility study. It also includes authorising resources for the project and reviewing the project progress from a corporate perspective. Accountants can play a key role in the steering committee in such areas as developing the business case, monitoring the level of expenditure on the project and ensuring that the information requirements of the finance function are not neglected.

The ERP project team will typically be a combination of staff from an external software company, consultants, and in-house staff. The project team is the group that actually implements the ERP system. The project team under the leadership of the project manager is responsible for delivering the system to specification, within budget and on time. As a member of the project team, a management accountant could play a number of roles including business process reengineering (BPR), mapping of business requirements, report designing, ensuring business controls, customisation of the package for the specific requirements, documentation, etc.

As process owners finance staff have an important role to play in ensuring that the migration to the new ERP system runs smoothly. This will include assisting with process mapping and measurement as well as providing inputs to process redesign. During testing they will be responsible for a significant element of the work programme and 'go-live' will see them taking primary responsibility for the systems. As the ERP enters a steady-state management accountants who are process owners will have a key role in identifying opportunities for benefits realisation.

Future challenges for accountants from ERP

In the future, ERP offers many opportunities for management accountants to move to the centre of information- and knowledge-based processes in the organisation. Businesses of the twenty-first century must have management processes in place to monitor and control the organisation while at the same time decentralising decision-making in order to react to competitive changes and take advantage of unexpected opportunities. One central element that supports this balance between control and flexibility is shared knowledge. Such knowledge, derived from both internal and external data sources, is converted to information that can be readily interpreted.

Improving the decision support architecture

By their own admission, management accountants and executives in large companies believe that their current decision support efforts are falling short. Many believe that the problem lies in the lack of a co-ordinated architecture for distributing clean, reliable data. A recent Forrester research report found that more than 60 per cent of IT executives said their systems need improvement or are awful (see Figure 1a). Seventy per cent expect that their decision support capabilities will improve over the next two years, but few are clear on how this will happen (see Figure 1b).

The Forrester report argues that effective decision support remains frustratingly out of reach. It points out that 'even when data can be pulled from the multitude of operational systems it is inconsistent, dirty, and late'. The reaction of business units and operating sites is to develop private databases or one-off data marts that quickly compound the problem by spreading low-quality data throughout the organisation. To bring the decision support chaos under control – and overcome the challenges of isolated data marts – management accountants are ideally placed to lead the efforts to improve decision support capability using ERP technologies. By using advanced data warehousing technologies combined with ERP systems they can begin to deliver to decision-makers. Forrester points out that, at present, only power users and business analysts get access to much of the organisational data. Complex tools and arcane data models block

Figure 1: The Fortune 1,000 rates decision support

(a) "How good are your company's decision support systems?"

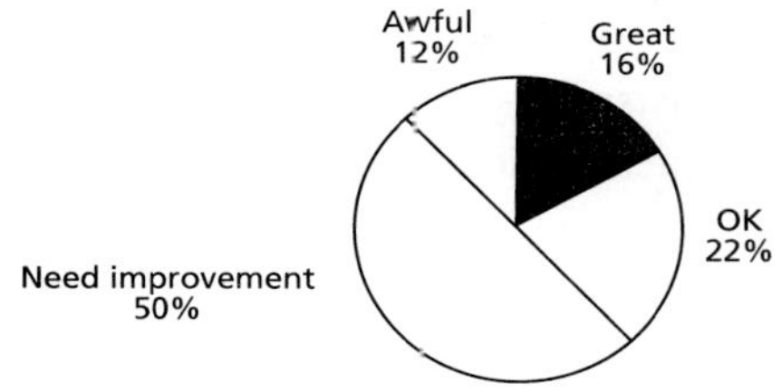

Per cent of 50 Fortune 1,000 companies interviewed

(b) "How will your decision support capabilities change over the next 2 years?"

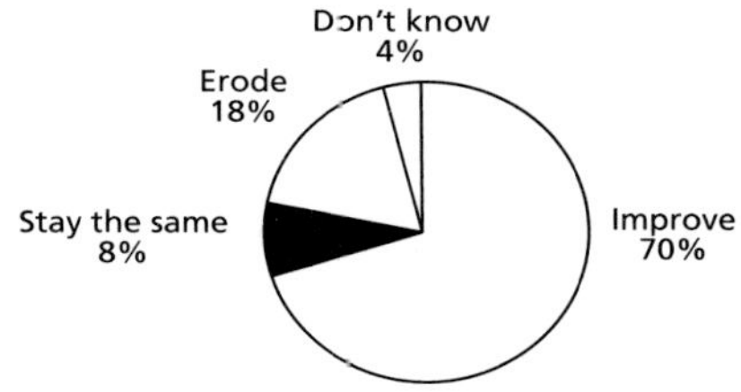

Per cent of 50 Fortune 1,000 companies interviewed

Source: Forrester Research, Inc.

decision-makers at all levels – from executives to customer service reps – from getting the data they need. To address these problems, management accountants need to begin to extend their role beyond the traditional data analysis and reporting to include taking responsibility for the firm's data warehousing and data mining capabilities.

As outlined in Figure 2 emerging decision support architectures combining ERP and data warehousing technologies allow firms to overcome the problems of poor data quality, unreconciled data definitions, and data spinning out of control. This approach enables better business performance measurement and enables analysts and decision-makers from all functional areas to identify exactly what is driving a business trend or an exception to that trend. Users of these systems are able to drill up and down on report text and graphics to get higher or lower levels of detail about the information they are assessing. In addition, they are able to 'slice and dice' various dimensions of business information – such as revenues, products, and time – so that they can easily customise existing reports to help uncover trends and better manage the business.

Figure 2: Emerging decision support architecture

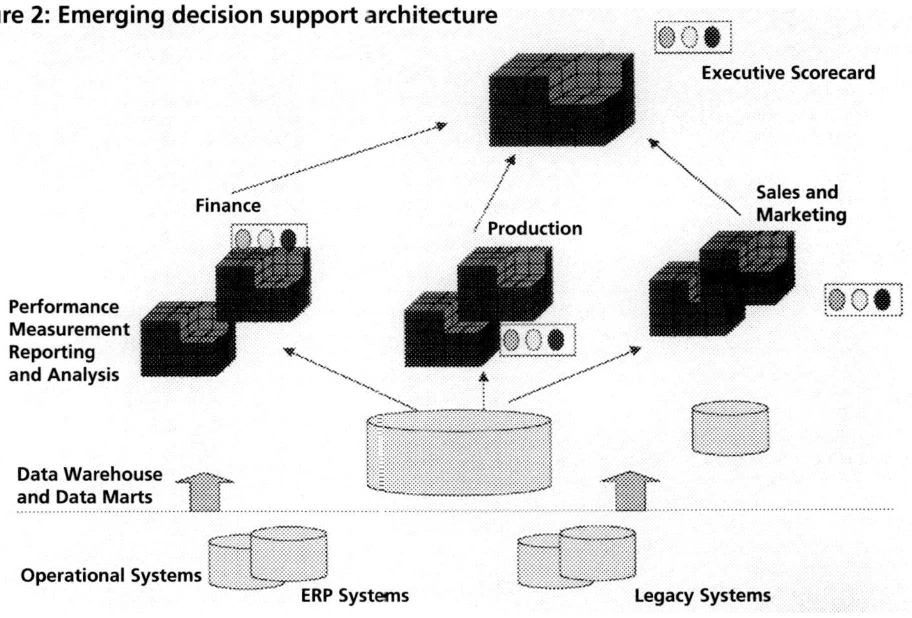

The following examples highlight the insights that can be uncovered with the suggested reporting architecture:

- *Measure business performance over time:* Time-based reporting allows users to quickly 'slice and dice' through multidimensional data to compare business results over time. With the click of a mouse, they can compare sales results from a particular region over a two-year period, instead of having to request this data from IT.
- *Track combinations of influences on the business:* Marketing managers can evaluate the impact of programs like advertising, trade shows, and Web events by region, sales channel, and product.
- *Conduct KPI tracking that traces performance indicators back to the source:* Sales managers who need to track the impact of margin discounts on their business may evaluate this KPI by examining the length of the sales cycle and the close rate at each discount increment.
- *Highlight exceptions:* Manufacturing managers can easily set both minimum and maximum inventory thresholds, by product, so that when they review stock-on-hand reports, anomalies are automatically flagged.

In these cases management accountants are facilitating the empowerment of managers across the organisation and enabling more effective business analysis and planning. Management accountants are therefore no longer merely a cost-based data processing and reporting function standing between decision-makers and inaccessible organisation data.

Enterprise application integration
Taken from 'Industry is about to reinvest itself', Rod Newing, *Finacial Times* survey, 15th December 1999. Reproduced by permission.

Electronic business is driving the need for enterprise application integration tools to connect ERP systems to the Internet. The enterprise application integration (EAI) market has grown up in response to the need to move from departmental or functional software architecture to a system that is more customer- and process-focused. This requires integrating bespoke software and packages from different vendors. EAI software replaces all interconnections between packages with a hub that integrates data from all the applications connected to it. In many respects, the success of ERP vendors in the past has been based on their ability to provide this integration already built into the software. However, the integration has often been problematic. Even within the core set of ERP modules, some have been obtained through acquisition and others have been written at different times using different technologies. Many organisations have different versions of the same package in use in different parts of the company. In order to create competitive advantage, organisations have always wanted to integrate their core ERP system with other packages, such as front office, electronic commerce and decision support systems. Acquisitions and mergers also require different ERP packages to be integrated.

The main driver of the EAI market is electronic business, which is causing organisations to open up their internal systems to suppliers, customers and consumers over the Internet. Organisations need to provide instantaneous inventory availability and follow up with details of transportation and delivery date within an hour. It puts tremendous stress on the link to the ERP system – overnight batch updates of inventory files do not work any more. The EAI market was formed by a number of small specialist vendors, but is now attracting the big operators.

Integration is complex, requiring five different layers. The physical links include message transport and data flow. In the software there is syntax mapping between formats, mapping between application programming interfaces and semantic mapping of business rules. The vendors take different approaches, based on their background. As well as transport, they use application servers, systems management, process modelling, message brokers and data movement. Because of the diversity and complexity, no single EAI tool can meet all an organisation's integration requirements. Some invest heavily in feature-rich tools, while others select the best tool for their highest priority integration problems. EAI software insulates ERP applications from all the other the interfaces. This allows organisations to build more flexible and cost-effective business processes.

Application service providers

The spectacular growth of the enterprise software industry has brought enterprise resource planning to a much wider market and refocused the familiar debate about the benefits of outsourcing. The first users of ERP were large companies which could dedicate a budget and staff to implement a new ERP system. Now, the ERP vendors are tailoring their offerings to the needs of small- and medium-sized enterprises (SMEs). This raises a problem, however, because enterprise software has a reputation as a complex and costly technology that can only be mastered by specialist staff. To counter this image, the ERP industry is heavily promoting a new business model in which the ERP vendor – or a third-party application service provider (ASP) – takes on the burden of installing and running the software and hosts the ERP application at a remote site in return for a monthly fee. The ASP model is different from traditional outsourcing because the role of the service provider is limited to hosting the ERP program externally; it does not get involved in the company's other IT systems. A full-blown outsourcing relationship requires the outsourcer to take some or all of the responsibility for the organisation's internal IT functions. SAP, the leading ERP vendor, has long offered a traditional outsourcing service for its R/3 software through partner companies. It recently unveiled an ASP service, called mySAP.com, which allows customers to 'test drive' solutions online using an Internet-based demonstration and evaluation service. If they decide to purchase, they can choose to implement their R/3 system in a hosted environment, from SAP or one of its partners. SAP sees outsourcing as a cost-effective alternative for SMEs that frees employees to concentrate on core business processes and allows the company to benefit from the partner's greater expertise in R/3. This problem of skills is particularly acute for SMEs which must compete with wealthier large companies to recruit specialist staff. The ERP industry therefore reasons that it makes more sense for SMEs to outsource this aspect of their business. JD Edwards, a leading ERP vendor for the manufacturing sector, has traditionally concentrated on the SME market with a relatively simple ERP offering. However, JD Edwards' latest product, called OneWorld, is more complex and designed to compete with the high-end ERP packages offered by SAP and PeopleSoft. One of the traditional reasons for outsourcing IT functions is cost savings. Oracle claims that potential savings of between 25 and 50 per cent can be achieved by using its new application hosting service, which is called Oracle Business OnLine. The service allows users to access any standard Oracle application hosting on a remote server via a standard web browser.

There is much debate in the industry over whether renting ERP software using the ASP model does save money. Cost analyses done by AMR Research, a specialist consultancy, found that in-house and outsourced ERP operations cost about the same to the end user.

The argument seems persuasive, but AMR Research points out that outsourcing addresses only part of the technical skill shortages. Even if the ERP application itself is outsourced, companies will have to employ staff in roles such as technical support, desktop PC management and client-side application maintenance. If they want to get the most from their ERP system, they will also need a business analyst who understands the capabilities of the ERP package.

ERP outsourcing is relatively knew and AMR Research estimates that only 200 mid-market ERP systems are outsourced today. Until the user base grows sufficiently, ERP outsourcing remains an interesting idea but companies should exercise caution.

CONCLUSION

The next five years will see the emergence of a mature ERP/E-Business technology environment in which customers, suppliers, employees and other stakeholders are integrated in real time. A key element of this integration will be the enterprise systems first implemented in the 1990s. If E-business and ERP are to achieve their promise we must recognise that they are evolving and continuously changing technologies that must be managed proactively. Management accountants must continue to embrace these technologies enthusiastically and take a proactive role in deploying them in pursuit of improved business analysis and planning. In the future, accountants will be increasingly involved in configuring and deploying not just new business processes but also new business models. In this regard management accounting may finally begin to fulfil its strategic potential in organisations.

Chapter 6

Strategic Enterprise Management

INTRODUCTION

The Internet has fundamentally changed the business landscape. As a result firms are changing competitive strategies and business processes, transforming traditional business models to more efficient, more flexible e-business models. As industries become deregulated and privatised, and companies extend their reach to global markets, the pressure to create increased shareholder value has never been greater.

As a direct consequence, businesses today must continuously adapt to this rapidly changing and highly competitive environment. The World Wide Web has caused a paradigm shift in consumer behaviour. Just when market growth was slowing down for most businesses, e-commerce expands the market by eliminating the geographic barriers. Research suggest that by 2003, 5 per cent of all sales around the world will be conducted online, opening the doors to a worldwide, 24-hour marketplace.

What does the future have in store for ERP systems? In the online 24*7 marketplace strategic business unit decision-makers need real time, and complete insight to what is happening at the operational level. The challenge is for ERP systems to deliver insights into day-to-day operational performance of decision-makers throughout the enterprise. Managers need to continuously monitor process performance, measure progress toward targets, and identify value-destroying activities and processes. In the global multinational corporation of the twenty-first century, decisions are made throughout the extended enterprise, not just at the executive committee level. Stakeholders and managers both internally and externally require up-to-the-minute decision support information that is designed to provide a quick, high-level view of performance.

Increasingly strategy formulation and execution has become an ongoing preoccupation for executives. In particular, firms are recognising that it is no longer sufficient for an organisation to revisit its strategic plan once or twice a year to compare actual versus projected performance. The complexity and competitiveness of the e-business environment requires a more dynamic approach to enterprise management than many firms have adopted in the past. If firms are to create significant shareholder value they need mechanisms which allow them to collect distributed budgeting and planning data from front-line managers and consolidate that data along with other pertinent internal and external information into a centralized resource for strategic management of the enterprise. In the absence of this information senior management are forced to rely on ad hoc and often spreadsheet-based IT solutions in their attempts to craft the strategic plan and fine-tune that plan in the face of changes in capital markets and competitor actions

To successfully generate shareholder value, executives must have access to:

- Performance measurement based on targets for each of the value drivers;
- Predictive value reporting;
- Value-based business appraisal;

- Integration of strategic, financial and operational information to support management processes;
- Transparency across the enterprise and to ensure continuity of information from strategy through to execution.

Transforming information into effective business decisions requires ERP-based solutions that provide timely and accurate access to information to support the key strategic management activities. In particular it should provide support for the direction setting in addition to the tracking and control roles of the management team. Strategic enterprise management (also referred to as enterprise performance management) systems are a new breed of analytic applications based on the premise that organisations succeed not through continually lowering costs, but by identifying and pursuing new and more profitable opportunities for creating shareholder value. Traditionally ERP systems have focused on improving transactional data collection and cost reduction at the level of operational processes. In contrast SEM is designed to improve the effectiveness of strategic management processes by providing managers with business performance monitoring, consolidation, and data warehousing/business intelligence capability. Alongside this data and information management capability, vendors such as SAP and PeopleSoft are also attempting to include analytical applications/techniques such as shareholder value management, balanced scorecard and activity-based management as part of their SEM offerings. As such, SEM is concerned with improving the strategy formulation/execution process and with helping organisations measure and manage performance and shareholder value in a wide variety of ways and then distributing the results in comprehensible, usable formats. The analytical applications, available, as part of SEM offerings, typically include:

- Balanced scorecard, which allows companies to communicate and monitor their critical key performance indicators to enable strategy alignment and execution throughout the enterprise;
- Workforce analytics, which helps manage employee compensation, goals, and competencies as well as retention;
- Shareholder value management, which helps identify value-destroying activities and processes and to develop effective business models;
- Activity-based management, including planning and simulation, which provides a tool for using goals and forecasts to drive the budget process and determine which resources and organisational structures need to be in place to meet the objectives.

The purpose of this chapter is to explore the implications of the emerging SEM offerings for management accounting and control activities in large organisations. In particular the chapter will demonstrate the potential of SEM and the importance of viewing SEM not just as a technological issue but instead as centring on integrating best practices in the key management process of planning, decision-making, implementation and measurement to maximise stakeholder value.

STRATEGIC ENTERPRISE MANAGEMENT – WHAT IS IT?

John Blackburn, PricewaterhouseCoopers.

At the heart of Strategic Enterprise Management lies a value-creation ambition driven by executives' desire to meet the growing demands for improved returns for stakeholders. Under the SEM approach, managers in organisations seek to configure a set of techniques, systems and processes in order to better implement business strategy at all levels of the enterprise. SEM sets out to support managers in solving three fundamental and interrelated questions:

- Where and how does the business create value for customers?
- Which enterprise business model most efficiently delivers that value?
- How is stakeholder value best maximised?

The ambition of SEM is to improve the quality and effectiveness of the strategic management processes by:

- Providing consistent data from internal and external sources as well as knowledge and insights created from simulation and scenario modelling;
- Providing managers with the capability to deconstruct value into its components;
- Providing improved information management and decision support processes;
- Providing a flexible modelling and analysis environment to support problem-solving and direction-setting ;
- Making relevant information easily available at the point of decision-making;
- Connecting top-down communication of strategic targets with bottom-up reporting of performance;
- Meeting the changing information requirements arising from dynamics of the organisational structures and processes;
- Combining both historic and predictive views to support the entire value management cycle;
- Keeping managers informed of changes in the extended value chain.

One of the criticisms of many performance improvement initiatives is that they require firms to abandon previous performance improvement techniques and systems and replace them with the latest 'silver bullet' solution. SEM explicitly recognises that there is valuable knowledge and learning embedded in existing techniques, systems and processes and that it is important that this value is not destroyed in the course of implementing new approaches. The SEM approach allows managers to leverage their existing insights and understanding and augments the value which firms have got from their efforts at process improvement to date. In particular, SEM draws on development in the areas of strategic analysis, data warehousing and other areas to deliver quantitative and qualitative information from internal and external sources to the executive desktop. Executives will be able to access this information using emerging technologies such as dashboards and management cockpits as well as through more conventional channels.

Why is this happening now?

The past decade has been a period of dramatic change in business and management. At the macro level we have seen the opening up of new markets, increased competition in existing markets as well as a relentless stream of technological innovation. Deregulation of capital markets and the liberalisation of many previously regulated industries has dramatically altered the business landscape. Other factors might include globalisation, changing barriers to entry in established markets (e.g. Internet) and compressed product life cycles. While many of these forces have led to positive benefits and increased wealth creation, it is important to recognise that it has also led to an extraordinarily high level of mortality in modern corporations. One-third of the 1980 Fortune 500 companies had disappeared by 1993. It is estimated that one-third of today's top 500 will have disappeared in ten years' time. With such a high rate of attrition firms are constantly struggling to reinvent themselves and compete in the global market.

Shorter windows of opportunity and the emergence of speed/time as a competitive dimension have led to a situation where managers are expected to make and implement decisions in shorter and shorter time periods. At the same time managers are faced with a deluge of information from both inside and outside the organisation. While the systems which organisations have implemented in the past have been effective in providing the hard quantitative information needed for operational control, they have been of limited value in supporting the activities of senior managers.

The most influential driver of change however has been the growing demands of individual and institutional shareholders for greater value creation. The increasingly mobile and demanding global investor expects a continuous and predictable growth in return on investment. As a result there is increasing dissatisfaction among senior manager with the quality of the strategic management processes (we use this term to mean both the determination and implementation of successful strategies) in their organisations. It appears that growing stakeholder demands and increasing organisational complexity have revealed a shortcoming in many organisations' ability to respond to the increased velocity of enterprise management.

Business models (the enterprise value chain) were once expected to last as long as ten years. A host of factors – including deregulation, globalisation, lower barriers to entry, free trade, increased speed to market and, above all, new technologies – have put paid to this comfortable situation. Today, a business model is good for five years at most. Soon, that time span will have shrunk to three or even two years. Businesses that do not change fast enough will become uncompetitive. They will be taken over or they will fold.

One dramatic example of the pace of change is the music industry, where the standard business model has been unaltered for a decade or more. An artist records tracks in a studio, the tracks are pressed into a solid form – first vinyl, then cassettes, then CDs and now minidisks – and sent to a distribution centre. From there, the product is passed to retail outlets, where customers buy it. Suddenly, the Internet is making this business model redundant. Now, the tracks can be placed directly on a web site. Customers can log on, listen to samples, choose their favourite tracks and download them to their MP3 player or equivalent technology. Conventional distributors and retailers will be cut out of the process. Music retailers will have to redefine how they create value for customers to survive. Some may become cyber cafés, where customers can drink coffee while sampling and choosing their tracks and even design and print their own cover sleeves. The retailers' business and value chain has been completely changed.

The same kind of thing is happening in every major industry, in every developed country in the world. Competition, technology and changing customer demands mean existing business models are unsustainable, whether in the aircraft industry, defence, automobiles, pharmaceuticals, financial services, food manufacturing, construction or electronics. In other words, the technical manuals which detail the business architecture need to be rewritten.

From ERP to SEM: a manual for change

Businesses must reassess themselves continually if they are to survive in the twenty-first century. And strategic enterprise management (SEM) will make this possible.

SEM will help every level of management within an organisation:

- to identify and evaluate alternative, more efficient ways of creating value for customers and shareholders;
- to find the best option;
- to implement that option;
- to track its progress as it is implemented.

SEM systems will sit on top of the enterprise resource planning systems widely introduced in the early 1990s by large corporations. ERP systems, such as those from SAP, Oracle, PeopleSoft and Baan, have helped to improve efficiency in big companies by using a set of system applications which contain existing best practices. Effectively, ERP systems have forced companies to modify and update their processes in order to meet defined standards. But ERP systems work at an operational rather than a strategic level. They do not show how a business can best create value for customers and meet its objectives, from maximizing shareholder value to fulfilling responsibilities to employees, business partners and the communities in which it operates.

Merging methods to create value

SEM will show how value can be maximised and how a company can meet its objectives.

It brings together three different methods of analysing information within an organisation (Figure 1):

- Shareholder value management – where the objective is to provide the owners of the organisation with the largest possible return on their investment;
- Activity-based management – where the objective is to discover what value is added or costs incurred at every stage of a company's existing processes;
- Performance management – where the objectives are to understand what is driving the performance of a business, how that performance is measured and reported, and how to set realistic targets for improvement.

Figure 1

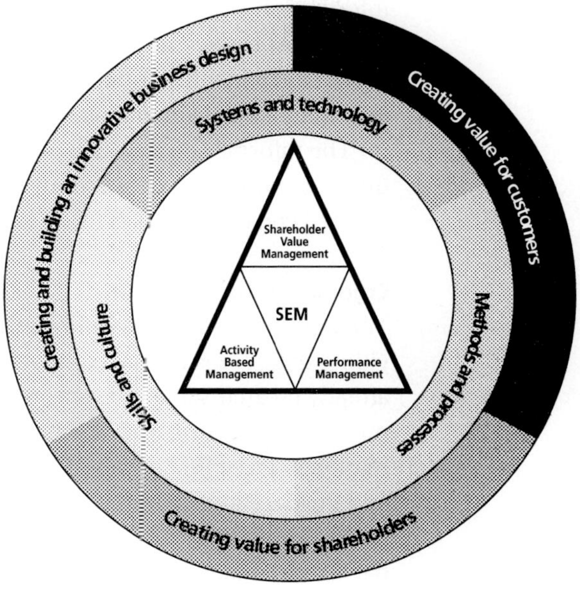

There are excellent and effective theoretical and practical approaches to each of these methods but, while the theoretical bases of each type of analysis have grown closer over the years, the techniques, processes and system tools used to provide relevant information have remained separate.

Mortgage lenders provide a simple example. A key driver of shareholder value is the quality of the mortgage portfolio. The longer a customer stays with the company, the greater the profit. The lenders recognise and measure this – but they also use the volume of new mortgage lending agreed in any period, irrespective of profitability, as a key performance measure for mortgage managers. It is easy to see how the two measures can conflict. SEM systems will allow the creation of performance measures, targets and reports that are aligned with shareholder value.

For payment card companies, the situation is more complex. Strategically, the main shareholder value measures are not sheer numbers of new cardholders and cardholder retention rates but the overall usage figures, loan portfolios, default rates and fraud rates. Activity-based management measures include the physical production and distribution of cards, the costs of processing transactions and the costs of marketing, set against the benefits of increased credit card loans and transaction fees.

The performance management measures will relate to the success of each part of a payment card business. SEM will integrate these three sets of measures; so predictive models can show the effects of changing any element of any one of the methods of measurement on the results of the other two methods. It will provide a unified view of an organisation, its objectives and its potential. At the same time, it can predict the consequences of any new course of action.

For example, if marketing is increased and results in a 10 per cent rise in spending volume, SEM will show the effects of that rise throughout the business model, pointing out where the model and the impact of alternative decisions – for example, through outsourcing – and judge the effect on overall profitability and other business objectives.

Lengthening the threads of management

At the same time, SEM will drive decision-making capabilities down an organisation's management structure by making relevant information freely available to those closest to any process that is creating an opportunity or problem.

SEM data warehouses will contain information about every aspect of a company, with additional inputs from outside the company. Each manager will receive only the information, opinions and predictions that are relevant to his or her job.

In most cases, executives will see the enterprise through a broad lens giving them the capability to identify and make better strategic decisions. Managers will get more detailed information relevant to their specialist areas and the decisions they need to make.

The information flow will be like a thick rope held by the top management team that unravels into cords throughout the business ensuring decisions are made and implemented consistently with the business's ambitions.

Ergonomics for the mind

The presentation of this information will also be important. There is little point in providing data if it is displayed in a form that is difficult to understand. ERP vendors have already created screen designs for SEM systems that effectively use ergonomics for the mind to marry form and function. Examples include Dashboard or SAP's Cockpit. Information is presented in ways that is most relevant to the actions that need to be reported and the decisions that need to be made.

The design and implementation of SEM will not be cheap – but it will become essential for any major organisation that wants to stay in business.

Building on the framework

Each SEM framework will exploit existing investment in an ERP system. Each aspect will be unique and will have to be individually configured. Businesses will also have to consider which type of SEM system best fits their needs. It is highly unlikely that any organisation will initially contain all the skills needed to set up and use SEM. Corporations installing ERP have needed external help to configure the technology. Those using SEM will need to use specialists who are experts in individual elements of the SEM framework. Most of these experts will not be technology experts but professionals in aspects of business such as shareholder value management, activity-based management, performance management and sub-groups including balanced scorecards, business economics and decision-making best practices.

Working together in inter-disciplinary teams, they will create a coherent overview of a corporation's aims and objectives, processes and value chains. Once this is in place, the results can be compared with the performance of other companies in the same type of business. Then new business models can be designed and their outcomes can be predicted. Above all, SEM provides managers with a complete view of their activities and clear insights into the choices available for the future of their companies. SEM will become a fundamental part of major corporations, allowing them to see processes, potential and results in the round for the first time, and helping them to posit alternative futures. Without SEM, many will have no future at all.

SEM EMBEDDING VALUE AND LEARNING IN THE BUSINESS

Jens Larsen, PricewaterhouseCoopers.

A successful business creates value for its shareholders by creating value for its customers and by maintaining its competitive advantage through an innovative business model. The increasing demand to create value for shareholders will force management to:

- Evaluate its own performance;
- Review its strategies continually;
- Re-examine the business model through which it competes;
- Implement new initiatives to achieve profitable growth.

The management of an organisation must understand where value is created and destroyed, whether its business model is operating effectively and how this can be improved. This is done by defining and evaluating the strategy, setting targets, measuring performance, forecasting and then re-evaluating the strategy (Figure 1).

Figure 1: Enterprise management

Corporations often find that their strategic decisions are not converted into the operational objectives of the business and that the strategic decisions are not understood or optimised at all levels. Strategy has to move out of the executive office and be integrated into the day-to-day work of each employee. The employee can then contribute to make strategy happen and provide feedback for further optimisation of the strategy. Only then can an enterprise really align its entire activities with the value expectations of the shareholders and other stakeholders (such as employees, business partners, customers, public interest groups), and thus ensure long-term profitability. The rapid pace of change and the fiercely competitive environment generated by the e-business revolution has created a new demand for timely and relevant management information. It has also meant that corporate strategies have to be altered far more often. These activities will in turn give rise to a large number of questions regarding the firm's performance. The questions that will recur include:

- How can we accelerate profitable growth in the future?
- How can we move from cost cutting to revenue growth?
- Which activities, products and customers are adding value and which are not?
- What customer needs are not met and how could we satisfy them profitably?
- What can we expect from the competition?
- How do we know if our strategy is working?
- How do we balance success today and success in the future?
- How can we obtain reliable information and perform the calculations to support these scenarios?

The role of SEM is to provide the enabling technologies to allow managers to access the information and analysis capabilities they need to answer these questions. As such, SEM should enable radical improvements in strategic management by providing managers with the knowledge and the insight to react quickly and effectively to the strategic challenges of the organisation. Although technology is a major component of SEM, it has to have a wider scope. SEM must also create an efficient, knowledge-sharing and learning enterprise that is focused on creating shareholder value.

The major software vendors such as SAP, Oracle and PeopleSoft are all developing integrated SEM tools to meet the challenges of the new environment. Companies that have invested in ERP systems already have a major information asset. They now need to fully exploit the potential of this asset through SEM.

SEM solutions typically provide an integrated framework to support the following core processes:

- Corporate strategy;
- Resource allocation and planning;
- Performance management;
- Compensation and rewards;
- Communication and stakeholder management;
- Consolidation;
- Business information sourcing.

These will support top-down translation of enterprise strategy into business unit, product and support centre targets as well as bottom-up performance monitoring and related decision support. The enterprise can anticipate and react promptly to impending changes in its business environment and at the same time actively manage the expectations of its stakeholders.

SEM enables organisations to implement SEM processes such as business planning and simulation, performance management and stakeholder communication based on the balanced scorecard concept. As we saw in the previous article, SEM sits on top of the existing ERP systems. It combines analysis techniques such as ABM and BSC with data warehousing and other technologies to deliver information and insights to the desktop. In the next section we will explore in depth the nature of these techniques and technologies.

SEM techniques

SEM encompasses three essential techniques (Figure 2):

- Shareholder value management to evaluate the strategy and set the objectives;
- Performance management to implement the strategic decisions by cascading detailed targets, by measuring results and by rewarding appropriate performance;
- Activity-based management to measure value creation and to forecast future performance .

Shareholder value management

To be effective, an organisation must be able to see the likely impact of specific decisions

Figure 2: SEM techniques

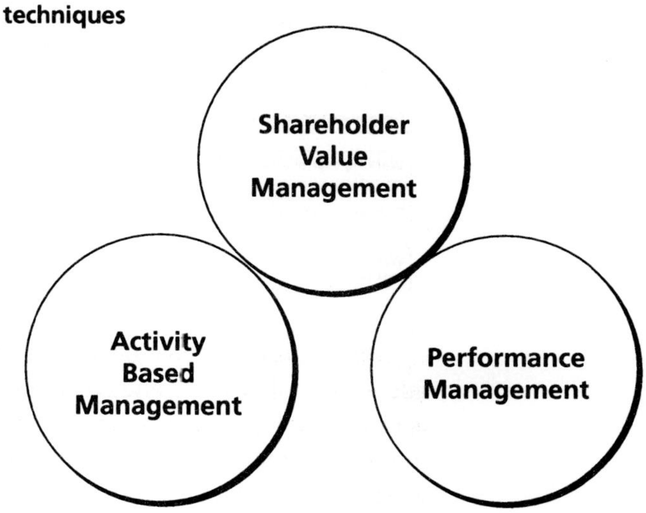

on the value of the business – not just major strategic decisions like mergers and acquisitions, but also operational decisions. For example, what will be the impact on shareholder value of reducing lead-time? To answer the question, 'How should we manage for value?', companies are now moving away from traditional targets such as return on capital employed and return on net assets towards value-based measures such as economic profit, residual income, and free cash flow. Each of these types has strengths and weaknesses and must be used appropriately in the value-creation process.

The broad acceptance of the shareholder value concept has meant that investors now play a significantly more active role in enterprises than was the case previously. Other stakeholder groups now also have a greater say in the enterprise strategy. Enterprises are rethinking the efficiency of their management processes, and are taking the principles of value-based management and the interests of stakeholders into greater account in their planning and performance monitoring processes.

Increasing shareholder value should be the basis of every organisation's strategy. Shareholder value management (SVM) recognises that the value of a business is based on its future stream of cash. It comprises:

- Development of strategies and techniques to evaluate these strategies in terms of future cash flows;
- Analysis of the drivers of value and where value is created;
- Allocation of resources to areas that will create value;
- Creation of performance measures to measure value creation;
- Devising incentives to reward success;
- Communication of the strategies to shareholders to realise the value.

Although cash flow measures of value have long been used for appraising capital projects, their use in the valuation of businesses is more recent.

Figure 3: Linking value drivers to key performance measures

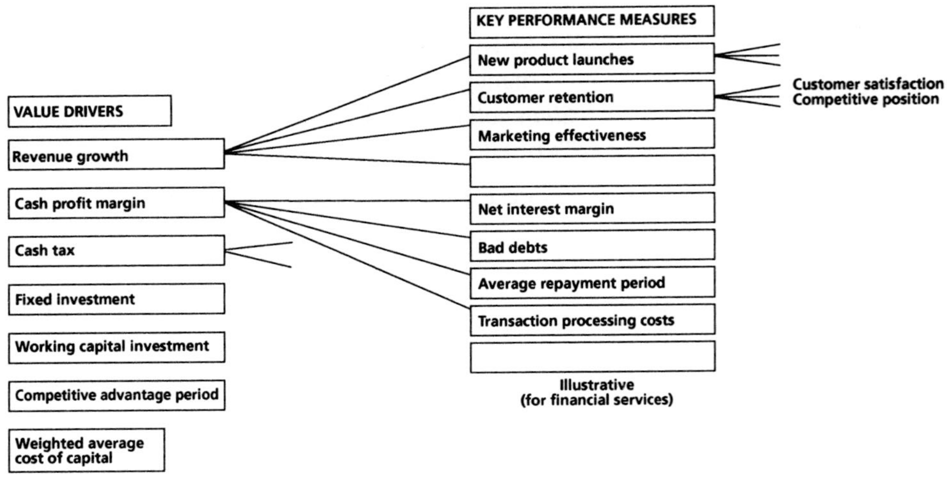

Many methods have been suggested for measuring value such as market value added, economic profit and cash flow return on investment. However, the approach that is most widely adopted is based on the free cash flow generated by a company. In this method shareholder value is the difference between the corporate value and debt, where corporate value is the sum of the free cash flows discounted at the weighted average cost of capital. Free cash flows are the cash flows adjusted for any change in the capital invested in the business and so in theory could be distributed to the shareholders. Discounting these flows takes account of risk and the time value of money.

Shareholder value management considers the seven value drivers of the free cash flow to be:

- Sales growth rate;
- Cash profit margin (earnings before interest, tax, depreciation and amortisation);
- Cash tax (i.e. the tax that will actually be paid);
- Fixed capital investment;
- Working capital investment;
- Weighted average cost of capital which is used as the discount rate;
- The competitive advantage period over which the discounted cash flows are summed.

These value drivers in turn can be linked to underlying strategies and then to performance measures, but some drivers will have a greater influence over value than others (Figure 3). By understanding what are the main drivers of performance in terms of shareholder value, management will be able to focus on the essentials when evaluating strategy.

Performance management

Performance management is based on a carefully selected set of measures derived from strategies of the business to communicate strategic direction to the organisation and for motivating change. These measurements are used by managers to plan and provide incentives and control results. The central theme of creating value for customers and of maintaining competitive advantage must be built into the strategy and then into the performance management system. Successful measures enable progress on strategy to be tracked, and provide information, through leading indicators and diagnostics, which help to determine corrective action. The strategy is more likely to be realised as a result. If a firm can understand and model the dynamics of the business and the cause and effect relationships it can use this to identify key business drivers. The key business drivers and their measures should then be assigned according to the ability of individuals, groups or departments to influence them. Balance is required to ensure that the full picture is obtained while avoiding 'measures overload' – not seeing the wood for the trees. To balance the scorecard, firms must ensure that the measures are defined using several perspectives: financial and non-financial, predictive and historical, external and internal, and set and cascade targets that together will deliver their strategy throughout the business. As financial measures tell only the story of the past, the balanced scorecard complements financial measures with measures of the drivers of future performance. Corporate executives can now measure:

- How their business units create value for the current and future customers, investors and other stakeholders;
- How they must enhance internal capabilities and the investment in people, systems and procedures necessary to improve future performance.

The information systems should be able to gather, synthesise and communicate the right information to the right people at the right time. This information should reflect the complexity of the business and of the type of decisions which are required. Much broader, more forward-looking information systems are needed for value-based decision-making. In these systems, external data can be balanced with internal data, predictive with historical data, and financial with non-financial data.

Leading organisations are beginning to move from a rigid, annual budgeting process that typically is painful and causes undesirable behaviours. They are introducing a business management mechanism which is based on rolling forecasts. The budgeting process becomes dynamic instead of static, leading instead of lagging.

Managing corporate performance by definition needs to affect all staff across all parts of the business. The biggest challenge for managing corporate performance is that it is no longer possible to change individual elements independently because the interrelationships and dependencies within today's complex business structures do not allow it.

IT vendors have responded by developing and releasing software to support executive decision-making using the balanced scorecard methodology. A key performance indicator (KPI) is assigned to each of the strategy objectives and these indicators enable planning and measurement of performance. Non-financial targets are also included such as the market, customers, product quality and human resources. The consideration of various areas of the business provides a balance between 'leading' and 'lagging', between internal and external, and between qualitative and quantitative performance indicators.

Many organisations misinterpret the concept of a balanced set of measures. Although their scorecards reflect different perspectives, the set of measures may not be causally linked to increasing shareholder value. This can because of poorly defined goals or can be the result of a scorecard metrics project rather than a performance project. A scorecard project searches for new ways to record or report a set of lagging indicators; a performance project is based on the prediction of outcomes and drivers. Another source of difficulty in developing a set of measures comes with too much of an inward focus. This results in a scorecard that tracks operational measures but does not link to external benchmarks. There is also a risk of creating too many measures, which will confuse managers instead of directing their efforts. Because many potential measures tend to overlap, care is needed to ensure that good coverage is achieved by each measure.

Activity-based costing/management

Activity-based management is an analytical approach to managing a business by planning and controlling the costs of activities in its own value chain and the value chains of its customers and suppliers. ABM enables an enterprise-wide view which can be used for:

- Planning through an understanding of cost behaviour;
- Gaining a common understanding and commitment to major changes in the way that resources are allocated.

Activity-based cost (ABC) systems calculate product and process costs by reflecting the consumption of resources. Firstly the cost of activities is calculated. Having gained a better understanding of activity costs as a first step, ABC then derives the true cost of a product or customer on the basis of the consumption of these activities by products or customers. Companies can then manage the profitability of products or customers and highlight re-engineering opportunities. This is important in itself to understand the drivers of process costs and to benchmark process costs internally across other parts of the company and externally versus 'world class' companies. This information can then be fed into the business planning and simulation. The objective of ABM is to discover what value is added or costs incurred at each stage of an organisation's existing processes. Figure 4 provides examples of the types of analysis which ABM facilitates.

Figure 4: ABM analysis

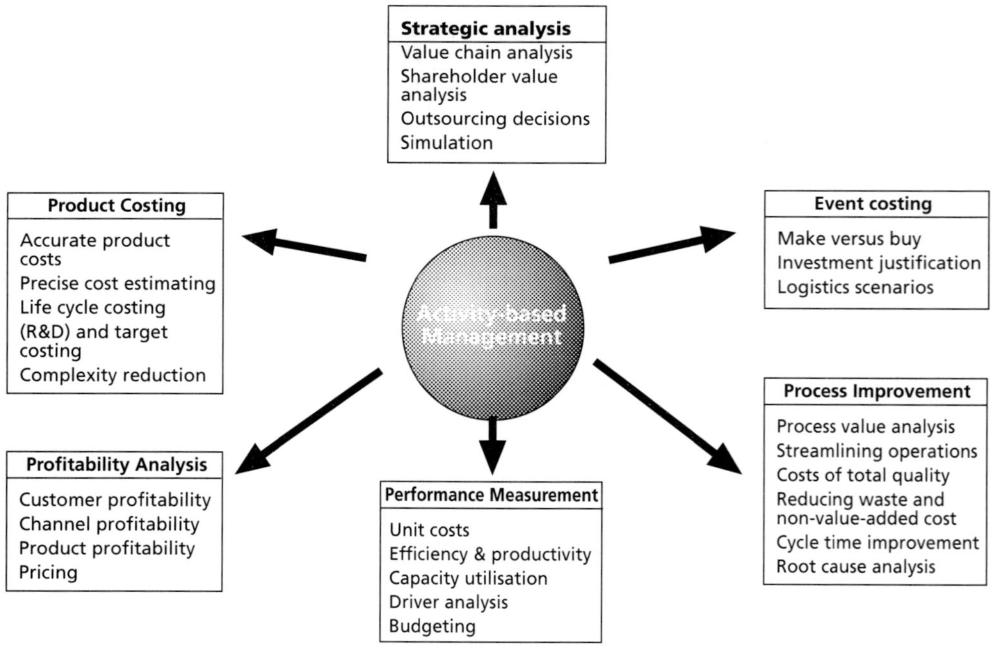

Other emerging SEM techniques

Business information collection. To provide unbiased business intelligence and a sound basis for decision-making, internal information must be viewed in context with information from external sources. For example, key figures from the ERP system could be merged with stock prices from commercial database providers via the Internet. The Internet is being used as a collection mechanism for necessary information. These may also be in the form of brokers' reports, press reports, or announcements on a competitor's home web page.

Business planning and simulation. The trend is away from key figures that focus on the past, such as those provided from the annual accounts. The trend is towards performance management that allows future focused enterprise management. This could be for strategic planning and specific operational problems. For example, to model and simulate the complex relationships between markets, competitors and your own enterprise. This links strategic planning and simulation with enterprise planning. The functions required include:

- Creation of dynamic linear business models;
- Modelling and simulation of various scenarios;
- Scenario planning and evaluation of these scenarios taking into account the business risks;
- Carrying out the resource allocation as part of business planning;
- Cross-functional enterprise planning;
- Rolling forecasting, triggered by strategic KPI targets;
- Modelling the business activities for each planning unit;
- Looking at planning such as sales volume, MRP, cost, capacity and headcount planning;
- Profit and loss and balance sheet planning.

Stakeholder relationship management. The long-term success of an enterprise depends increasingly on its ability to establish a solid relationship with its various stakeholder groups. SEM provides support for communicating enterprise strategy, current plan data and strategic initiatives to these different stakeholder groups. Different stakeholders require different levels of information. For example, private investors may demand a great deal of financial information.

The communication is not all one-way however. Stakeholders such as employees, shareholders and customers inform the enterprise of their expectations. This enables the enterprise to receive, organise and effectively evaluate this feedback. Increasingly the Internet is seen as the facilitator and the perfect tool for this communication.

SEM technologies

SEM brings together a number of technologies which are designed to support managers and provide an environment for decision-making through an accessible source of consistent information, i.e. a data warehouse and a suite of flexible systems for consolidation, analysis, planning and communication (Figure 5).

Ideally the systems for SEM should draw upon a common pool of consistent data (the single version of the truth) which is accessible by all authorised users for decision-making and which allows drilling down to the detail required. Above this warehouse should be a set of analytical application systems. Since these systems will share common definitions and sources, there should be greater reliability and accessibility. Users will be able to combine data from different sources to produce new information.

Figure 5: SEM technologies

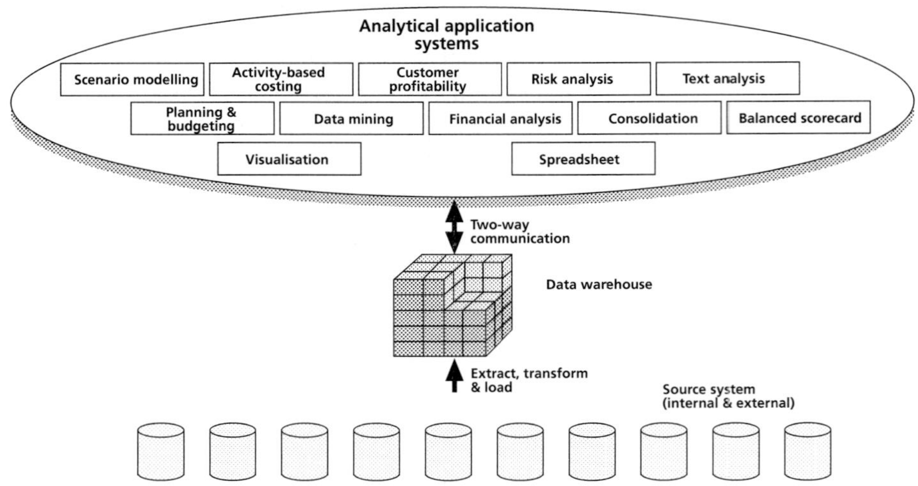

The systems should also require the users to do more than merely look at information that is presented to them. The ideal system should require input such as revised forecasts and feedback or should allow the user to forward the information for someone else's action. These requirements for new information or for action have to be tracked and controlled.

At present there is a wide variety of suppliers of software but many only meet some of the requirements. A key task is to identify an architecture that provides the user-friendliness, speed and flexibility that decision-making requires, whilst minimising the diversity of definitions, interfaces and databases.

In many organisations, essential management information is created and locked away in spreadsheets. Spreadsheets are useful general-purpose tools, but often they should be replaced by specialist software which is easier to maintain and which provide the features needed as standard. The information in spreadsheets may also be inconsistent, inaccessible to those who need the information, manually updated and so prone to error. The concept of SEM is based on a single version of the data and metadata that is accessible to authorised people and that can be used for each of the analytical applications.

The applications that use the data warehouse must be updated by changes to the data and metadata. They must give the users flexibility to model, add new elements and create new views. This is in contrast with ERP systems where processes are not expected to change. Unless the decision support systems can change quickly and unless this change can be made by the users, they will move back to becoming islands of information once more.

Few organisations have a homogeneous set of source systems. Although some information will always be input manually, the aim should be to automate the collection of routine information, some of it from Internet sources. The challenge is to extract this data from diverse sources, transform it, correct it and load it into the data warehouse with as little human intervention as possible. Each additional interface will need maintenance and consequently the analytical applications should be integrated with the data warehouse, either by selecting the same supplier or by using industry-standard links.

Most organisations are more than just a single business. There may be many divisions, subsidiaries, locations, products and customers, each of which may require a different level of detail for strategic decision-making. The detailed information required at the lowest levels should be compatible with the summarised requirements needed higher up the organisation. The need to creating a flexible environment for detailed decision-making has to be balanced against the need for consistency throughout the group and the need to take decisions that will affect several parts of the organisation at once.

An effective data warehouse must be structured to allow efficient storage of information and simple and quick access. Most of the leading business warehouses from the ERP vendors support strategic enterprise management. These include products such as:

- SAP's Business Warehouse;
- Oracle's Intelligent Webhouse and;
- Peoplesoft's Enterprise Warehouse.

These all utilise user tools to enable graphical modelling and multi-dimensional storage of data.

Additional Tools

Advanced features are made available for performance optimisation and management of the database. The system must monitor and adjust table space and allow for growth of the stored data. In a fast-moving age a business data warehouse must be easily scalable to cope with the increasing demands made of it.

The diverse range of information needed to support an enterprise requires the gathering of data from outside of the traditional arena of the finance and logistics systems. To be competitive a business warehouse must be able to access these systems from across a range of vendors.

To access existing ERP systems within an organisation the simplest option is to align the business warehouse vendor with that of your existing ERP system vendor. With the systems diversity within individual companies (often resulting from mergers and takeovers), this is not always possible.

To address this issue the major players utilise different technologies to enable the extraction, transformation and loading of data into the warehouse from a variety of sources. Peoplesoft's EW relies on third-party tools with built-in capability to 'read' non-Peoplesoft database structures. Similarly Oracle's 'transparent gateway' allows access to non-Oracle databases as if they were Oracle, enabling the use of standard oracle query tools to extract data.

The ability to extract data from diverse sources is becoming increasingly important, bearing in mind the volumes of data being made available through the Internet.

New Sources of Data

In addition to this growing Internet array of available market information, 'back door' market research also can lie unused and wasted in the log and registration files of many companies' Internet sites. Site hits and clickstream data provide the volumes of information about customer preferences and behaviour that traditional market research could never hope to achieve with random sampling methods. The extraction and transformation of this freely available web data is a challenge many warehouse vendors are only starting to come to terms with and incorporate into current releases of warehouse designs.

Figure 6 illustrates SAP's toolkit and integration to third-party products. This is typical of the approach for all major ERP vendors.

Figure 6: Multi-vendor SEM platform

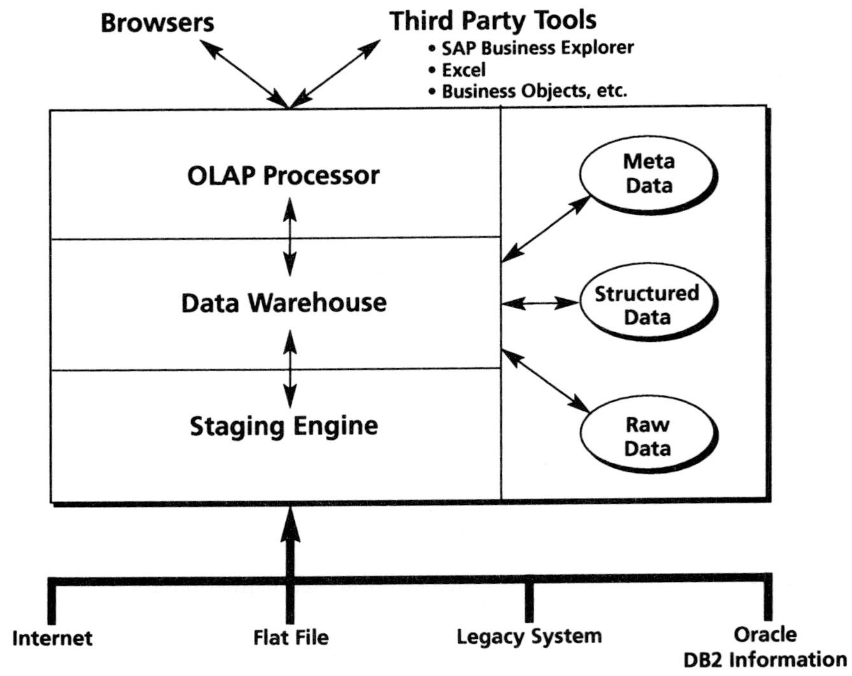

The Demands of the User Interface

Conversely the move towards more balanced measures of assessing performance has necessitated capturing and displaying information not readily available within existing systems. Such indicators as employee satisfaction can only be accessed through direct feedback from employees. Market position data may only be available in graphical form on web pages. User friendly and easily accessible front ends for data capture and display are therefore becoming equally crucial to the formulation and implementation of a corporate data strategy.

The approach to the user interface is also changing:

- Access (including entry and analysis of data) is becoming heavily reliant upon third-party tools with a familiar look and feel to make the user feel 'at home'. In some cases extensive use is made of well-known applications such as Microsoft Excel.
- More radically there is a move towards the complete elimination of the dedicated ERP user interface. This newer approach uses traditional Internet browser formats to perform function calls and to present data. The browser-based interface is now increasingly familiar to a range of users and is particularly useful in large organisations where strategic initiatives seek the involvement of a broad range of employees.

One technique used to enable executive managers to monitor the enterprise is the use of key performance indicators (KPIs). These can be updated on a daily or hourly, basis if required. They can extract indicators of where problems lie and where management attention should be focussed. These KPIs can be drawn together into 'management dashboards' and 'cockpits'. The leading ERP vendors' strategic enterprise suites support these and allow 'at-a-glance' traffic light style reporting.

Competitive advantage requires more than technology

The technologies which underpin SEM will continue to evolve and it is likely that the next two years will see a growing number of ERP vendors and niche software firms offering SEM capability. In the long term, competitive advantage from SEM will arise not from the widely available software or techniques but from an organisation's ability to adopt these technologies and techniques to the unique operating and decision-making culture of the organisation.

How does SEM benefit organisations?

1. *Improving business performance management.* The SEM approach seeks to effectively link performance measurement and control to strategic objectives, in an attempt to ensure that operational decision-making is fully focussed on delivering strategic objectives. Under SEM the drivers of stakeholder value are the key performance evaluation criteria and the traditional approaches to performance measurement and control are extended to include competitors, customers, products and relative market position. SEM thus supports decision-makers' information needs, provides seamless integration of strategic, financial and operational information and provides transparency across the enterprise to ensure continuity of information from strategy through to execution.

2. *Improving business problem-solving.* Senior managers in organisations are faced with a continuous stream of complex and non-repetitive business problems. These problems are in most cases significant in terms of their organisational implications and are often concerned with issues such as supply chain management, investment appraisal, margins, and market share. Unlike previous approaches to decision support, SEM recognises that the provision of information processing and analysis capabilities is only a small part of improving decision-making. SEM supports business problem-solving by providing managers not just with access to the technology and data they need but it also provides them with tools for improving problem definition, problem analysis, alternative evaluation and choice. It eliminates the excess of irrelevant information that threatens thinking by providing managers with a flexible environment in which to explore ideas and alternatives.

3. *Improving business learning.* Enterprises are faced with an increasingly complex and bewildering business environment. Fundamental changes in markets, technologies, stakeholder expectations, and developments such as the Internet, have left managers struggling to make sense of their environment. These relentless changes have manifested themselves most clearly in a dramatic increase in the velocity of organisational decision-making. SEM supports business intelligence by putting in place the systems and processes to allow organisations to effectively gather and filter the information that senior executives need in order to make sense of their environment.

4. *Strategic management as a core competency at all levels.* SEM allows firms to make strategic management a core competency and to develop strategic management at all levels of the firms' operations. In the past, firms have often relied on external consultants to inform their strategy formulation process, with strategy implementation remaining the domain of internal staff. As the velocity of business increases it is no longer possible to outsource the foresight aspects which external consultants bring; instead, firms will have to provide this themselves. It allows the firm to manage internal processes with an external mind-set. Managers thus have the insight of those involved in business execution with the foresight of external consultants and stakeholders.

5. *Deploying responsive information systems to allow organisations to exploit the increasing velocity of the business environment.* Shorter product life cycles, risk and globalisation, technology, etc. have all led to an increase in the velocity of business decision-making. The number of incidences requiring management to make important changes in its strategic posture has increased dramatically. In order for managers to cope with the continuous stream of decision points, they need a responsive information system to support learning. This information system must keep them informed of the outcomes of previous decisions but also alert them to changes in the wider competitive environment. In the past, firms have relied on a range of systems to support this. SEM attempts to do this more effectively.

6. *Improving business direction setting.* The evidence to date suggests that successful corporations have superior strategic management processes. Successful organisations are those which are capable of charting a course which maximised stakeholder value in the face of a hostile environment. SEM operationalises value-based management, by helping managers:

- Understand what drives value;
- Find where value is created or destroyed
- Establish value as the criterion for decision-making;
- Embed value into the firms' culture.

7. *Institutionalising stakeholder value as a plank in strategic management.* SEM allows the firm to institutionalise shareholder value as the key guiding factor in decision-making resource allocation and direction setting. In addition it exposes the drivers of shareholder value and provides a unifying theme for appraising alternative views and perspectives. This is particularly important in the light of the plethora of business performance metrics which arose in the 1990s.

   Managers need to appreciate that SEM is not a quick fix for fundamental flaws in the firm's strategic management processes. Without a talented and committed executive team SEM will not yield the long-term increase in shareholder value which firms are looking for. Before making the commitment to a large SEM solution, firms should ask themselves how effective are their current strategic management processes. Ultimately SEM is only as good as the executive team it supports.

CONCLUSION

Strategic enterprise management helps managers to create value for stakeholders by allowing them to create and build innovative business which meets the customer's needs. As such, SEM integrates stakeholder value management, activity-based management, and performance management in pursuit of greater strategic management capability. This combination creates views of the profitability of products and customers over their lifetimes.

A firm needs to be sure that it is delivering sustainable customer value to the right customers; customers around whom a business can be built that creates sustainable shareholder value. These are the basic elements of an effective SEM. All elements must be covered to meet the central challenge. The result should be business decisions that create value for current and future customers which translates into financial performance commensurate with your shareholder value targets.

Chapter 7

Making a Strategic Impact with ERP

INTRODUCTION

The last eighteen months has seen the coming together of two of the key technologies of the last decade; ERP systems and the World Wide Web. Firms quickly realised that a successful e-business model requires a stable and robust underlying transaction and information processing infrastructure. In particular, firms recognised that to effectively exploit the opportunities of the WWW they needed to have superior information and knowledge-based processes. As a result ERP is increasingly seen as a prerequisite for e-business. Businesses in particular are looking to so-called 'off-the-shelf' ERP, systems to provide them with the systems functionality they need to exploit the virtual market space. Alongside this, ERP vendors have recognised the enormous opportunities which e-business brings for them. In particular they see an opportunity for their systems to become the back-office engine that powers e-business.

The Internet will soon be a become a trillion dollar marketplace, resulting in a fundamental change in the dynamics of supply chains and distribution channels. To succeed in this new environment firms are moving mission critical operations and processes/transactions to the web. By 2003, 5 per cent of all sales around the world will be conducted online, opening up a worldwide, 24-hour marketplace. The statistics speak for themselves:

- The number of global users of the Internet is doubling every 100 days, with 70,000 new users logging on to the Internet each day;
- Internet users in the UK alone rose from 500,000 in 1998 to 11 million in 1999;
- In 1997 it was predicted that Internet commerce would reach US$327 million by 2002; this estimate was recently increased to US$1.3 trillion by 2003.

The Internet has fundamentally changed competitive strategies and business processes, transforming traditional business models to more efficient, more flexible e-business models. As industries become deregulated and privatised, and companies extend their reach to global markets, competition for customers increases at a dramatic rate. Large firms in particular can be susceptible to low-cost competition from so-called virtual firms. Without the heavy burden of investment in fixed assets, smaller and leaner virtual operators are able to undercut traditional operators, particularly in the business-to-consumer market, for items such as cds books, airline tickets, etc. Established market leaders that do not seize the online opportunity may lose market share to startups emerging from nowhere.

Under an e-business approach firms will no longer buy and sell their products using traditional manually and often paper-based processes. Instead firms use the Internet to create a seamless and fully automated electronic network to link buyers, suppliers, capital markets and other stakeholders. As a result, transaction processing becomes largely automated and the traditional supply chain relationships are moved to a closed loop virtual setting. The benefits to organisations are impressive and take many forms; service levels are improved; and significant transaction processing costs are eliminated and processes move from being cost-focused to revenue enhancing.

Firms are recognising that e-business has the potential to transform the entire value chain. A recent report suggests that the return on investment for e-procurement can be dramatic, with the average ROI in excess of 300 per cent. To date, three basic e-business models have emerged:

Business-to-business (B2B) involves firms in a particular industry or sector, creating virtual marketplaces where they conduct their purchasing and sales with business counter parties over the web. Examples include the pharmaExchange in the pharmaceuticals industry and the Exostar in the Aerospace sector.

Business-to-consumer (B2C) involves the online seller presenting their products or services to consumers over the web. A key part of the B2C model is the use of experience gained from previous transactions to form a one-to-one relationship with each customer. The growth of these markets is expected to increase rapidly as an increasing number of consumers gain access to the Internet through advances in mobile phone technology in the forms of so-called 3G phones.

Business-to-workforce (B2W) uses the web to facilitate transactions with the workforce, including expenses and remuneration. Most significantly, it allows information to be assimilated and easily accessed, creating knowledge throughout the organisation.

In this chapter we explore the opportunities which exist for firms to create sustainable value from the convergence of ERP and e-business. The chapter begins by exploring the challenges which ERP vendors face in the e-business arena and the way in which they are responding. This is followed by a detailed examination of the way in which e-business and ERP are transforming the enterprise. The chapter concludes with a review of the challenges which face management in the e-business environment in the coming years.

ERP RIP

Enterprise resource planning is not dead, but it will have to live with the Internet. "ENTERPRISE resource planning is kind of a wasteland. The back-office market is just horrible. It's saturated. Everybody has it and the store is closed." So says Tom Siebel, the chairman and founder of Siebel Systems, the hottest firm in the hot business of selling sales-force automation and customer-relationship management (CRM) software. And yet for much of the 1990s ERP was just about the biggest thing in business software. It changed the way companies worked by bringing together all their operational parts into one smoothly functioning whole (or so it was claimed). A complete system could take several years and several hundred million dollars to deploy. The market leader, a German software firm called SAP, was seen as a second Microsoft, apparently able to increase its revenues by more than 60 per cent a year indefinitely. Oracle, the number two player in ERP, but the dominant supplier of relational databases to the Windows NT and Unix markets, became the second-largest independent software company in the world. Other ERP high-fliers, such as Baan and PeopleSoft, also became huge software successes.

But in the past nine months, ERP has lost its glamour and its swagger. Baan seemed close to collapse after an accounting scandal, and PeopleSoft has been in disarray. Even mighty SAP has seen its share price plunge since its much-heralded debut on the New York Stock Exchange last summer. One reason is that year-2000 fears first artificially boosted the market and then undermined it when time ran out to tie in a millennium overhaul with an ERP deployment. But another reason is that the ERP vendors seem largely to have missed the first e-business wave, lacking front-office applications (in essence, everything that involves dealing with customers) such as Siebel's and, except for Oracle, being generally slow to adapt their client/server architecture to the rigours of Internet computing.

To make things still trickier for the ERP players, their underlying business model is being challenged by a radically different alternative offered by the web. At present, ERP works on the assumption that a fairly small proportion of the workforce (typically less than 10 per cent in large global companies) will need access to an application for a particular department, so the licence fees for each user will be set at a high level. That makes sense when deployment on client/server systems is costly, and staff require extensive training to cope with clunky and obscure systems.

But the Internet has made possible a different model in which applications sit on web servers to which anyone on the intranet has access, using a point-and-click browser running on anything from a PC to a hand-held computer or a smart phone. Since any number of people can get into the system without incurring extra costs, and anyone can use it with ease, high licence fees for each user are no longer appropriate; what is needed is a volume pricing model. Moreover, once the information is put in a central place where it can be reached by anyone who needs it, it becomes more valuable in itself. And if it can be shared much more widely within a firm, it should also become far less difficult to provide selective access to suppliers and customers through extranets and the public Internet.

Wrong address

Companies that have looked to their traditional ERP vendors for the means of turning themselves into e-businesses have had little luck. To get what they want, they have had to buy separate components from a mass of competing software houses. Their round might include Ariba and CommerceOne for procurement; AOL /Netscape, Broadvision, IBM, Calico and Sterling Commerce for e-commerce platforms; Siebel, Vantive and Onyx for front-office applications that help find, service and sell to customers; and Business Objects, Oracle and i2 for analytical tools that search databases and supply-chain systems for critical business intelligence. They would also have to search out "middleware" companies such as Iona, CrossWorlds, TSI and Active that specialise in application integration to tie everything together and form bridgeheads into legacy ERP systems.

According to Harry Tse, a senior analyst at the Yankee Group, a consultancy, companies need to understand that e-business requires something quite close to building a second "backbone" system on top of ERP. They should also realise that it will be neither quick nor easy. IBM estimates that "70 per cent of all code written today consists of interfaces, protocols and other procedures to establish linkages among various systems." Marshall Senk, a software analyst at BancBoston Robertson Stephens, explains: "Enterprise application integration is where I spend 50 per cent of my time. EAI is trying to create virtual homogeneity across systems, creating a common layer so that we can think about systems in the way we think about our business. The key thing is that we don't want to rewrite our systems. We want to leave everything that's working where it is and build bridges without writing custom code."

But is all this fragmentation in the software market in the customer's interest? The Butler Group, a British IT consultancy, says it has seen "a backlash against the inadequacies of monolithic application packages", and argues that techniques to integrate applications can lead to better solutions "without the stranglehold of inflexible functionality". The implication is that if you do it right, you should get a decent return on your investment, which was not always true for ERP.

The absence of a standard set of e-business solutions means you should be able to gain competitive advantage from selecting the right applications, integrating them seamlessly and building a robust infrastructure that is able to grow with your business. Small, fast-growing software houses are in a better position than giants such as SAP to provide the kind of environment, and stock options, that attract the best and most creative talent. And there are now plenty of tools available to make different systems work together: the Java programming language to link applications across platforms, increasingly sophisticated "integrationware", and the growing Internet and e-business skills of the systems integrators. There is no reason why a pick-and-choose approach, if properly thought through, should not deliver results.

Equally, however, it would be a grave mistake to count out the ERP powerhouses too soon, particularly Oracle and SAP with their huge installed bases (over 20,000 SAP R/3 deployments worldwide, and Oracle databases in nearly every one of the world's top 500 companies). Both intend to be leaders in turning businesses into e-businesses, and know what they have to do to regain their momentum.

Oracle has moved fast to take advantage of the advantages of the Internet computing platform over client/server systems. Release 11, its latest suite of applications, is designed to run only within an Internet-style architecture. Larry Ellison, Oracle's founder and chairman, is frank about the deficiencies of client/server platforms. Talking not just about Oracle but computing in general, he says: "We blew it in the 1990s. By running applications on the client, client/server was meant to put information at your fingertips. But all we did was to create distributed complexity and fragmented data. CEOs have come to hate IT because they can't get what they want from it. Burger King put an SQL Server database in every hamburger store, but they still couldn't answer the question, 'how many Whoppers are we selling each day?'. ERP as an industry missed the boat. It focused on automating processes, not on getting information to key decision makers. Every CEO wants to understand profitability per customer and to be able to detect dissatisfaction before the customer leaves.

So how do we do it now? We've learned from the Internet that you don't put shared applications on the client and that you centralise complexity. You consolidate your data. The unchanging appliance accesses the dynamic applications of the network."

Along with "web-centricity", Oracle has identified business intelligence and customer-relationship management as the applications everyone needs to extract value from their ERP systems, and has launched a CRM package that will integrate smoothly with its Release 11 applications. Oracle freely concedes that its principal target is Siebel, a few miles south on the other side of Highway 101. Mr Ellison claims that Siebel has insufficiently embraced the Internet and that, with "the wrong technology foundation", it will be knocked off its market-leader perch by the middle of next year. The new incumbent, he predicts, will be Oracle. He wants a substantial slice of a front-office market that is expected to be worth nearly $12 billion in 2002.

Beauty competition

Not surprisingly, Tom Siebel begs to differ. He insists that the latest release of his own software, Siebel 99, is a great deal nearer to the web ideal than anything produced by Oracle, and that he will believe Oracle has a competitive package for managing customer relations when he sees it in the market. In his view, the ERP firms have a problem: they may have identified the front office as a faster-growing, less crowded market than their own, but they lack the "domain expertise" to succeed. "This isn't simply something you can throw a thousand software programmers at," he says. "It's something that somebody in the organisation has to know something about."

He agrees, however, that integration with ERP is important. To allow companies to exploit every available distribution channel simultaneously, Mr Siebel says it is essential to have a web-based architecture "hooked into the same common information system. Using an extranet, we can reach out and just bring customers into the information system and let them engage in product configuration, selection and Internet self-service."

Like Oracle, but running a few months behind, SAP too is about to enter the front-office market with a number of new web-based applications covering business-to-business procurement, business-to-consumer selling and business-to business selling – all designed to integrate with its market-leading R/3 suite. SAP believes this will be the key to extending its franchise into e-business.

Chuck Phillips, an analyst with Morgan Stanley, cites at least two reasons for agreeing:

One: process cohesiveness – the logical view of the chain of commerce isn't disjointed because of technical incompatibilities. The user thinks of the process as one function with a series of related steps and would prefer not to traverse through dissimilar systems with inherent data leakage between them. *Two:* technical simplicity – the integrated view for better decision-making is achieved without the brittle, custom links built between front-office and back-office systems not designed to work together. Staying with the same system to capture or initiate an order or track and prosecute a settlement has an appeal to anyone who's gone through an integration exercise.

Not content with relying on their existing big company-installed bases to ensure their e-commerce success, both Oracle and SAP are using the Internet to offer smaller firms (which might in the past have opted for a low-price Microsoft solution) web-based applications to rent on a per-user, per-month basis – "apps on tap", in the jargon. Part of the cost-efficiency, according to Gary Bloom, who is responsible for Oracle's Business Online, is that small and medium-sized companies no longer need to compete for expensive IT professionals. A small team of experts can serve many customers from a single data centre. It is also ideal for the needs of young, fast-growing e-businesses because it can meet their needs as they expand, and will not absorb precious venture capital.

Both SAP and Oracle also intend to become fully fledged business-to-business portals. MySap.com, which will be launched later this year, is intended to be a meeting place and business centre for all the companies using SAP software. A new web-based interface will give SAP users access to applications and content that run on the portal, such as travel-reservation systems and online procurement engines. SAP says the site will help to identify trading partners, and will be a central point for negotiating the sale of goods and services. According to Mr Ellison, Business Online will also quickly evolve into a web-based business community. PeopleSoft, another ERP company, has announced similar plans to become a horizontal business portal, and Siebel has recently launched Sales.com, a portal for mobile users of its software providing sales leads, company profiles and other services.

The broad model which all four are following was established earlier this year by Ariba, a company that makes procurement software. In partnership with Hewlett-Packard, Ariba has established the Ariba.com network for its customers, a business-to-business portal that acts as a middleman, managing the procurement of office supplies for 33 big technology companies, including Cisco and Hewlett-Packard.

Without the automated processes that ERP provides, large-scale e-business would be next to impossible, so it is hard to believe that the big ERP vendors have had their day. Indeed, ironically, it may be that only when a company commits itself to becoming an "extraprise" that it will start to see a return on its earlier ERP investment.

Nor is the ERP market as saturated as Mr Siebel claims. It may be true that a third of the world's top 1,000 companies are knee-deep in ERP, but industries such as financial services and telecoms are only just getting tailor-made applications. Renting will also extend ERP into small and medium-sized businesses; and the Internet will hugely increase the number of ERP users in each company.

However, not every customer will be happy about the ERP companies' insistence on owning every software link in the integrated value chain. Some companies will want to "pick-and-mix" applications to gain competitive advantage in their industry and avoid becoming the prisoner of a single vendor. Because the value of e-business rests so squarely on the ability to extend processes and integrate with other companies, customers will demand open interfaces and a commitment to support both formal and informal standards and protocols. If there is one industry where the values of the new business ecosystem might be expected to apply, it is surely IT.

E-BUSINESS AND ERP – TRANSFORMING THE ENTERPRISE

John Blackburn and Martin Osborn, PricewaterhouseCoopers.

Introduction

The last few years have seen significant acceleration in the importance of E-business to organisations across the world. In the 1990s ERP was in vogue and demanded investment in order to position business for the future. ERP focused on cost reduction and internal integration. Major organisations revamped their global supply chains but focused mainly on stock management, ordering or distribution within the organisation or along traditional distribution channels. As Figure 1 illustrates, firms were slow to exploit ERP for market collaboration and it was not until the late 1990s that the focus shifted from cost reduction and efficiency to value creation and collaboration.

Newer themes have embraced further distribution channel effectiveness and co-operation along the supply chain with the main businesses partners.

There are now strong signs that the whole concept of doing business is changing. Customers have far more access to a range of suppliers. Suppliers are gaining direct access to customers. Market communities are springing up that could transform existing supply chains and alter the buying balance of power. Organisations must find how to operate effectively in the new market places and must find a resilient niche for medium- to long-term business.

Figure 1: The evolution of business to E-business

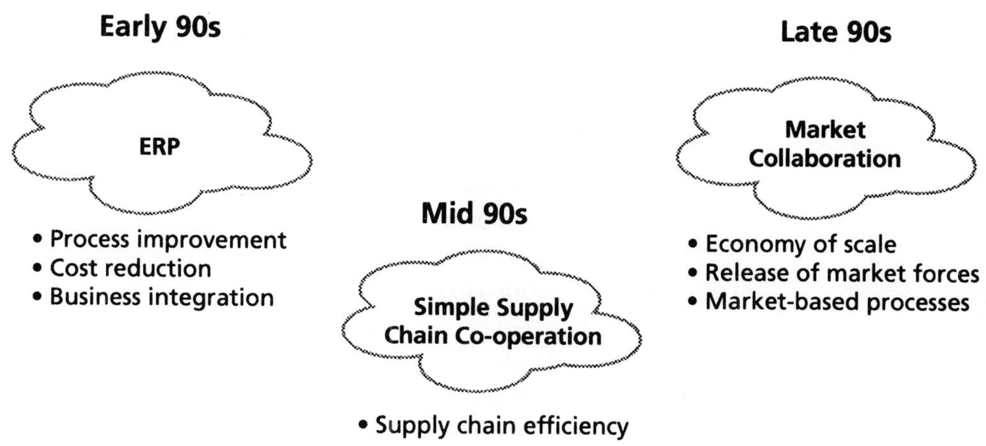

The Experience with ERP

When properly designed and implemented ERP gave significant benefits but proved hard work and costly to implement.

- It was supposed to bring best business practice but the workforce often found it complex and difficult to use.
- ERP helped organisations to feel on safer ground as they went through year 2000 but the cost was often seen as extreme and the move from well fitting, if ageing, legacy systems was not universally welcomed.
- Some processes became more complex or demanded more care with data maintenance.
- ERP promised to reduce manual intervention and to order stock or plan production automatically but organisations struggled to trust the automation and found data accuracy was too low for consistent results.
- Common ERP systems swept away a mish-mash of legacy systems and gave maintenance benefits and common systems across multiple businesses but then the E-business revolution hit!

The early days of the E-business revolution

With the advent of the Internet, companies felt that they had to respond to the challenge. Some responses were a protective move aimed at learning the technology and processes or getting positioned to respond to major inroads on their market place by new entrants or existing competitors. New entrants often focused on the ability to take orders via the Internet but some discovered that they did not have the back office administration and delivery capability – often provided by ERP – to meet growing customer demand. Similarly, even organisations with good back office systems found that merely adding Internet technology did not solve the whole problem. Accurate delivery promises, that optimised the potential from the whole supply chain, demanded more integration and fundamental process redesign. The notion that a company could transform itself into an E-business by simply buying a piece of software and adding it to its existing infrastructure was shown to be wrong and dangerous.

Businesses learnt what the Internet alone could and could not do:

- **It promised to lower the effort and cost of integration but integration proved to be more than giving customers direct access to existing applications;**
- **It promised to compare product offering from diverse sources but it proved a challenge to get at information from each company to make the comparison;**
- **It promised to let knowledge content and information flow freely but it resulted in an information glut;**
- **It promised to make markets more competitive but the efficiency was often only gained in low value activities.**

Businesses learnt that transformation required the whole process to be transformed and that this transformation must run from customer contact and throughout the whole value chain.

Transforming the customer contact experience?

What are the opportunities for transforming the customer contact experience with E-business? Some organisations are installing CRM systems such as Siebel, Clarify or SAP's CRM. SAP are also pushing MySAP.com workplace as a means of integrating the customer contact agent's user interface. A typical scenario might be:

- A customer rings up and the system displays in one window the customer data picked up from the caller id telephone number. (This is not always possible. They may be ringing from home or work or a mobile! All valid alternatives may not be on the system);
- Other windows display the history of products ordered, deliveries made or in progress and invoices and payments;
- Data mining technology has examined the buying patterns of other people who have bought the same products and displays items to suggest at the right time. Alongside each suggested product is an indication of current stocks and predicted delivery dates;
- The caller enquires about a product that is on the suggested list but wants more stock than is available currently. The customer agent can "drag & drop" the product id into another window that shows the current stocks and predicted deliveries for the product within the supply chain. This is achieved by routines that make separate real time enquiries to (1) warehouse and distribution systems from the out-sourced distribution agent; (2) sales and stock system of the supplier of the product that will be resold to the customer. The routines access the remote system by using application programming interfaces supplied by the vendor of the remote system;
- The customer contact agent is able to have a meaningful discussion and negotiation about product availability and delivery as well as the clearance of outstanding debts and payment.

To support these requirements the ERP vendors are integrating both telephone and internet access into their core ERP applications. To support the internet dimension vendors want to allow direct access to internal systems to order or inquire. The technology must support product catalogues, order taking, on-line credit check, integration to banks and credit cards and have high security features. It must also feature auto response and auto forwarding of e-mails. The efficiency of the whole process is based on slick design and the elimination of internal staff from all administrative aspects of the sales process. However, customer requirements are often not satisfied without a human touch. There is an increasing demand to be able to conduct live voice conversations with customers whilst they access company web sites or systems. This is taking telephone and system integration one step further. Already the telephone integration or CTI (Computer Telephone Integration) allows queue management, auto response, fax back, caller identification, changed routing or system processing driven by the number dialed and automatic access to basic customer information. This processing is typical of what is required by businesses and in major call centres. The design of the queuing process can have a major impact on the perception of customer service and customer irritation. Does the customer have an immediate option to request operator assistance or must they always wade through key pad response information? While they are waiting, does the system calculate average waiting time and manage their expectations and offer alternative means of communication? Does the system make good use of the customer's time by collecting vital information that will speed the rest of the process? Does the operator ask the customer to repeat the information keyed in? Finally the CRM systems may need to support the full range of outbound customer contact required, whether by diary managed calling, response calling, planned out bound campaigns or the equivalent by paper or electronic mail. The system must integrate into fulfillment and distribution functionality to give quick response. No element of this functionality is entirely new. The main change is the degree and reach of integration and the willingness and ability of other partners in the supply chain to participate.

What about the growth of "marketplaces"?

Product suppliers like Commerce 1, Ariba and SAP Markets are creating other transformations. They are allowing the creation of markets "owned" by customers or suppliers. Every one who wants to supply must integrate their systems into the marketplace or the marketplace catalogue. The marketplace must be able to respond to a request for a product from a customer and indicate the price and delivery date from each supplier. The customer is able to choose manually or automatically the combination that meets their need. The order and payment can be processed automatically. The supplier can tune the price according to supply and demand. The owners of the marketplace can value all orders placed with each supplier over the period and expect a commission or volume discount that could be passed onto the customers. Suppliers who decide not to integrate into the market lose the chance to sell.

The business dynamics of such trends are significant. It is dangerous not to compete. If you compete, victory goes to the most efficient and speediest competitor. All of the traditional arguments for ERP flood back into the frame. In order to be cost competitive, internal efficiency must be maximised. This requires integration and automation. The challenges of trusting the system to process orders automatically and the challenge of data accuracy have to be overcome.

The key point is that the marketplace now owns the customer. The marketplace dictates the terms of engagement.

A number of new business models pick up the themes above and will become stronger over the next few years. These include:

Infomediaries, which consolidate buyers and sellers in fragmented markets. Travelocity.com is an example in the travel world, providing airport, hotel, and rental car information to buyers on-line, and representing a host of different sellers.

Aggregators, which pull together fragmented markets for buyers. They aggregate the products of dozens of non-production supply companies and produce e-catalogues customised to the buying company. Individuals within the buying company can buy only from those companies whose products are in the intranet-based catalogue. Orders are consolidated at the buying company and sent via the Internet; The marketplace system forwards orders to individual companies and disaggregates the payment from the buying company to all of the selling companies.

Auctioneers, which provide reliable channels for sellers. Auctioneers are very popular in business-to-consumer (B2C) e-business, eBay being the most well known. In the B2B world, they provide a way for companies to sell excess product and may be an important way for companies to buy commodities. CheMatch and ChemConnect are providing this service to the chemicals industry.

Exchangers, which match bid and ask prices as a neutral third party on a stock exchange model.

Over time, these different types of market will increasingly be able to transform industries. Power will shift to buyers as product and price information become more available and widely used. As more companies integrate into the markets, the cost of changing suppliers will be reduced. Transaction costs and cycle times will also become compressed. Speed, range, accessibility, and low cost of information will create opportunities for more competition.

Table 1 illustrates some "aggregator" markets focused on particular industries.

Table 1

Industry	eMarket
Aerospace and Defence	Exostar
Auto Manufacturing	GM/Covisint
Consumer Products	Transora
Energy/Petrochemicals	Petrocosm
Energy/Petrochemicals	Trade Ranger
High Tech	e2open
High Tech	Ehitex
Pharmaceuticals	PharmaExchange
Retail	GlobalNetXchange
Retail	WWRE
Telecommunications	Telco Exchange
Utilities	Pantellos

The aggregation of demand and the auction capability have given major benefits but some organisations have also gained major benefits from collaborative product development via the e-market. In this buyer and seller co-operate together to exchange product information and specifications electronically and achieve significantly faster time to market for new products. This has great value in the internet age.

The efficiency of operation of these markets has attracted many early users but some have realised that the process of aggregation is removing the chance for differentiation from their competitors. This has led to the growth of equivalent private exchanges that give many of the benefits of e-markets but are owned by one company.

Transforming the supply chain with collaborative planning

Collaborative planning requires buyers and sellers throughout the supply chain to develop a:

- single shared view of stocks;
- forecast of demand;
- plan of supply to support this demand.

These must be updated regularly.

Key supply chain partners should all have real-time access to point-of-sale or order information, stocks and forecasts. They should share forecasts so all parties work to a schedule aligned to a common view. Schedule, order, or product changes trigger immediate adjustments to all schedules. Surprises and emergency actions are minimised. Pricing decisions do not create surprises for suppliers and "end of range" pricing decisions are made on the basis of the whole supply chain not just the immediately visible stocks.

Collaborative planning is designed to synchronise plans and product flows, optimise resource utilisation over an expanded capacity base, increase customer responsiveness and reduce inventories. The resource capacities could include production, administrative, distribution fleet, warehouses, warehouse personal and stock rooms. The approach offers many additional benefits when full integration has been achieved:

- The distribution from major distribution centres could be synchronised more closely with supplier deliveries to "flow through" (i.e. cross-docking from the supplier vehicle to the distribution vehicle with no entry into storage and minimal repacking. This can be done providing deliveries and despatches are synchronised and the pack sizes match the delivery drop quantities!). In the longer term this can reduce the capital investment in warehouses as well as stocks but will mean redesign of the warehouse facilities;
- Supplier vehicles delivering to your sites and your own distribution fleet often criss-cross the country. If there is visibility of supplier orders and the trips of your own distribution fleet then trucks returning empty from customer deliveries could pick up supplies from vendors and reduce carriage charges with minimal extra cost.

ERP and advanced planning and scheduling (APS)

Advanced planning and scheduling (APS) systems are often required to supply the "intelligence" for the collaboration. APS functionality ranges from strategic (network optimisation) and tactical (supply planning) to operational (line scheduling). Most APS systems use mathematical algorithms (such as linear programming) to identify optimal solutions to complex planning problems that are bound by such constraints as materials, labour, or capacity resources.

APS systems are particularly well suited to solving the challenges associated with supply-chain management for three reasons:

1. They focus on critical capacity constraints;
2. They provide modelling to run different scenarios and "what-if" analyses;
3. They highlight exceptions and recommend a course of action.

They are designed to develop an optimisation plan for the supply chain and to receive and process data from other databases and transaction-based applications such as ERP systems.

Companies as varied as Ford in motor vehicles, Black & Decker in hand tools, Coca-Cola in beverages, and Frito-Lay in snack foods have used APS tools to transform their supply-chain management. They have used products such as Manugistics, i2, Chesapeake, and Red Pepper (purchased in 1999 by PeopleSoft) and SAP's APO.

Companies using APS software have reduced inventory between 20 and 70 per cent, lowered cost by up to 12 per cent, and trimmed capital by up to 15 per cent. More importantly, however, they have increased sales due to better customer service by between 2 and 15 per cent; improved production throughput by 2 to 6 per cent; and increased customer response, at lower total cost.

Optimising the supply chain has now become a major area of investment to gain competitive advantage.

To date, the standalone APS providers have had far better solutions to meet APS needs than main ERP vendors. However ERP vendors are:

- forming alliances with the main APS software providers (such as the alliance between Oracle and Manugistics);
- buying good APS product companies and integrating the solutions with their own offerings (like PeopleSoft with Red Pepper);
- building their own solutions aggressively (like SAP with APO).

Organisations wishing to implement APS can also integrate best of breed products using enterprise application integration software but in the end a single integrated supplier must be the best solution.

Many organisations are realising that they must significantly change collaborative relations, business processes and internal skills and disciplines as well as face the challenges of integrating the technology. This is a significant project and a major learning curve for any organisation.

CONCLUSION

The current focus on e-business results from an instinct for intimate customer and supplier relationships. It is also driven by the realisation of untapped capability to develop and deliver products and services faster, extend geographic reach further, and increase process efficiency and effectiveness.

As Figure 2 illustrates, E-business is a disruptive technology which raises many challenges. In particular it raises the following issues for management:

- How can we best leverage our product across emerging distribution channels?
- How might E-business change the paradigm of my business?
- What changes are needed in my processes, skills, organisation and systems?
- How is the Internet going to affect various revenue streams or cost structures?
- What will be the impact and where is the return on investment of the electronic commerce revolution?
- How can I develop even closer relationships with my trading partners?
- How best can we leverage and protect intellectual property?
- How do we integrate mergers and acquisitions to recognize and capture new business opportunities?
- What must characterise my internal systems in order to be a success in these new markets?

- How can we best leverage our product across emerging distribution channels?
- How might E-business change the paradigm of my business?
- What changes are needed in my processes, skills, organisation and systems?
- How is the Internet going to affect various revenue streams or cost structures?
- What will be the impact and where is the return on investment of the electronic commerce revolution?
- How can I develop even closer relationships with my trading partners?
- How best can we leverage and protect intellectual property?
- How do we integrate mergers and acquisitions to recognize and capture new business opportunities?
- What must characterise my internal systems in order to be a success in these new markets?

Figure 2: E-business is a disruptive technology

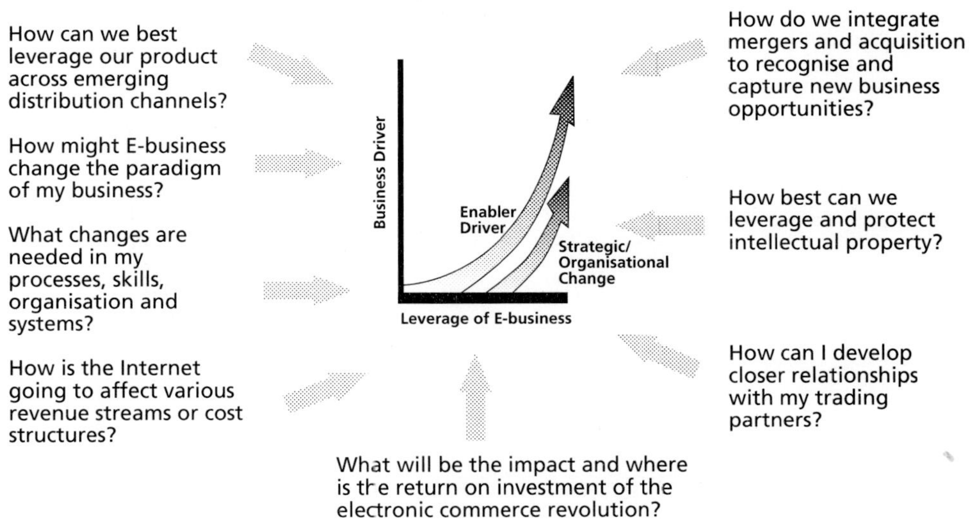

When ERP and e-business are properly implemented, each one supercharges the other. A well-implemented, integrated ERP system is the best core to provide the quality of information, efficient processes and adequate integration within and across enterprises. Companies that try to integrate within an extended value chain before implementing their own ERP systems will find the benefits of value-chain integration to be elusive. Organisations who decide not to integrate into the market lose the chance to compete. Victory goes to the most efficient and speediest competitor. What is your ERP and e-business strategy?

Enterprise Resource Planning Systems

Further Reading

Bingi, P., Sharma, M.K. and Godla, J., "Critical issues affecting an ERP implementation", *Information Systems Management*, Summer 1999, Vol. 16, Issue 3, pp. 7–14.

Black, A., Wright, P. and Davies, J., PricewaterhouseCoopers (2000). *In Search of Shareholder Value.* London: FT-Prentice Hall.

Booth, R. (1999), "Enterprise-wide performance management", *Management Accounting*, October 1999, Vol. 77, Issue 9, pp. 16–17.

Cooper, R. and Kaplan, R.S. (1998), "The promise of Peril of Integrated Cost Systems", *Harvard Business Review*, July/August 1998, pp. 130–5.

Cooper, R. and Slagmulder, R. (1998), "Strategic cost management: Introduction to enterprise-wide cost management", *Management Accounting*, August 1998.

Dauphinais, G.W., Means, G. and Price, C., PricewaterhouseCoopers (2000). *The Wisdom of the CEO.* Chichester: John Wiley & Sons.

Davenport, T. (1998), Putting the enterprise into the enterprise system, *Harvard Business Review*, July/August, Vol. 76, No. 4, pp. 121–31.

Deloitte Consulting, *"ERP's second wave, maximizing the value of ERP-enabled processes,"* Deloitte Consulting, 1998.

Means, G. and Schneider, D., PricewaterhouseCoopers (2000). *Meta-Capitalism.* Chichester: John Wiley & Sons.

Norris, G., Hurley, J.R., Hartley, K.M., Dunleavy, J., Balls, J., PricewaterhouseCoopers (2000). *E-Business and ERP – Transforming the Enterprise.* New York: John Wiley & Sons Inc.

Scapens, R. (1998), SAP: Integrated information systems and the implications for management accountants, *Management Accounting*, September, Vol. 76, No. 8, pp. 46–8.